Practical Android

14 Complete Projects on Advanced Techniques and Approaches

Mark Wickham

Apress®

Practical Android: 14 Complete Projects on Advanced Techniques and Approaches

Mark Wickham
Dallas, Texas, USA

ISBN-13 (pbk): 978-1-4842-3332-0   ISBN-13 (electronic): 978-1-4842-3333-7
https://doi.org/10.1007/978-1-4842-3333-7

Library of Congress Control Number: 2017964267

Cover image by Freepik (`www.freepik.com`)

Managing Director: Welmoed Spahr
Editorial Director: Todd Green
Acquisitions Editor: Steve Anglin
Development Editor: Matthew Moodie
Technical Reviewers: Jeff Friesen and Chaim Krause
Coordinating Editor: Mark Powers
Copy Editor: Mary Behr

Distributed to the book trade worldwide by Springer Science+Business Media New York, 233 Spring Street, 6th Floor, New York, NY 10013. Phone 1-800-SPRINGER, fax (201) 348-4505, e-mail `orders-ny@springer-sbm.com`, or visit `www.springeronline.com`. Apress Media, LLC is a California LLC and the sole member (owner) is Springer Science + Business Media Finance Inc (SSBM Finance Inc). SSBM Finance Inc is a **Delaware** corporation.

For information on translations, please e-mail `rights@apress.com`, or visit `www.apress.com/rights-permissions`.

Apress titles may be purchased in bulk for academic, corporate, or promotional use. eBook versions and licenses are also available for most titles. For more information, reference our Print and eBook Bulk Sales web page at `www.apress.com/bulk-sales`.

Any source code or other supplementary material referenced by the author in this book is available to readers on GitHub via the book's product page, located at `www.apress.com/9781484233320`. For more detailed information, please visit `www.apress.com/source-code`.

Printed on acid-free paper

To my parents, who helped me discover computers and software when I was young.

Contents

About the Author

Mark Wickham is a Dallas-based Android developer who has lived and worked mainly in Beijing since 2000. Mark has led software development teams for Motorola in China, and also worked with product management and product marketing teams in the Asia-Pacific region.

Mark has been involved in software and technology for more than 30 years and began to focus on the Android platform in 2009, creating private cloud and tablet-based solutions for the enterprise.

Mark majored in Computer Science and Physics at Creighton University, and later obtained an MBA from the University of Washington and the Hong Kong University of Science and Technology.

Mark can be contacted via his LinkedIn profile (www.linkedin.com/in/mark-wickham-94b3173/) or Github page (www.github.com/wickapps).

About the Technical Reviewers

Jeff Friesen is a freelance teacher and software developer with an emphasis on Java. In addition to authoring *Java I/O, NIO, and NIO.2* (Apress) and *Java Threads and the Concurrency Utilities* (Apress), Jeff has written numerous articles on Java and other technologies (such as Android) for JavaWorld (JavaWorld.com), informIT (InformIT.com), Java. net, SitePoint (SitePoint.com), and other websites. Jeff can be contacted via his website at JavaJeff.ca. or via his LinkedIn profile (www.linkedin.com/in/javajeff).

Chaim Krause presently lives in Leavenworth, KS, where the U.S. Army employs him as a Simulation Specialist. In his spare time, he likes to play PC games; he occasionally develops his own games as well. He has recently taken up the sport of golf to spend more time with his significant other, Ivana. Although he holds a BA in Political Science from the University of Chicago, Chaim is an autodidact when it comes to computers, programming, and electronics. He wrote his first computer game in BASIC on a Tandy Model I Level I and stored the program on a cassette tape. Amateur radio introduced him to electronics while the Arduino and the Raspberry Pi provided a medium to combine computing, programming, and electronics into one hobby.

Acknowledgments

Everybody has a story about their first computer. Mine was built by my father. It had 8K RAM and was powered by the mighty Intel 8080 CPU. It allowed me to learn programming using 8080 machine language, and later, MITS Altair BASIC. I have been writing software ever since.

I would like to thank Steve Anglin, Mark Powers, Matthew Moodie, Jeff Friesen, Chaim Krause, Mary Behr and the rest of the team at Apress without whom this book could not have been possible.

Thanks to Mary Sue Wickham for her help in editing the original manuscript, and to Tim Dimacchia for his help at Android conferences and for collaboration on software projects dating all the way back to college. A special shout out to Lily's American Diner in Beijing for the images shown in the Lazy Loading app, and to Nogabe, the band, for the live recording used in the Music Service app.

Preface

I have taught a series of popular classes at Android development conferences since 2013. This book covers content from my most popular classes. Each chapter covers an important concept and provides the reader with a deep dive into the implementation.

The book uses a project-based approach. Unlike most books on the market today, *Practical Android* provides complete working code for all of the projects. Developers will appreciate this approach because it enables them to focus on their apps, and not waste time trying to integrate code snippets or troubleshoot environment setup issues.

Practical Android is an ideal resource for developers who have some development experience but may not be Android or mobile development experts. Each chapter includes at least one complete project to show the reader how to implement the concepts. In Android, there are always multiple ways to accomplish a given task. *Practical Android* will help you choose the best approach for your app and let you implement solutions quickly by leveraging complete projects.

Audience

This book is intended for software developers who want to create apps for the Android platform.

Because you are developing for Android, in addition to mastering the Java programming language, you must also master the intricacies of the platform itself.

It's not easy to create commercial apps for the Android platform. You can easily become frustrated for a variety reasons:

- Project setup is not trivial in Android. Whether you are using the latest version of Android Studio or an alternative development environment such as Eclipse, it can sometimes be frustrating making sure all of the libraries, manifest, and project assets are set up correctly.

- When you identify the requirement for a specific functionality in your Android app, it is often difficult to find working code or to integrate the code snippets that are readily available from various online resources.

- The Android platform and the Java programming language offer a lot of functionality. There are often multiple approaches to implementing a particular desired feature. The book helps you decide the best approach for your apps.

- You often need to make architecture decisions when writing Android apps, especially when you require a server connection. It takes experience to implement solutions to meet the right architecture, and you can be faced with a code rewrite or refactoring effort after the app is launched.

- There are a lot of code fragments available online. However, it is often not easy to integrate these assets into your own project. They may be incomplete, or they may contain errors and thus can't be compiled. The book contains 14 compete Android projects. It is easy to get the projects up and running.

Introduction

Chapter Layout

Each chapter in the book follows a consistent structure which includes

- Introduction
- Project(s) Summary
- Overview
- Detailed Section(s)
- References

Each chapter includes several detailed sections. The detailed sections explain the concepts to be implemented. In many cases, the detailed sections explain the different approaches available in Android and which one might be best depending on your app requirements.

Each Android project includes

- App introduction
- App screenshot
- Project setup and app overview
- Technical description of how the app works, including the key code. Not all of the code is reproduced in this book. Typically only the key code is presented. Readers are encouraged to download and view the full project source code to see the complete working implementations.

A reference section is included at the end of each chapter. It is broken into subsections based on the chapter contents. The reference section includes URL links to related technical information.

Project Summary

This book intends to help beginning and experienced Android developers overcome typical difficulties by providing complete Android projects for each of the chosen topic areas. These projects can be imported into your development environment and tailored to meet your specific requirements.

Table 1 contains a summary list of all 14 of the projects covered in the book, including a snapshot of the main layout screen.

Table 1. *Project Summary and Setup Notes*

Chapter 2: Connectivity

Connections App:

A configurable app that shows current device connection status and can repeatedly test reachability of servers. The app is configurable by a JSON file. Reachability can be tested using two different methods, as specified in the configuration file.

Splash App:

A splash screen implementation that downloads a large file when the app first starts, while displaying the download progress information. When the download is finished, a second activity is launched.

Chapter 3: Lazy Loading

Lazy Loading App:

This project connects to the server and downloads a JSON configuration file which provides details for the images that will be lazy loaded into the app. The app supports three different views for the images: *ListView*, *GridView,* and *Gallery*.

(continued)

Table 1. (continued)

Chapter 4: Remote Crash Logs

Remote Crash Log App:

This project displays a map and performs a location lookup to show the current device location. The main view contains a button that will force a crash of the app. When the app crashes, a crash log will be sent up to the server using the ACRA library.

Chapter 5: Uploading, Downloading, and Emailing

Server Spinner App:

The project implements a server-based version of the Android Spinner widget. The server spinner contents are downloaded from the server. The contents of the spinner can be dynamically updated. The app demonstrates how to upload files. Pictures can be taken with the camera and then uploaded to the server.

Emailing App:

When including email functionality within an app, there are three different approaches that can be used. The Emailing app demonstrates how each of them can be implemented.

(continued)

Table 1. *(continued)*

Chapter 6: Push Messaging

FCM Push Messaging App:

A complete implementation of push messaging using the popular Firebase Cloud Messaging (FCM) library. Google recently integrated its popular Google Cloud Messaging (GCM) library into the Firebase suite.

MQTT Push Messaging App:

MQTT (Messaging Queuing Telemetry Transport) is an open source protocol which has been ported to Android. This project will implement a complete push messaging solution using MQTT. The protocol requires a broker to be set up on a server to handle the routing and delivery of messages to all devices. MQTT uses a publish/subscribe model, which is very scalable.

Chapter 7: Android Audio

Audio Buffer Size App:

An adaptation of Google's Audio Buffer Size app, which shows optimal audio settings for your device. The app has been extended to provide a simple test to estimate the output latency of your device. The app also has been extended to display the built-in audio effects supported by the device.

Playing Audio App:

A configurable app that can play audio assets using the three main Android audio playing APIs. The app is built using a JSON configuration file. All of the samples that can be played by the app are displayed in a *GridLayout*.

(continued)

Table 1. (continued)

	Music Service App: Demonstration of how to play music or sounds using a background service. The background service loads an .mp3 song into a MediaPlayer object. The playing of the song can then be controlled from the foreground activity.
	Recording Audio App: Demonstration of how to record audio and store the recording as an uncompressed .wav file.
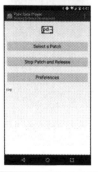	Ringdroid + App: An open source Google app that demonstrates how to handle all aspects of audio including recording and encoding into compressed formats such as AAC (.mp4). The app has been extended so the user can also save files as uncompressed .wav files.
	Puredata Player App: A player app that can load Puredata source files (.pd) and play them using the Puredata audio synthesis engine.

Table 2 includes a summary of the key setup notes for each of the apps.

Table 2. App Setup Notes

Chapter 2: Connectivity

Connections App

Res ➤ Raw ➤ connectfile.txt

Specify the JSON configuration file in the project resources.

Splash App

SplashActivity.java

```
String getURL = "http://www.yourserver.com/english-proper-
names.txt";
String ip204 = "http://www.yourserver.com/return204.php";
```

Chapter 3: Lazy Loading

Lazy Loading App

MainActivity.java

```
String serverFileBase = "https://www.yourserver.com/";
String serverPicBase = "https://www.yourserver.com/fetch800/";
String fileName = "lazyloadconfig.txt";
```

Chapter 4: Remote Crash Logs

Remote Crash Log App

MyApplication.java

```
formUri = "http://www.yourserver.com/crashed.php",
```

Chapter 5: Uploading, Downloading, and Emailing

Server Spinner App

MainActivity.java

```
String serverPath = "http://www.yourserver.com/index.html";
String serverPicBase = "http://www.yourserver.com/";
String listFilesScript = "http://www.yourserver.com/listfiles-a.php";
String uploadFilesScript = "http://www.yourserver.com/uploadfile.php";
String deleteFileScript = "http://www.yourserver.com/deletefile.php";
```

Emailing App

MainActivity.java

```
String sendEmailScript = "http://www.yourserver.com/sendmail.php";
String email Account = "yourAccount@gmail.com";
String emailPassword = "yourPassword";
```

Chapter 6: Push Messaging

FCM Push Messaging App

Global.java

```
String SERVER_URL = " http://www.yourserver.com/register.php";
String SENDER_ID = "your Google Sender Id"; FCM.PHP
```

```
define("GOOGLE_API_KEY", "yourAPI");
```

MQTT Push Messaging App

Global.java

```
String MQTT_BROKER = "your broker URL or IP address";
```

(continued)

Table 2. *(continued)*

Chapter 7: Android Audio

Audio Buffer Size + App	The package name of this project is com.levien.audiobuffersize and it cannot be changed due to dependencies on a Native library call.
Playing Audio App	Project resources *Res ➤ Raw ➤ soundfile.txt* *Res ➤ Raw ➤ all of the .mp3/wav/ogg/m4a sound files*
Music Service App	Project resources *Res ➤ Raw ➤ nogabe.mp3*

Recording Audio App	*RecordWavActivity.java*
	
	`String AUDIO_RECORDER_FOLDER = "media/audio/music";`
	`String AUDIO_RECORDER_TEMP_FILE = "record_temp.raw";`

Ringdroid + App	None

Puredata Player App	*PdPlayer.java*
	
	`filesDir=new File (android.os.Environment.getExternalStorage`
	`Directory(),"PDPatches");`
	
	This project depends on the following 2 library projects:
	`PdCore`
	`AndroidMidi`

Conventions

Each chapter in the book uses a mix of figures, tables, and code blocks to explain the chapter concept. Figures and tables are identified by a chapter-derived sequence number and are referred to in the accompanying chapter text.

The *technical italic* font is used to represent technical terms. This includes Android-specific terms, URLs, or general technical terms.

Reference URLs are included at the end of each chapter. Occasionally, a URL will be included within the chapter details.

Code examples are presented within boxes as shown by the following example. The code blocks do not have identifiers. They represent key code that will be discussed in the text that immediately precedes or follows them.

```
switch (type) {
    case 0:
        // Release any resources from previous MediaPlayer
        if (mp != null) mp.release();
        mp = new MediaPlayer();
        Uri u = Uri.parse("android.resource://com.wickham.android.playaudio/" + resid);
        mp.setDataSource(MainActivity.this, u);
        mp.prepare();
        mp.start();
        break;
```

In order to help you locate the code within the associated project resources, the filename associated with the code block will normally be included as a section header in the text preceding the code block. The code blocks are not complete. They are often simplified to help explain a key concept. Refer to the actual project source code to see the full Java code implementation.

Development Environment

Increasingly, Android developers are migrating to Google's Android Studio development environment. This book will not cover the specifics of Android Studio. Rather, the focus remains on the code. In the chapters that require an external library to be included, the instructions are included to help you set up the library dependencies in Android Studio and with external library files.

The complete Android projects are included as a companion asset for the book and are available on GitHub. These projects can easily be imported into Android Studio.

Software License

Android is a trademark of Google Inc.

Most of the software contained in this book is licensed under the Apache 2.0 license.

Unlike many Android books, you are free to use and modify the code in its entirety according to the terms of the license.

The projects written by the author include the following Copyright notice:

```
/*
 * Copyright (C) 2016 Mark Wickham
 *
 * Licensed under the Apache License, Version 2.0 (the "License");
 * you may not use this file except in compliance with the License.
 * You may obtain a copy of the License at
 *
 * http://www.apache.org/licenses/LICENSE-2.0
 *
 * Unless required by applicable law or agreed to in writing, software
 * distributed under the License is distributed on an "AS IS" BASIS,
 * WITHOUT WARRANTIES OR CONDITIONS OF ANY KIND, either express or implied.
 * See the License for the specific language governing permissions and
 * limitations under the License.
 *
 */
```

For full details of the license, please refer to the link referenced above.

Some of the projects in the book are derived from existing open source projects, which already include their own copyright.

The Audio Buffer Size, Ringdroid, and FCM Quickstart projects are open source and

Google holds the copyright. They have been modified by the author to include additional functionality. In such cases, the original copyright is included and a reference to modifications made by the author is noted in the source code.

The book includes discussion of some open source apps whose code is not modified, such as the Circle of Fifths, Csound, and K-9 Mail apps.

Chapter 1

Introduction to JSON

1.1 Introduction

It may seem unusual to start an Android book off with a chapter on JSON, but writing great apps is all about having great software architecture. Throughout the book, I will be using projects to help teach key concepts, and one function that almost all of the projects have in common is connectivity. Our apps need to connect to the Internet, and we need a simple yet sophisticated way to interchange data with the server.

This is where JSON comes in. JSON, or JavaScript Object Notation, is a lightweight data-interchange format. JSON has several important properties that have helped to make it hugely popular across the Internet and especially within mobile app development.

- JSON is easy for us to read and write and is easy for machines to parse and generate.

- There is a JSON library available for almost every platform and language.

- JSON is based on a subset of the JavaScript programming language, hence its name.

- JSON is a text format and is language independent.

- JSON uses conventions that are familiar to programmers of the C- family of languages.

Many of the projects in this book will use JSON for configuration files. Using JSON as the interchange format with your application server creates a flexible and expandable architecture for your apps.

© Mark Wickham 2018
M. Wickham, *Practical Android*, https://doi.org/10.1007/978-1-4842-3333-7_1

1.2   Chapter Projects

This chapter contains no projects.

However, several of the chapters in this book use the JSON code and principles described in this chapter to accomplish their server connectivity for configuration.

Table 1-1 shows the JSON usage summary for the projects in this book.

Table 1-1. JSON Project Usage Summary

Chapter	Project	Use
2	Connections	The app loads a configuration file called *connectionfile.txt* from the server.
3	Lazy Loading	The app loads a configuration file called *lazyloadconfig.txt* from the server.
7	Playing Audio	The app loads a configuration file called *soundfile.txt* from the server.

Note: The table does not include the projects that do not use JSON in their implementation.

1.3   JSON Overview

As a data-interchange format, JSON provides a method for us to communicate with the server. JSON is built on two data structures that are common in nearly all programming languages: a collection of name/value pairs, and an ordered list of values.

In JSON, there are two primitives that are used to represent these data structures. Using only these primitives, you will be able to construct complex structures that can represent almost any type of data relationship.

  ▓ *JSONObject*: An unordered set or collection of name/value pairs

  ▓ *JSONArray*: An ordered list of values

Both JSON objects and JSON arrays contain values. A value can be a string in double quotes, or a number, or true or false or null, or another JSON object or JSON array. These structures can be nested, which is why JSON is so powerful for data structures.

Figure 1-1 shows a graphical representation of the JSON syntax. The most important thing to notice is the usage of the [(left bracket) and] (right bracket), and { (left brace) and } (right brace) identifiers.

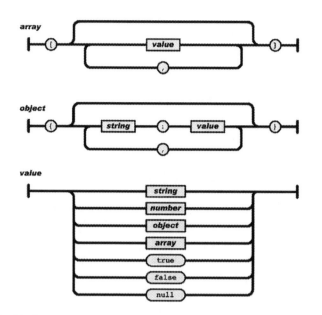

Figure 1-1. JSON building blocks

A summary of the formatting:

▓   Objects begin with { (left brace) and end with } (right brace).

▓   Arrays begin with [(left bracket) and end with] (right bracket).

▓   Values can be of multiple types and are separated by , (comma).

The power and flexibility of JSON is established by the fact that values can be comprised not only of strings, numbers, and Booleans, but also can contain arrays and objects themselves.

1.4   JSON and Android

JSON has been included in Android since the earliest release of the SDK. Table 1-2 shows a list of the Android JSON classes including the exception handler.

Table 1-2. Android JSON Package Summary (org.json)

Classes	Description
JSONArray	A dense indexed sequence of values
JSONObject	A modifiable set of name/value mappings
JSONStringer	Implements *JSONObject.toString()* and *JSONArray.toString()*
JSONTokener	Parses a JSON-encoded string into the corresponding object
JSONException	Thrown to indicate a problem with the JSON API

You shall see, in several of the projects in this book, how to use JSON to handle the app's configuration. This makes it easy to change the app without the need to recompile the code.

The *JSONArray* and *JSONObject* objects are all you need to manage JSON encoding and decoding. The following code sample shows how these objects are defined and used in Android:

```
// Define a new JSON Object
// Remember that JSON Objects start with { (left brace) and end with } (right brace)

JSONObject jsonObject = new JSONObject(myJsonDataString);

// Define a new JSON Array
// Remember that JSON Arrays start with [ (left bracket) and end with ] (right bracket)

JSONArray jsonArray = new JSONArray(myJsonDataString);
```

The trick to using JSON effectively lies in defining a JSON data structure to represent your data.

1.5   Designing JSON

The recursive nature of the JSON syntax makes it suitable to represent almost any type of data.

Let's take an example of a customer ordering application. When a customer orders items from a menu, a ticket is generated to represent key aspects of the transaction. Think about the receipt you get from a restaurant or coffee shop. It probably contains a number of important data related to the transaction, including

- ID of the transaction
- Date/time of the transaction
- Name of the wait staff handling the transaction
- Number of guests on the ticket (important because restaurants frequently calculate the amount spent per customer)
- Sale type identifier, such as take-out, in-restaurant, or internet-order
- Delivery information if the sale type is a take-out order

Order total, which is a sum of the individual totals of each item on the ticket

Details of all the individual items for the order

Let's represent this data in JSON. JSON is ideal because once you have all the details encoded, it is easy to pass the details off to other consumers of the data. For example, you may have another internal activity that is responsible for printing out tickets, or you may wish to upload or download tickets to and from cloud storage over the network.

JSON Sample File

The code block below shows how you might wish to represent the ticket in JSON. Note that whitespace does not have meaning in JSON, but I have included indenting in this JSON example to show the nesting levels within the JSON structure.

At its simplest form, the JSON required to represent this order ticket is a single array of 11 objects. Note that the main array starts and ends with square brackets, and each of the 11 objects within the main array start and end with curly braces. Also, note that the first 10 objects are simple name/value pairs.

```
[ { "orderid": "151001-101300-9" },
  { "customername": "" },
  { "tablename": "9" },
  { "waiter": "Mark" },
  { "guests": "2" },
  { "saletype": "0" },
  { "time": "101940" },
  { "ticketnum": "15297" },
  { "ordertotal": 70 },
  { "deliveryaddress": "" },
  { "dishes": [
            [ { "dishId": 45 },
              { "dishName": "Vegetarian Burger" },
              { "categoryName": "Burgers" },
              { "qty": 1 },
              { "price": 35 },
              { "priceDiscount": 100 },
              { "specialInstruction": "" },
              { "options": [] }
            ],
            [
              { "dishId": 61 },
              { "dishName": "Spaghetti" },
              { "categoryName": "Italian" },
              { "qty": 1 },
              { "price": 35 },
              { "priceDiscount": 100 },
              { "specialInstruction": "" },
              { "options": [
                            [ { "optionId": 0 },
                              { "optionPrice": 0 },
```

```
                              { "optionName": "pesto" }
                            ]
                        ] }
                ]
            ] }
]
```

The last object, named "dishes", is different. Its value is an array of dishes because each ticket could contain multiple dishes. In this example, two dishes are included in the array.

Each dish itself has several name/value pairs, including the dish name, the dish category, the dish price, quantity, special instructions, etc.

Note that there is a third level of nesting because each dish can have options. The first dish has no options, but the second dish has one option, which defines "pesto" as the type of dish and indicates that this option has no extra cost. Of course, a dish could have more than one option, so this is a very flexible structure.

Validating JSON

JSON structures can become complicated, and it is important to validate them when you are designing them for use within your apps. There are several web-based JSON validators available.

Figure 1-2 shows the JSON validator available at `http://jsonlint.com`. The site does a nice job of telling you if the JSON is valid. When the validator detects problems, it can highlight the problems so you can correct them.

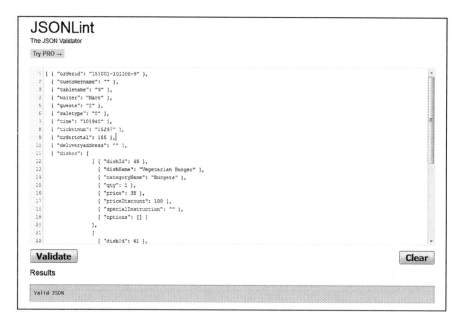

Figure 1-2. Web-based JSON validation using `http://jsonlint.com`

When designing JSON structures for your Android apps, it is important to validate them before writing the code that will parse them. There is nothing more frustrating than trying to debug JSON code that is trying to operate on invalid JSON structures.

Text File Encoding

JSON files are text files. They can be stored remotely on a server or internally within your apps. They often use the extensions of .txt or .json.

JSON text files can use any type of encoding. I recommend always using UTF-8 encoding. The advantage of UTF-8 is that it is a multi-byte encoding and thus can handle special characters such as Chinese, Kanji, Latin, or many others. Using UTF-8, you can easily embed these non-ASCII characters inside your JSON strings. Almost all text editors, including Windows Notepad, will allow you to specify the encoding when you save a file.

Android apps also allow you to set the default character encoding for text files. It is important to set this to UTF-8 so it will match your UTF-8 encoded JSON text files.

Depending on your IDE, the character encoding can be set in the project *Properties* under the *Resource* setting. There are typically two choices for text file encoding:

- Inherited from container (Cp1252)
- Other

If you select the drop-down box associated with "Other," you will be able to choose UTF-8 character encoding from the list.

1.6   Common JSON Operations

Now that you know you have a valid JSON structure, let's take a look at how to implement a number of common JSON operations, including

- Setting a JSON value in a JSON object
- Getting a JSON value from a JSON object
- Creating a JSON file programmatically
- Reading in a JSON file and parsing it into Java ArrayLists
- Printing out JSON strings
- Removing a JSON array from within a JSON structure

You will see these operations used in several of the projects later in this book.

JSON is a low-level library. You will see at the end of this chapter that GSON (Google JSON) is an alternative external library used for data interchange. GSON allows us to work with Java objects rather than JSON objects.

Since you are working directly with JSON without external libraries, let's write some simple helper functions that will allow you to access the data inside your JSON objects. You will see these helper functions used in several projects in the book that incorporate JSON. The first two operations, for setting and getting Object values, will use a helper function.

Setting a JSON Value in a JSON Object

Recall that JSON objects begin and end with curly braces: { and }. The JSON order ticket contains 11 JSON objects. You are going to define a helper function called *jsonSetter* to help you set a value for any of the JSON objects in the JSON order ticket.

jsonSetter Helper Function

The first helper function is called *jsonSetter*. It is passed a *JSONArray*, a key String, and a replace Object. This function iterates over the JSON string and allows you to set the value of a specific *JSONObject*.

```
private void jsonSetter(JSONArray array, String key, Object replace) {
    for (int i=0; i<array.length(); i++) {
        try {
            JSONObject obj = array.getJSONObject(i);
            if (obj.has(key)) {
                obj.putOpt(key,replace);
            }
        } catch (JSONException e) {
            // log("jsonSetter exception");
        }
    }
}
```

For example, in the JSON order ticket, you may want to set the value of "customername" to "Hungry Person".

This can be accomplished with the following single line of code using the helper function and passing it the object name and the new desired value:

```
// Assume JSONTicket is a JSONArray assigned to the sample JSON order ticket shown earlier
// Call the helper function to set the value of the "customername" Object

jsonSetter(JSONTicket,"customername","Hungry Person");
```

Recall that the JSON order ticket is an array that contains 11 objects. The helper function traverses over each of the objects until a key match is found. The function then replaces the value for that key with the newly specified value.

Getting a JSON Value from a JSON Object

You can also use a helper function to retrieve values from JSON objects. The *jsonGetter* helper function below returns an object that is the value of the corresponding key that was passed in.

jsonGetter Helper Function

This function allows you to retrieve the value of a specific *JSONObject*. The *jsonGetter* helper function is passed a *JSONArray* and a key String.

```
private Object jsonGetter(JSONArray json, String key) {
    Object value = null;
    for (int i=0; i<json.length(); i++) {
        try {
            JSONObject obj = json.getJSONObject(i);
            if (obj.has(key)) {
                value = obj.get(key);
            }
        } catch (JSONException e) {
            // log("jsonGetter Exception=" +e);
        }
    }
    return value;
}
```

For example, in the JSON order ticket, you may want to get the value of "waiter". This can be accomplished with the following single line of code using the helper function:

```
// Assume JSONTicket is a JSONArray assigned to the sample JSON order ticket shown earlier
// Call the helper function to get the value of the "waiter" Object

String waiter = jsonGetter(JSONTicket,"waiter").toString();
```

Recall that the JSON order ticket is an array that contains 11 objects. The helper function traverses over each of the objects until a key match is found. The function then retrieves the value of the specified key and returns it as a Java object, which is then converted to a String value.

Creating a JSON File Programmatically

It is common when designing or creating JSON files to do so offline and then validate the JSON using tools. However, you can also programmatically create a JSON file using the *JSONArray* and *JSONObject* methods.

Recall that the order ticket consisted of 11 objects. The last object held the dishes of the ticket, which itself was a JSON array. The following code shows how to set up a blank JSON structure to represent the order ticket. It is a good practice to identify JSON variables as arrays or objects within the name, such as *ticketAry* or *dishesAry* or *tmpObj*. This makes it easier to work with the structures in your code.

```
// Create a blank JSON Order Ticket
try {

    JSONArray ticketAry = new JSONArray();
    JSONArray dishesAry = new JSONArray();
    JSONObject tmpObj = new JSONObject();

    ticketAry.put(tmpObj.put("orderid",""));
    ticketAry.put(tmpObj.put("customername",""));
    ticketAry.put(tmpObj.put("tablename",""));
    ticketAry.put(tmpObj.put("waiter",""));
    ticketAry.put(tmpObj.put("guests",""));
    ticketAry.put(tmpObj.put("saletype",""));
    ticketary.put(tmpObj.put("time",""));
    ticketAry.put(tmpObj.put("ticketnum",""));
    ticketAry.put(tmpObj.put("ordertotal",0));
    ticketAry.put(tmpObj.put("deliveryaddress",""));
    ticketAry.put(tmpObj.put("dishes",dishesAry));

} catch (JSONException e) {
    // log("JSONException Intial e=" + e);
}
```

Once you have the JSON structure set up using the *put* method, you can use the *jsonSetter* helper function to update any of the values in the structure or the *jsonGetter* helper function to retrieve object values from the structure.

Reading and Parsing a JSON File

Several of the projects in this book read a local JSON configuration file. The file could just as easily be downloaded over the network using HTTP. Reading and parsing JSON files is a three-step process.

1. Read in the JSON UTF-8 encoded text file as a string.

2. Assign the string to a JSONArray.

3. Iterate over the JSONArray and extract values into *ArrayLists* or other local variables.

The following code shows how this is accomplished. In this example, the local file is named *Resources/Raw/jsonfile.txt* and contains a simple array of values. There are no JSON objects (name/value pairs).

Note that the required JSON and file exception handling are not included in the following code.

```
// This code will parse a JSON Array of values, such as the following:
// jsonfile.txt = [ "value1","value2","value3","value4","value5" ]
```

```
// Define the ArrayList that we will populate from the JSON Array
private ArrayList<String> myArrayList = new ArrayList<String>();
myArrayList.clear();

// Step 1.
// Read in the JSON file from local storage and save it as a String
Resources res = getResources();
InputStream in_s = res.openRawResource(R.raw.jsonfile);
byte[] b = new byte[in_s.available()];
in_s.read(b);
String fileTxt = (new String(b));

// Step 2.
// Assign the text file String to a JSONArray
JSONArray fileJsonAry = new JSONArray(fileTxt);

// Step 3.
// Build the ArrayList by iterating over the JSON Array
for (int i=0; i<fileJsonAry.length(); i++){
    String value = fileJsonAry.get(i).toString();
    myArrayList.add(value);
}
```

Printing JSON Strings

Printing out JSON strings is accomplished using the *toString* method. The *toString* method can be invoked on JSON objects or JSON arrays. It encodes the content into a human-readable JSON string, which can be useful for debugging or passing up to a server using HTTP.

In the example of the JSON order ticket, the whole structure can be printed out or saved as a string with the following code:

```
String jsonText = ticketAry.toString();
```

The *toString()* method can also accept an integer parameter called *indentSpaces*, which represents the number of spaces to indent for each level of nesting. This makes the string larger in size, but much more readable if you have many levels of nesting.

The following example sets a spacing of four spaces for each level of nesting:

```
String jsonText = ticketAry.toString(4);
```

Removing JSON Arrays

JSON structures can become complex. Sometimes it is necessary to remove a JSON array from a JSON structure that may contain multiple arrays.

For example, recall that the order ticket example contained a JSON object named "dishes". The value of this object is an array of arrays representing all of the dishes on the order ticket. In your example, there were two dishes.

What if you want to remove one of the dishes? In the next example, you will delete a single dish from the "dishes" object.

Deleting an array is pretty straightforward in newer versions of the Android SDK because you can make use of the *JSONArray remove*() method. However, the *remove()* method is not available on devices prior to Android SDK 4.4. You do not wish to exclude users of those devices from using your app, so you need to write a helper function to handle the operation for older devices.

The following helper function, *removeJSONArray*, will delete a JSON array. It takes two parameters: the higher level input JSON array, and an integer position identifying the sub-array to delete. It returns a new JSON array excluding the specified item.

```java
public static JSONArray removeJSONArray(JSONArray inJSONArray, int pos) {
    JSONArray newJsonArray = new JSONArray();
    try {
        for (int i=0; i<inJSONArray.length(); i++) {
            if (i != pos)
                newJsonArray.put(inJSONArray.get(i));
        }
    } catch (Exception e) {
        e.printStackTrace();
    }
    return newJsonArray;
}
```

You can perform a check for the device SDK version to determine if you can use the built-in JSON function or if you need to invoke the helper function.

In either case, before you can remove the array, you need to access the JSON dishes array inside the structure. Follow these steps to access and delete the desired dish:

1. Use the *jsonGetter* helper function to grab the "dishes" object.

2. Define *JSONdishesAry*, which is the JSON array that is the value of the "dishes" object.

3. *JSONdishesAry* contains all the dishes. You pass *JSONdishesAry* along with the position ID of the dish to delete the *remove()* function.

These steps are accomplished by the following code:

```java
try {
    // The next two lines access the dishes array assigned to the value of the "dishes" object
    JSONObject JSONdishObj = JSONOrderAry.getJSONObject(jsonGetter(JSONOrderAry,"dishes"));
    JSONArray JSONdishesAry = JSONdishObj.getJSONArray("dishes");

    int position = 1; // ID of the dish we want to remove

    // Check for SDK version to see if we can use the JSON .remove function directly
    if (Build.VERSION.SDK_INT >= Build.VERSION_CODES.KITKAT) {
        JSONdishesAry.remove(position);
```

```
    } else {
        // We need to do it with a helper function
        JSONdishesAry = removeJSONArray(JSONdishesAry,position);
    }
```

JSON takes a while to get used to. But once you grasp the concept of arrays and objects and how they can be nested and arranged, the possibilities are endless!

1.7   JSON Alternatives

Both the *JSONObject* and *JSONArray* classes follow the DOM (Directory Object Model) method of parsing. Thus, they require you to load an entire JSON data/response into a string before you can parse it. This is the main weakness of JSON and it becomes inefficient when there are large JSON structures to be parsed.

The GSON and Jackson libraries can help to overcome this weakness if you have large JSON files and performance is a concern for your app.

GSON

GSON is a lightweight library that was developed by Google. It can be used to convert Java objects into their JSON representation. It can also be used to convert a JSON string to an equivalent Java object.

In other words, GSON is a JSON serialization and deserialization library that uses reflection to populate your Java objects from JSON objects.

According to Google, there were several goals for GSON:

- Provide easy-to-use mechanisms like *toString*() and constructors to convert Java to JSON and vice-versa.
- You can customize GSON by adding your own serializers and deserializers.
- Allow pre-existing unmodifiable objects to be converted to and from JSON.
- GSON can work with arbitrary Java objects including pre-existing objects for which you do not have source code.
- Allow custom representations for objects.
- Support arbitrarily complex objects.
- Generate compact and readable JSON output.

In order to use GSON in your Android projects, you need to import the GSON library file called *gson-2.2.4.jar*. The file is available at `https://github.com/google/gson`.

The following serialization and deserialization examples give you an idea of how to use the GSON *toJson* and *fromJson* methods:

```
Gson gson = new Gson();

Serialization Examples:

String str = gson.toJson(myObj);
String str = gson.toJson(1);
String str = gson.toJson("abcd");
String str = gson.toJson(new Long(10));
String str = gson.toJson(values);

Deserialization Examples:

int one = gson.fromJson("1", int.class);
Integer one = gson.fromJson("1", Integer.class);
Long one = gson.fromJson("1", Long.class);
Boolean false = gson.fromJson("false", Boolean.class);
```

Jackson

Jackson is a relatively fast streaming JSON parser and generator. It is a multipurpose open source Java library for processing the JSON data format. According to its website, Jackson aims to be the best possible combination of fast, correct, lightweight, and ergonomic.

You can download the Jackson library from `https://github.com/FasterXML/jackson`.

Jackson version 1.6 and above contains the following six .jar files:

- *Core.jar* contains streaming JSON parser and generator interfaces and implementations.

- Optional *Mapper.jar* contains functionality for data binding, including *TreeMapper* and *ObjectMapper*.

- Optional *jax-rs.jar* contains the class(es) needed to make a JAX-RS implementation.

- Optional *xc.jar* contains the classes needed to add XML compatibility support.

- Optional *MrBean.jar* contains functionality for materialized beans.

- Optional *Smile.jar* contains support for JSON-compatible binary format called Smile.

There is also a newly added *jackson-all.jar* that contains contents of all the jar files, making it more convenient to use and upgrade.

1.8   References

Android JSON

- Android JSON Objects: http://developer.android.com/reference/org/json/JSONObject.html

- Android JSON Arrays: http://developer.android.com/reference/org/json/JSONArray.html

- Android JSON Package Summary: http://developer.android.com/reference/org/json/package-summary.html

- JSON RFC Standard RFC 4627: www.ietf.org/rfc/rfc4627.txt

Google GSON

- GSON User Guide: https://github.com/google/gson/blob/master/UserGuide.md

- GSON GitHub: https://github.com/google/gson

Third Party

- JSON Validator: http://jsonlint.com

- Jackson Library Download and Documentation: https://github.com/FasterXML/jackson

Chapter 2

Connectivity

2.1 Introduction

The single most important characteristic of a successful app is connectivity. You can accomplish most of your connectivity requirements with the ubiquitous HTTP protocol, which makes up the backbone of all Internet communications. In this chapter, I will cover the HTTP options available within Android.

Sometimes more specialized protocols are required. In Chapter 6, I will cover push messaging and the unique protocols used for its implementation.

Let's begin with the three important aspects of connectivity to determine the following:

- Is your device *connected?*
- Is your network *available?*
- Is your server *reachable?*

You will see that the reachability test is not trivial. To help you understand the key aspects of connectivity, you will implement the Connections app. The Connections app is a useful tool that will help you view your connectivity status and make decisions about how you can best determine the reachability of your server.

You will also implement a simple splash screen, a useful and common pattern for apps typically used to download content in the background when the app first launches.

2.2 Chapter Projects

This chapter will present the apps shown in Table 2-1.

© Mark Wickham 2018
M. Wickham, *Practical Android*, https://doi.org/10.1007/978-1-4842-3333-7_2

Table 2-1. Chapter Projects

Title of Project	File Name	Description
Connections	*connections.zip*	A configurable app that shows current device connection status and can repeatedly test reachability of servers specified in the configuration file using multiple methods.
Splash	*splash.zip*	A splash screen implementation that downloads a large file when the app first starts, while displaying a graphical image and progress information.

The Connections app is a useful tool that can be used to explore the reachability of server endpoints. It is configurable via a JSON file, and it implements a timer to repeatedly check multiple connections using two different techniques.

Many apps use a splash screen display, a graphic, or text introduction while performing network activity in the background at launch time. The splash app provides an example of this common pattern.

2.3   Connectivity Basics

It is important to know the connectivity status of your device at all times for two main reasons:

- You need to let your users know the connectivity status so they can take action if the connectivity becomes degraded, such as enabling mobile data if a hotspot is not available, or logging into a WiFi service if this is required by the WiFi service provider.

- You may need to make logic decisions within your app based on the connectivity status of the device. For example, you may want to prevent users from downloading large files when they are connected by mobile data, due to unfavorable data rates.

Of course, the nature of a mobile device is to be on the move, so the connectivity status can change at any time, which is a fundamental difference from network programming for a static connected device such as a server or workstation.

Let's take a look at the networking model and see how it applies to you as an Android developer. Figure 2-1 shows a typical network connection layer model.

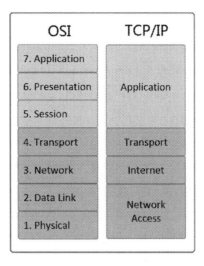

Figure 2-1. *Digital communications network layer model*

The traditional seven layers of the OSI are shown in the left column, while the right column shows a collapsed version that is typically used to represent TCP/IP communications.

At the lowest layer, network access, there are two possibilities on mobile devices:

▨ Mobile data

▨ WiFi

These two different access methods are important for the users of your apps because data rates are typically billed differently by the network operators. Luckily, in Android there are several APIs that make it simple to detect the status of these access methods.

At the higher application layer in Android, you are going to be primarily using the HTTP protocol over TCP/IP, the transport and Internet layers, for all of your communications.

You will implement the HTTP protocol at the application layer for both the Connections app and the Splash app in this chapter.

2.4   Android HTTP Options

Historically, there are two HTTP stacks available internally in Android:

▨ *HttpURLConnection*

▨ *AndroidHttpClient*

The Google Android team has recently discontinued support for the *AndroidHttpClient* class. This was primarily due to the large size of the stack and the inability to provide ongoing support for it. So today it is best to go with the *HttpURLConnection* unless there is a particular feature you require that is not supported by this popular built-in stack.

In addition to these two choices, there are also external HTTP stacks, which can be included in your projects. The two most popular and powerful external HTTP stacks are

- *ApacheHttpClient*

- *OKHttp*

Table 2-2 shows a summary of the HTTP stacks for Android along with a description and major points for each stack.

Table 2-2. Android HTTP Stack Comparison

HTTP Stack	Internal	Notes
AndroidHttpClient	Y	Supports *HttpBasicParams, Get, Post, HttpResponse, CookieStore, AuthenticationHandler, RedirectHandler.* Supports multithreaded connection pools. Has many methods, but is no longer supported by Google and is no longer included in Android as of Android 6.0.
HttpUrlConnection	Y	Includes extensive session and cookie managers. Simpler API with much smaller size than *AndroidHttpClient*. Some major issues prior to Android 2.2. Supports *basicHttpAuthentication*, and SSL. Can use *getURL()* to check for WiFi redirects (up to 5). Input and Output streams are unbuffered.
OKHttp	N	Open source HTTP client from Square. It was forked from *URLConnection* in Android 4.0 and maintains same API. Designed for efficiency and to work well on mobile networks, which are not always stable. Supports Android 2.3 and above.
		HTTP/2 support allows all requests to the same host to share a socket. Integrated cache, response compression, and sophisticated connection pooling. Support for multipart forms.
ApacheHttpClient	N	Very large size. The library is 50K lines of code, but provides lots of bells and whistles. *HttpGet* is included in SDK API 10+. Supports MIME MPE (multipart encoding), which is useful for uploading binary files and file entities. Supports *HttpRequestRetryHandler,* which is useful if you are dealing with unstable networks.

Using the built-in *HttpURLConnection* stack is generally the best choice. Refer to Figure 2-2 for a summary of the HTTP stacks and a decision process. If you do decide to use one of the external HTTP stacks, you will need to download the library files or set up the Gradle dependency to include them in your project. Check the reference links at the end of the chapter for download links.

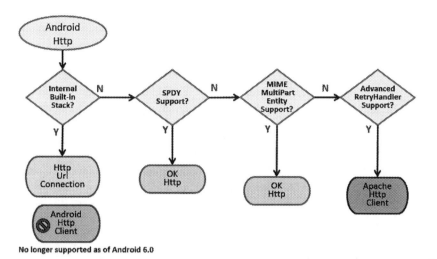

Figure 2-2. *HTTP stack decision criteria*

The external *OkHttp* or *ApacheHttpClient* libraries are useful if you want to use multipart forms for uploading files or if you want to use the advanced *RetryHandler* method, both of which are not available in the *AndroidHttpClient* or *HttpURLConnection* stacks.

The *ApacheHttpClient* consists of the following four files that must be included in your project setup:

- *httpclient-4.1.jar*
- *httpcore-4.1.jar*
- *httpmime-4.1.jar*
- *httpmime4j-0.6.jar*

Using the *ApacheHttpClient* also requires some additional setup because the package names are identical to the internal *AndroidHttpClient*.

One of the advantages of using the external *ApacheHttpClient* library is the support it has for some advanced features of the protocol, such as the ability to handle retries using the *HttpRequestRetryHandler* interface.

The following code block shows how you can utilize this functionality:

```
httpclient.setHttpRequestRetryHandler(new DefaultHttpRequestRetryHandler() {
    @Override
    public boolean retryRequest(IOException exception,int executionCount,HttpContext context) {
        if (executionCount >= 4) {
            ... do your retry exceeded work here
        return false;
        }
        if (exception instanceof NoHttpResponseException) {
        return true;
        }
```

```
        if (exception instanceof SSLHandshakeException) {
        return false;
        }
        if (exception instanceof java.net.SocketTimeoutException) {
        return true;
        }
        return false;
    }
});
```

OkHttp is an excellent HTTP stack from the team at Square. It is an open source project and was forked from *HttpURLConnection.* It is very stable and loaded with features. I highly recommend it, especially if you are just getting started with HTTP in your apps.

Using the *OkHttp* external library is very easy. Check the Square GitHub page at `https://square.github.io/okhttp/` for the Android Studio Maven and Gradle setup instructions. For other development environments, the *OkHttp* library consists of two files that must be included in your project:

- *OkHttp-3-9-0.jar*: The main library

- *OkIo.jar*: Used for fast I/O and resizable buffers

According to Square, *OkHttp* was designed to be efficient by default and includes the following features:

- HTTP/2 support allows all requests to the same host to share a socket.

- Connection pooling reduces request latency (if HTTP/2 isn't available).

- Transparent GZIP shrinks download sizes.

- Response caching avoids the network completely for repeat requests.

Square has many examples and recipes on its site to show you how to implement *OkHttp*.

2.5   Connectivity Status

Using the Built in APIs

In Android, you can make use of the built-in APIs to determine network available and connectivity type.

The following code shows how to use the *ConnectivityManager* and the *NetworkInfo* object to obtain the connection type, and also to let the user know if the network is available and connected:

```
ConnectivityManager cm = (ConnectivityManager) getSystemService(Context.CONNECTIVITY_
SERVICE);
NetworkInfo netInfo = cm.getActiveNetworkInfo();

if (netInfo.getTypeName().equalsIgnoreCase("WIFI")) {
    // Wifi connectivity
}
```

```
if (netInfo.getTypeName().equalsIgnoreCase("MOBILE")) {
    // Mobile data connectivity
}
if (netInfo.isAvailable()) {
    // Network is available
}
if (netInfo.isConnected()) {
    // Network is connected
}
```

Obtaining the connection type is achieved by using the *getActiveNetworkInfo* method to populate a *NetworkInfo* object.

The connection status is obtained by using the *isAvailable* and *isConnected* methods. To understand what these terms mean, let's take a look at the definitions.

▓   *Available* means connectivity *is possible* and the radio is *turned on.*

▓   *Connected* means connectivity *exists* and you are able to *pass data.*

While helpful, you can see from these definitions that they do not guarantee that you are able to reach your server or even the wider Internet.

You will need to implement the equivalent of a *ping test* to know if your network destination is actually reachable. But before you do that, let's review another important method for connectivity status: the WiFi *BroadcastReceiver.*

WiFi Broadcast Receiver

Another powerful construct for determining connectivity status in Android is the *BroadcastReceiver* class. The *onReceive* method of the *BroadcastReceiver* will be called each time there is a change in the WiFi state. The following code shows a basic implementation:

```
BroadcastReceiver wifiStatusReceiver = new BroadcastReceiver() {
    @Override
    public void onReceive(Context context, Intent intent) {);
        SupplicantState supState;
        WifiManager wifiManager = (WifiManager) getSystemService(Context.WIFI_SERVICE);
        WifiInfo wifiInfo = wifiManager.getConnectionInfo();
        supState = wifiInfo.getSupplicantState();
        if (supState.equals(SupplicantState.COMPLETED)) {
            // wifi is connected
        } else if (supState.equals(SupplicantState.SCANNING)) {
            // no wifi is available, but scanning is in progress
        } else if (supState.equals(SupplicantState.DISCONNECTED)) {
            // wifi not connected
        }
    }
};
```

Each time you implement a *BroadcastReceiver*, you need to register it in the *onResume* method of your app and unregister it in the *onPause* method, as follows:

```
@Override
protected void onResume() {
    super.onResume();
    IntentFilter filter = new IntentFilter(WifiManager.SUPPLICANT_STATE_CHANGED_ACTION);
    this.registerReceiver(wifiStatusReceiver, filter);
}
@Override
public void onPause() {
    this.unregisterReceiver(wifiStatusReceiver);
    super.onPause();
}
```

You will be using each of these APIs later in the Connections project to give the user a look at the device's connectivity state.

2.6   Server Reachability

You saw in the previous example how using the *ConnectivityManager* makes it easy for you to determine if your device has connectivity. However, you need to do additional work to determine if your server is reachable.

Determining reachability is important because if your server is not reachable, you will likely be forced to provide your users a degraded user experience, and you should notify them of this condition while it exists.

Pinging a server is the approach you would typically take in an operating system to see if a server or IP address is reachable. Android, of course, runs Linux. However, the Linux ping function is not available unless the device is rooted. This is not something you can expect from your users, so you need to look for alternative methods to implement the ping test.

There are two approaches you can use to implement a ping in Android. Recall from Figure 2-1 that there is a transport layer and a protocol layer. The two approaches will use different protocols on these two layers.

- Ping using ICMP (Internet Control Message Protocol) on layer 3. This will be implemented in Android using the Java *InetAddress* class.

- Ping using HTTP on layer 4. This will be implemented in Android using the Java *HttpClient* class. In the Splash app, you will use the recommended *HttpURLConnection* class to determine reachability.

These two protocols typically are assigned to specific ports on TCP/IP. HTTP resides on port 80, while ICMP resides typically on port 7.

Pinging with ICMP

ICMP is one of the main protocols of the Internet. It is used to send error messages and can also be used to relay query messages. The related Linux ping utility is implemented using the ICMP "Echo request" and "Echo reply" messages.

In the Java world, the *java.net* package contains the *InetAddress* class, which provides the *IsReachable* method you will use to implement a ping solution. This method can be invoked by host name or by host address.

If you have a known fixed IP address for your server, you can implement the ping directly using the IP address. This has the added advantage of bypassing any DNS (Domain Name System) lookups, which will improve performance by reducing overhead.

The *java.net.InetAddress.isReachable* call uses the ICMP "Echo request" command and falls back to TCP "Echo request" both on port 7. The method accepts a timeout and returns either a Boolean or throws an *IOException*.

Pinging IP addresses using ICMP with the *.isReachable* method is accomplished with the following code. The Android implementation shown here occurs inside an *AsyncTask*, which is recommended for long running networking tasks.

You will see this example implemented in the Connections app.

```
public class PingIP extends AsyncTask<. . .>{
public PingIP(String ip, int i) {
    ip1 = ip;
    in1 = null;
    item = i;
    code = false;
}
protected Integer doInBackground(Void...params) {
    try {
        in1 = InetAddress.getByName(ip1);
    } catch (Exception e) {
        code = false;
    }
    try {
        if (in1.isReachable(timeoutReachable)) {
            code = true;
        } else {
            code = false;
        }
    } catch (Exception e) {
        code = false;
    }
return 1;
}
```

Note that a timeout parameter is included with the call to the *.isReachable* method. The timeout value units are milliseconds. The *.isReachable* method is invoked on the IP address, which is set up using the *InetAddress.getByName* method.

Pinging a server using this approach occurs at the transport layer (layer 3) and is a lower level approach than using a layer 4 protocol such as HTTP, which I will discuss next.

The main issue with relying on a lower level protocol like ICMP is that it may be blocked by routers between your source and destination points. Unless you have a deterministic path to your network destination, using ICMP for reachability testing will likely not be a reliable approach.

Pinging with HTTP

HTTP is the main protocol of the Internet and you can use it to implement a ping function in Android.

The following code block shows how to implement a ping using the Android *HttpURLConnection* class running inside *AsyncTask*. The *AsyncTask* is again used so you can perform the network operation on a background thread.

```
public class PingHTTP extends AsyncTask<. . .> {
public PingHTTP(String ip) {
    boolean pinged = false;
    int response = -1;
    ip1 = ip;
}
protected Boolean doInBackground(Void...params) {
    URL url = new URL(urlString);
    URLConnection conn = url.openConnection();

    HttpURLConnection httpConn = (HttpURLConnection) conn;
    httpConn.setAllowUserInteraction(false);
    httpConn.setInstanceFollowRedirects(true);
    httpConn.setRequestMethod("GET");
    httpConn.connect();
    try {
        response = httpConn.getResponseCode();
        if (response == HttpURLConnection.HTTP_OK) {
            pipnged = true;
        }
    } catch (Exception e) {
        // Handle exception
        Pinged = false;
    }
Return pinged;
}
```

Pinging the server is as simple as performing the following steps:

1. Setting up the URL to the IP address, which can be a name or be represented in octet dot notation.

2. Setting up the *Get* request.

3. Executing it on the *httpURLConnection* object.

Using this approach, you can simply check the return response status code to know what has happened to the request.

This method is efficient "over the wire" because you do not have to download the webpage body content to see the response status code. HTTP has many response status codes that can tell you if your server is reachable, and if not, why it was not reachable.

HTTP Status Codes

Table 2-3 shows the valid HTTP response codes. There are many response codes that cover a large set of circumstances. Normally, you are looking for a response code of 200 to indicate that the response was received correctly. 300, 400, and 500 level response codes indicate a variety of delivery failure scenarios.

Table 2-3. HTTP Response Codes

Status Code	HTTP Response Code Reason
100	Continue
2xx	Success
200	OK
201	Created
202	Accepted
203	Non-Authoritative Information
204	No Content
3xx	Redirection
300	Multiple Choices
301	Moved Permanently
302	Found
303	See Other (since HTTP/1.1)
4xx	Client Error
400	Bad Request
401	Unauthorized
402	Payment Required
403	Forbidden
404	Not Found
405	Method Not Allowed
406	Not Acceptable
5xx	Server Error
500	Internal Server Error
501	Not Implemented
502	Bad Gateway
503	Service Unavailable
504	Gateway Timeout
505	HTTP Version Not Supported

Using HTTP as a ping approach seems simple enough. But does a response code of 200, as shown in the following code, really indicate that your server is reachable?

```
(httpResponse.getStatusLine().getStatusCode() == 200)
```

Unfortunately, it does not. You are going to need a more robust solution to determine reachability.

Blocked Protocols and URL Redirects

You saw that ICMP has some good low-level messaging capabilities to determine if a server is reachable. However, the issue with ICMP is that you can't rely on the protocol to be available throughout the network because, unlike HTTP, ICMP is often blocked by service providers.

HTTP also has a fatal flaw: the URL redirect situation. When you connect your devices to public WiFi, you may often be behind a firewall or connected to a wireless access point that requires a login to gain network access. This is often the case at coffee shops or public places such as airports. In such situations, until you successfully authenticate, almost any HTTP request you send will receive a response code of 200, even though you are certainly not able to send packets beyond the internal router control point.

Service providers who require authentication before connectivity redirect the HTTP requests to a local page yet still return a response code of 200. In this scenario, the HTTP response header should indicate that the request was redirected, but this is often not correctly flagged. So, you have no way of knowing that you do not have a reachable destination just by checking the response code.

In addition to incomplete or incorrect redirect flags in the HTTP header, URL redirects do not work across protocols. HTTP and HTTPS are considered different protocols, so if your HTTP request is forwarded to HTTPS, any redirect flags will be lost.

Given these complications with ICMP and HTTP approaches, how do you know if a server is really reachable?

The Android source code provides the solution. Figure 2-3 shows a message in the notification bar that you may have seen many times on your Android device.

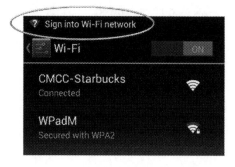

Figure 2-3. Android WiFi detection

The Android Open Source Project contains code for the WiFi State Machine. It provides this indication for you when you are behind a firewall or access point and must authenticate before you have network connectivity.

But how does it know this condition given the issues you saw with ICMP and a false HTTP response code 200? If you look at the Android source code, you will see that the following HTTP request is being sent to determine if you have reachability:

▓ `http://connectivitycheck.gstatic.com/generate_204`

This script generates a HTTP response code of 204, which indicates "NO CONTENT". If a 204 is received, you know the server was reachable. If a 200 is received, you know the server is not reachable and that a URL redirect has occurred.

Generating 204 Responses

A generate 204 script is very easy to implement on a server. The simple PHP code follows. It is just as easily implemented in any server-side scripting language.

```
<?php
http_response_code(204);
?>
```

Using this approach, determining if you have network connectivity becomes a simple two-step process:

1. Hit a known server page that generates a 204 return code with no content.

2. Check for return status code = 204.

If you have a match for the response code = 204, you know that your server is reachable and you have full connectivity.

You can make use of the google *generate_204* pages, like the Android system does, or place your own script onto your server.

2.7   Connections App

The Connections app will put all of the previous concepts together to create a useful tool that will allow you to monitor the connected status of your device and the reachability status of a list of servers that you can specify in a configuration file.

Connections App Overview

Figure 2-4 shows a screenshot of the Connections app. It includes three informational sections that are populated based on the connectivity status of the device.

- Update Status: The app implements a timer that specifies the update interval for the reachability test. The current device time and the last refresh time are displayed. The default update status interval is 10 seconds (10,000 milliseconds).

- Connection Status: The device connection status is displayed, including connection type, network available, connected, and WiFi broadcast receiver status.

- Reachability: The app processes a list of server destinations and tests them for reachability using either the ICMP or HTTP ping method.

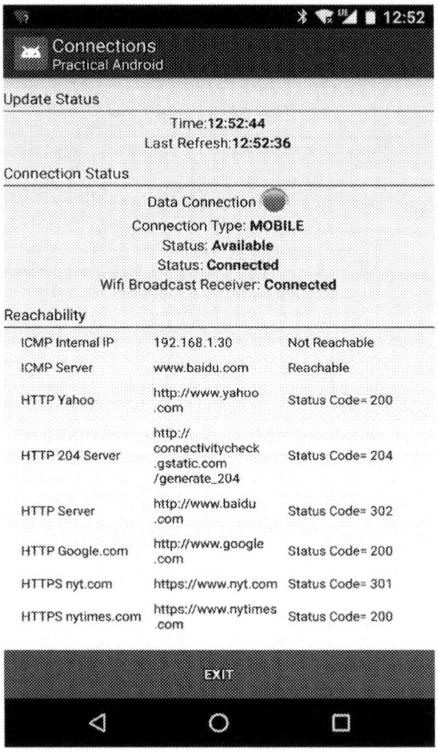

Figure 2-4. *Connections app screenshot*

Connections Project

Table 2-4 displays the project structure of the app. The app consists of a single Java file and a single XML layout file. All of the code is contained within *MainActivity.java*.

Table 2-4. Connections Project Setup

Sources	Resources/layout	Resources/raw
MainActivity.java	main.xml	connectionfile.txt

The layout file for the screen is contained in *main.xml*. Note that the reachability section is built dynamically based upon the configuration file contents. This way, you don't need to make modifications to this file if you change the server reachability list.

The app requires the following permissions in the manifest file, which are typical for a networking app with local storage access required to read a configuration file:

```
<uses-permission android:name="android.permission.INTERNET"/>
<uses-permission android:name="android.permission.ACCESS_NETWORK_STATE"/>
<uses-permission android:name="android.permission.WRITE_EXTERNAL_STORAGE"/>
<uses-permission android:name="android.permission.ACCESS_WIFI_STATE"/>
<uses-permission android:name="android.permission.CHANGE_CONFIGURATION"/>
```

Connections App Configuration

The app has a main timer named *updateInterval*, which is set at 10,000 milliseconds (10 seconds), which controls the refresh cycle of the app. Each time it expires, all of the connections that are being tested for reachability will be reset and tested again.

The *timeoutConnection* and *timeoutSocket* are used by the HTTP reachability test, while the *timeoutReachable* is used by the ICMP reachability test. These timers are set at 5 seconds. The values can be adjusted depending on how frequently you want screen updates and how long you want to wait for server responses. It is generally a good idea to keep the screen updates at 2x the connection and socket timeout values.

A summary of the default timer values that are set internally in the code:

```
private static int timeoutConnection = 5000;
private static int timeoutSocket = 5000;
private static Integer timeoutReachable = 5000;
private static Integer updateInterval = 10000;
```

Aside from these timeout values, the most important configurable parameters in the app are the server addresses that you would like to test for reachability. In order to provide a flexible and expandable architecture, you will use a JSON configuration file to store the server list information. Using this approach means you can easily make changes to the server list without modifying the app source code.

Each connection contains the following four fields, which can be set or updated by modifying the *connectionfile.txt* text file. The *connectionfile.txt* file is stored internally in the app *Resources/raw* folder. This file could easily be moved out of the app onto the SD card, or even downloaded externally over the network.

- "type": The type of ping used to test for reachability. Two ping types are supported in the app: *AndroidHttpClient* and ICMP *Inet.isReachable*. A "0" value indicates ICMP and a "1" value indicates HTTP. This could easily be expanded to include more types, such as *OKHttp*, *HttpURLConnection*, or even *ApacheHttpClient*.

- "name": The name of the server, which is displayed along with the results in the reachability section of the app user interface view.

- "url": The URL of the server that will be tested for reachability.

- "res": The response code or result from the ping test. This field should be left blank in the JSON file, but will be displayed in the app user interface view when ping results become available.

The following code block shows a complete JSON configuration file for the app:

```
[
    [{"type":0},{"name":"ICMP Internal IP"},{"url":"192.168.1.30"},{"res":""}],
    [{"type":0},{"name":"ICMP Server"},{"url":"www.baidu.com"},{"res":""}],
    [{"type":1},{"name":"HTTP Yahoo"},{"url":"http://www.yahoo.com"},{"res":""}],
    [{"type":1},{"name":"HTTP 204 Server"},{"url":"http://connectivitycheck.gstatic.com/
                                         generate_204"},{"res":""}],
    [{"type":1},{"name":"HTTP Server"},{"url":"http://www.baidu.com"},{"res":""}],
    [{"type":1},{"name":"HTTP Google.com"},{"url":"http://www.google.com" },{"res":""}],
    [{"type":1},{"name":"HTTPS nyt.com"},{"url":"https://www.nyt.com"},{"res":""}],
    [{"type":1},{"name":"HTTPS nytimes.com"},{"url":"https://www.nytimes.com"},{"res":""}]
]
```

The JSON configuration file will be read in and parsed by *MainActivity.java*. Android *ArrayLists* will be used to store the information when the JSON file is parsed.

MainActivity.java

When the app is launched, the first thing you need to accomplish is to read in the configuration file and parse the JSON into *ArrayLists* that will be used to perform the reachability testing.

The following code demonstrates how to accomplish this. The four *ArrayLists* are defined, the JSON file is read into a string called *connectionFileTxt*, and finally the four *ArrayLists* are built inside the *for()* loop. The *jsonGetter2* function is a JSON helper function that was covered in the first chapter.

```
// Array List Definition:
//
// pingType (int) 0=isReachable 1=httpclient
// connName (Str) Name of the connection to test
```

```
// connURL  (Str) URL or IP address of the connection
// Response (Str) Response back from ICMP or HTTP

ArrayList<Integer> pingType = new ArrayList<Integer>();
ArrayList<String>  connName = new ArrayList<String>();
ArrayList<String>  connURL  = new ArrayList<String>();
ArrayList<String>  response = new ArrayList<String>();

private static JSONArray connectionFileJson = null;
private static String connectionFileTxt = "";
// Read in the JSON file
Resources res = getResources();
InputStream in_s = res.openRawResource(R.raw.connectionfile);
byte[] b = new byte[in_s.available()];
in_s.read(b);
connectionFileTxt = (new String(b));

// build the Array lists
connectionFileJson = new JSONArray(connectionFileTxt);
for(int i=0; i<connectionFileJson.length(); i++){
    int type = (Integer) jsonGetter2(connectionFileJson.getJSONArray(i),"pingType");
    pingType.add(type);
    String cname = jsonGetter2(connectionFileJson.getJSONArray(i),"connName").toString();
    connName.add(cname);
    String url = jsonGetter2(connectionFileJson.getJSONArray(i),"connURL").toString();
    connURL.add(url);
    String resp = jsonGetter2(connectionFileJson.getJSONArray(i),"response").toString();
    response.add(resp);
}
```

With the four *ArrayLists* set up, the app starts a periodic timer and then begins to display device connectivity status and server reachability status. The "Update Status" section of the app is continuously updated with the timer status so you can see when the last refresh occurred.

The "Connectivity Status" section of the user interface is refreshed each time the timer is reset. As you saw earlier, the Android *ConnectivityManager* supplies all of the information for you. It displays a green or red icon depending on if connectivity exists. You are showing the connectivity type as either "WiFi" or "Mobile Data," and according to the *ConnectivityManager*, you are also showing the "Connect" and "Available" status.

Finally, if WiFi is enabled on the device, the *BroadcastReceiver* displays the latest status. This update does not rely on the timer, but rather is updated in real time whenever the *BroadcastReceiver onReceive* is sent an update by the system.

The "Reachability" section of the user interface is also updated each time the timer is reset. The main loop for handling the server pings is found in *updateConnectionStatus()*. The following code block shows the key code that takes care of updating the WiFi status and performing the pings and updating the results.

The view on the user interface is created dynamically. If you wish to see the entire code for how the layouts are built, refer to the project code because the code block below shows only the connectivity aspects in the main loop.

A simple *if* statement is used to determine which type of ping will be utilized for each of the servers in the list. Note that the *AsyncTask.THREAD_POOL_EXECUTOR* is used so that the network ping background tasks can all run concurrently.

```java
private void updateConnectionStatus() {

    // update the wi-fi status
    img = (ImageView) findViewById(R.id.image1);
    img.setBackgroundResource(R.drawable.presence_invisible);
    if (checkInternetConnection()) {
        img.setBackgroundResource(R.drawable.presence_online);
    } else {
        img.setBackgroundResource(R.drawable.presence_busy);
    }

    // See the project files for full code of the following 4 sections
    // Grab the LinearLayout where we will dynamically add LL for the ping Work List
    // Set a LayoutParams for the new Layouts we will add for the ping Work List items status
    // LayoutParams for the TextViews
    // Setup a screen proportional font size

    // Loop through the work list, fire off a ping for each item based on the Type
    for(int i=0; i<pingType.size(); i++){
        if (pingType.get(i) == 0) {
            // send the ping with ICMP
            new PingICMP(connURL.get(i),i).executeOnExecutor(AsyncTask.THREAD_POOL_EXECUTOR);
        }
        if (pingType.get(i) == 1) {
            // send the ping with Http
            new PingHTTP(connURL.get(i),i).executeOnExecutor(AsyncTask.THREAD_POOL_EXECUTOR);
        }
    }

    // update the refresh time
    TextView textRefr = (TextView) findViewById(R.id.textUpdate);
    textRefr.setText(GetTime());
}
```

The code block for the *PingICMP* routine is shown next. A new *AsyncTask* will be started each time a server with *pingType* = 0 is encountered. Note that the *Inet.isReachable* method is used. The *AsyncTask* includes an *onPostExecute* method that gets called when the *AsyncTask* completes. At this point, the user interface will be updated with the proper color-coded result for the ping test. With ICMP there is no response code, so you can just indicate whether the server was reachable or not reachable.

```java
// check for connectivity using ICMP
public class PingICMP extends AsyncTask<Void, String, Integer> {
    private String ip1;
    private boolean code;
```

```
        private int item;
        private InetAddress in1;

        public PingIP(String ip, int i) {
            ip1 = ip;
            in1 = null;
            item = i;
            code = false;
        }
        protected void onPreExecute(Void ...params) {
        }
        protected Integer doInBackground(Void ...params) {
            try {
                in1 = InetAddress.getByName(ip1);
            } catch (Exception e) {
                code = false;
            }
            try {
                if (in1.isReachable(timeoutReachable)) {
                    code = true;
                } else {
                    code = false;
                }
            } catch (Exception e) {
                code = false;
            }
            return 1;
        }
        protected void onProgressUpdate(String msg) {
        }
        protected void onPostExecute(Integer result) {
            if (code) {
                pingTextView[item][2].setText("Reachable");
                pingTextView[item][2].setTextColor(Color.parseColor(textColor[0])); // green
            } else {
                pingTextView[item][2].setText("Not Reachable");
                pingTextView[item][2].setTextColor(Color.parseColor(textColor[1])); // red
            }
        }
    }
}
```

The code block for the *pingHTTP* routine is shown next. A new *AsyncTask* will be started each time a server with *pingType* = 1 is encountered. Note that in this case, you are setting up the HTTP Get request and the *AsyncTask onPostExecute* method uses the HTTP response code to determine the reachability result. If the response code = 200 or the response code = 204, you will mark the results in green text (success). All other response codes will be presented in red text (not reachable).

```
// check for connectivity using HTTP
private class pingHTTP extends AsyncTask<Void, String, Integer> {
    private String urlString;
    private boolean ping_success;
```

```
    private int item;
    private int status;

    private pingHTTP(String ip, int i) {
      ping_success = false;
      item = i;
      urlString = ip;
    }
    protected void onPreExecute(Void ...params) { }
    protected Integer doInBackground(Void ...params) {
      try {
        URL url = new URL(urlString);
        HttpURLConnection httpConn = (HttpURLConnection) url.openConnection();
        httpConn.setAllowUserInteraction(false);
        httpConn.setInstanceFollowRedirects(true);
        httpConn.setRequestMethod("GET");
        httpConn.connect();
        status = httpConn.getResponseCode();
        // Check for successful status code = 200 or 204
        if ((status == HttpURLConnection.HTTP_OK) || (status == HttpURLConnection.HTTP_NO_
        CONTENT)) ping_success = true;
      } catch (Exception e) {
        // Handle exception
        ping_success = false;
      }
      return 1;
    }
  protected void onProgressUpdate(String msg) { }
  protected void onPostExecute(Integer result) {
    if (ping_success) {
      pingTextView[item][2].setText("Status Code= " + status);
      pingTextView[item][2].setTextColor(Color.parseColor(textColor[0])); // green
    } else {
      pingTextView[item][2].setText("Status Code= " + status);
      pingTextView[item][2].setTextColor(Color.parseColor(textColor[1])); // red
    }
  }
 }
}
```

Interpreting Reachability Results

The Connections app is a useful tool to understand how to best manage connectivity in your apps.

If you wish to understand how available ICMP is as a protocol in your network locality, you can set up a server list and test each of them for connectivity using *pingType* = 0. You may find that ICMP is more often available over mobile data access than WiFi. You might also determine that ICMP is almost never available over commercial WiFi services such as at coffee shops and airports.

Figure 2-5 shows typical results over a WiFi connection before authentication (left panel) and after authentication has been completed (right panel).

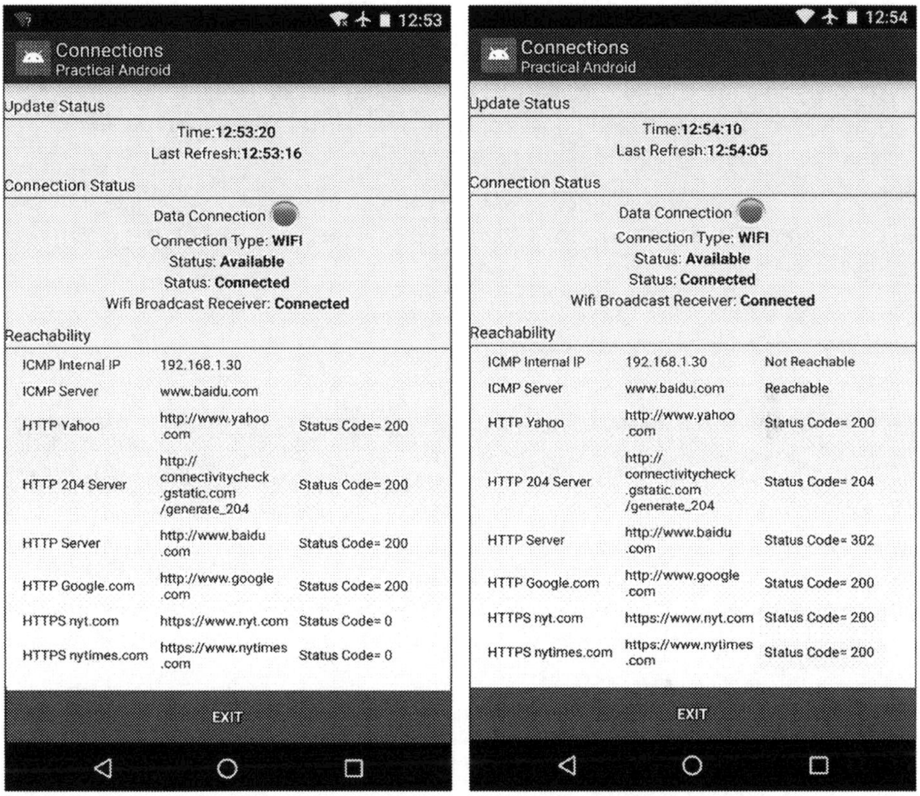

Figure 2-5. *Connection app left panel: WiFi connectivity with no reachability (response code = 200 when 204 was expected). Right panel: WiFi connectivity with reachability (response code = 204).*

Look specifically at the fourth entry using *pingType* = 1 (HTTP) and hitting a server with a *generate_204* script. Before authentication is complete, you can see that the response code was 200, which means the server was not reached, but rather instead a WiFi redirect has taken place. On the right panel, after authentication is complete, you can see a response code of 204, which indicates that the server was successfully reached.

2.8   Splash App

Now that you know how to determine if a server is reachable, let's put together the pieces and implement a splash screen.

Splash App Overview

Splash screens are initial displays, usually graphical, that appear temporarily when an app first launches. Splash screens can serve dual purposes:

- Provide an initial welcome or branding message for an app.

- Allow you a short time, usually just a few seconds, to take care of some background tasks that the app requires, such as downloading required content or setting up the app's resources.

Typically while the splash screen is displayed, a progress indicator is provided, which gives the user some idea about how long the splash will be displayed before the main app functionality is available.

Figure 2-6 shows a screenshot of the Splash app, which includes the startup splash screen activity and the secondary main activity.

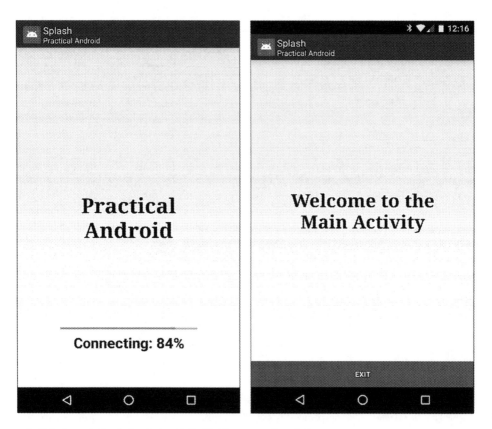

Figure 2-6. Splash app left panel: splash activity. Right panel: main activity.

While the splash screen is displayed, a large file is downloaded from the server. The progress of this download is shown via a progress bar using the Android *ProgressBar* widget and a *TextView* object, which together indicate the percentage of the download that has been completed.

Once the download has been fully completed, the splash screen is replaced by a new screen, which displays "Welcome to the Main Activity."

Splash Project

Table 2-5 shows the structure of the project.

Table 2-5. Splash Project Setup

Sources	Resources	Libraries
SplashActivity.java	splash.xml	
MainActivity.java	main.xml	

There are two activities, one for the splash screen and the second to handle the main activity, which is executed after the splash operation completes. Each of the activities has a layout XML file. No external libraries are used in this project.

In this app, you use the *HttpURLConnection* class to handle the network downloading of the large file while the splash screen is displayed.

Splash.xml

The layout of the splash screen is defined in the *splash.xml* file, as shown:

```
<?xml version="1.0" encoding="utf-8"?>
<RelativeLayout xmlns:android="http://schemas.android.com/apk/res/android"
    xmlns:tools="http://schemas.android.com/tools"
    android:id="@+id/relLayout"
    android:layout_width="fill_parent"
    android:layout_height="fill_parent">

    <TextView
        android:id="@+id/title"
        android:layout_width="wrap_content"
        android:layout_height="wrap_content"
        android:layout_centerInParent="true"
        android:text="Android Software Development"
        android:textColor="#111111"
        android:textSize="34sp"
        android:layout_gravity="center"
        android:gravity="center"
        android:layout_margin="40.0dip"
        android:textStyle="bold"
        android:typeface="serif" />"
```

```
<ProgressBar
    android:id="@+id/progBar"
    style="?android:attr/progressBarStyleHorizontal"
    android:layout_width="fill_parent"
    android:layout_height="wrap_content"
    android:layout_alignParentBottom="true"
    android:layout_gravity="center"
    android:layout_marginBottom="100.0dip"
    android:layout_marginLeft="50.0dip"
    android:layout_marginRight="50.0dip"
    android:focusable="false"
    android:maxHeight="20dip"
    android:minHeight="20dip"
    android:paddingLeft="28dp"
    android:paddingRight="28dp" />

<TextView
    android:id="@+id/text"
    android:layout_width="wrap_content"
    android:layout_height="wrap_content"
    android:layout_alignParentBottom="true"
    android:layout_centerHorizontal="true"
    android:layout_marginBottom="65.0dip"
    android:text="Connecting"
    android:textColor="#111111"
    android:textSize="24sp"
    android:textStyle="bold"
    android:typeface="sans" />

</RelativeLayout>
```

You are using a *RelativeLayout*, which allows you to more easily provide a centered layout for the elements of the splash screen. The splash screen consists of three elements:

- The text displayed during the network operation is defined in the *TextView*. This could just as easily be an *ImageView* if you wanted to show a graphic image.

- A progress bar to display the completion status of the download. This element is aligned to the bottom of the screen using the *layout_alignParentBottom* attribute.

- A text view to display the message "Connecting:" followed by a numerical representation of the percentage of the download that has been completed. This element is also aligned to the bottom of the screen, placed just below the progress bar using the *layout_marginBottom* attribute.

The splash screen layout is used to display the splash screen inside the splash activity. It is displayed immediately when the app is started by the *onCreate* method of *SplashActivity.java*.

SplashActivity.java

SplashActivity displays the splash screen and then performs a network download of a file in the background. During the download, the progress is updated on the splash screen.

The file *english-proper-names.txt* will be downloaded from the server and its URL will be stored in the string variable named *getURL*.

In this example, you are going to check if your server is reachable before you start the download. The URL of the *generate204* script is stored in the string variable named *ip204*.

Additionally, *connection* and *read* timeout values are set for the HTTP operation.

When the activity first starts, there is a simple check to see if your device has a network connection. If the check passes, the HTTP download proceeds; otherwise, a message is displayed and the user is forced to exit the app and resolve the device connection issue.

```java
public class SplashActivity extends Activity {
    int i;
    String getURL = "http://www.yourserver.com/ARH/english-proper-names.txt";
    String ip204 = "http://www.yourserver.com/return204.php";
    public static int ConnectTimeout = 10000;
    public static int ReadTimeout = 10000;

    @Override
    public void onCreate(Bundle savedInstanceState) {
        super.onCreate(savedInstanceState);
        getWindow().setFlags(
            WindowManager.LayoutParams.FLAG_FULLSCREEN,
            WindowManager.LayoutParams.FLAG_FULLSCREEN);
        this.setContentView(R.layout.splash);
        if (haveNetworkConnection()) {
            new HttpDownload().execute();
        }
        else {
            noConnection();
        }
    }
}
```

Note that because this is a splash screen, you are setting the flags for *LayoutParams. FLAG_FULLSCREEN* on the window. This allows the notification bar and the title bar to be hidden for the splash screen; they would normally be present at the top of the screen. The *MainActivity* does not set this flag, so the notification bar and title bar will reappear after the splash activity completes and control is handed off to the *MainActivity*.

The HTTP download of the file is handled in Android *AsyncTask*. Within the *AsyncTask* you are following a two-step process:

1. Connect to the server and check for a 204 response using the *setRequestMethod("HEAD");*.

2. Open a connection to the server and retrieve the file using the *OpenHttpConnection(getURL);*.

Once the file download is started, the progress bar on the splash screen is updated each time a buffer is read from the server.

The following code block shows how the *HttpDownload* is implemented:

```
public class HttpDownload extends AsyncTask<Void, String, Void> {
    @Override
    protected Void doInBackground(Void... unused) {
        publishProgress("Connecting","0");
        String fromServer = "";
        int BUFFER_SIZE = 2000;
        float fsize = 890000;
        InputStream in = null;
        try {
            // Check for reachability
            URL url = new URL(ip204);
            HttpURLConnection conn = (HttpURLConnection) url.openConnection();
            conn.setConnectTimeout(ConnectTimeout);
            conn.setReadTimeout(ReadTimeout);
            conn.setRequestMethod("HEAD");
            in = conn.getInputStream();
            int status = conn.getResponseCode();
            in.close();
            conn.disconnect();
            if (status == HttpURLConnection.HTTP_NO_CONTENT) {
                // Server is reachable, so initiate the download
                publishProgress("Reachable", "0");
                in = OpenHttpConnection(getURL);
                InputStreamReader isr = new InputStreamReader(in);
                int charRead;
                char[] inputBuffer = new char[BUFFER_SIZE];
                while ((charRead = isr.read(inputBuffer))>0) {
                    //---convert the chars to a String---
                    String readString = String.copyValueOf(inputBuffer, 0, charRead);
                    fromServer += readString;
                    inputBuffer = new char[BUFFER_SIZE];
                    //---update the progress
                    float ratio = (fromServer.length() / fsize) * 100;
                    int num = (int) ratio;
                    publishProgress("Connecting: " + String.valueOf(num) + "%",
                                                    String.valueOf(num));
                }
                in.close();
            } else {
                publishProgress("Not Reachable", "0");
                failedReach();
            }
        } catch (IOException e) {
            failedDownload();
        }
        publishProgress("Completed","100");
        return null;
    }
}
```

Note that there are three separate failure cases that will result in a pop-up dialog being displayed on the device when the conditions occur. When this happens, the user will be forced to exit the app and correct the problem.

- Failure Case 1: *noConnection()* indicates that the device has no connectivity.

- Failure Case 2: *failedReach()* indicates that the server was not reachable.

- Failure Case 3: *failedDownload()* indicates that the download failed before it could be completed.

The Splash app uses the recommended HTTP stack, *HttpURLConnection*. The following code block shows how this connection is set up. The HTTP *GET* method is used to retrieve the network file requested. This is slightly different from the reachability check where you used the HTTP *HEAD* method to check for a 204 response code in the header without downloading the file contents.

```
public static InputStream OpenHttpConnection(String urlString) throws IOException {
    InputStream in = null;
    int response = -1;
    URL url = new URL(urlString);
    URLConnection conn = url.openConnection();
    if (!(conn instanceof HttpURLConnection)) throw new IOException("Not an HTTP connection");
    try {
        HttpURLConnection httpConn = (HttpURLConnection) conn;
        httpConn.setAllowUserInteraction(false);
        httpConn.setInstanceFollowRedirects(true);
        httpConn.setRequestMethod("GET");
        httpConn.connect();
        response = httpConn.getResponseCode();
        if (response == HttpURLConnection.HTTP_OK) {
            in = httpConn.getInputStream();
        }
    } catch (Exception ex) {
        throw new IOException("Error connecting");
    }
    return in;
}
```

Perhaps the most important function of the splash activity is to update the user of the download progress. To accomplish this, you are going to use the *onProgressUpdate* method of the *AsyncTask* that is performing the download. This method takes an array of strings as its argument. The following two values are passed into the method for updates back to the user on the splash screen:

- *Item[0]*: A string that will be displayed in the *TextView* so you can keep the user informed about what is happening. This will be updated, for instance, when the download is started, completed, in progress, if the server is not reachable, or if the download fails.

▦ *Item[1]*: An integer that represents the percentage of the download that has been completed. This value is set to "0" before the download starts and "100" when the download is complete. It is calculated and updated during the downloading of the file.

The following code shows how the *onProgressUpdate* method is implemented using these two values:

```
@Override
protected void onProgressUpdate(String... item) {
    TextView txt = (TextView) findViewById(R.id.text);
    txt.setText(item[0]);
    ProgressBar progressBar = (ProgressBar) findViewById(R.id.progBar);
    int num = Integer.parseInt(item[1]);
    progressBar.setProgress(num);
}
```

The calculation is performed by creating a ratio, which is defined as the total bytes downloaded divided by the total file size. The file is downloaded in 2,000 byte blocks and the total file size is fixed, as shown here:

```
int BUFFER_SIZE = 2000;
float fsize = 890000;
```

Typically in a splash screen, you have a fixed size of data you are downloading, so defining it in this way is acceptable.

However, if you need to download a file of unknown size, you can obtain the size of the file before you download it using the *Content- Length* attribute of the HTTP response header. If the *Content-Length* header is not present in the server reply, the only way to determine the size of the content on the server is to download it.

Two approaches for getting the file size from the server are as follows:

```
// Approach #1
URL myUrl = new URL("http://yourserver.com/file.mp3");
URLConnection urlConnection = myUrl.openConnection();
urlConnection.connect();
int file_size = urlConnection.getContentLength();

// Approach #2
URL myUrl = new URL("http://yourserver.com/file.mp3");
myConnection = myUrl.openConnection();
List headersize = myConnection.getHeaderFields().get("Content-Length");
```

2.9   Essential Tools

It can be difficult to debug network communications. HTTP is a robust protocol, and when things are not working properly, you need a way to analyze what is happening over the wire. This is when protocol analyzers become essential.

Wireshark is a very popular free network protocol analyzer. It lets you see what is happening on your network at a low level. Figure 2-7 shows a snapshot of the Wireshark interface.

Figure 2-7. Wireshark protocol analyzer

Wireshark is available for most platforms. It allows you to look at live traffic over the network, or to save traffic to files for offline analysis. Wireshark makes it easy to see HTTP traffic, including response codes coming back from the server.

If you have an app that submits HTTP form data to the server, Wireshark makes it easy to see the name/value pairs as they are sent over the wire.

2.10   References

Android HTTP and Connectivity

▓ Android HttpClient Removal: *http://developer.android.com/about/versions/marshmallow/android-6.0-changes.html*

▓ HttpURLConnection: *http://developer.android.com/reference/java/net/HttpURLConnection.html*

▓ Connectivity Manager: *http://developer.android.com/reference/android/net/ConnectivityManager.html*

▓ Determining and Monitoring Connection Status: *http://developer.android.com/training/monitoring-device-state/connectivity-monitoring.html*

ApacheHttpClient

▓ Configuring Apache Http Client for Android: *https://hc.apache.org/ httpcomponents-client-4.3.x/android-port.html*

OkHttp

▓ OkHttp for Java and Android Applications: *http://square.github.io/okhttp/*

▓ Okio library for OkHttp: *https://github.com/square/okio*

▓ OkHttp jar file: *https://square.github.io/okhttp/#download*

▓ OkHttp Recipes: *https://github.com/square/okhttp/wiki/Recipes*

▓ SPDY Chromium Project: `www.chromium.org/spdy`

Tools

Wire Shark: `www.wireshark.org/`

Chapter **3**

Lazy Loading Images

3.1   Introduction

Lazy loading images is a very common pattern in mobile application development. You may not be familiar with the term, but you will have certainly experienced it when navigating almost any app. It is implemented whenever images are displayed inside lists or other views that can be navigated with a "fling" motion.

"Lazy loading" describes the process of dynamically downloading and displaying images when a user scrolls down or across a sequence of images on the device screen.

The *ListView* is possibly the most commonly used widget in app development. When images are included within the *ListView*, it delivers a very powerful user experience.

Unfortunately, such a common and powerful pattern is not trivial to implement in Android. There is no built-in library to accomplish lazy loading, and there are many factors that must be considered, including threading, HTTP requests, memory management, and caching.

In this chapter, you will take a look at the lazy loading options available on the platform and you will implement a lazy loading app that combines the best features of the available approaches.

3.2   Chapter Projects

The chapter contains the project shown in Table 3-1.

Table 3-1. Chapter Projects

Title of Project	File Name	Description
Lazy Loading	*lazyloading.zip*	This project connects to the server and downloads a JSON configuration file that provides details for the images that will be lazy loaded into the app. The app supports three different views for the images: *ListView*, *GridView*, and *Gallery*.

© Mark Wickham 2018
M. Wickham, *Practical Android*, https://doi.org/10.1007/978-1-4842-3333-7_3

3.3   Lazy Loading Libraries

Despite the complexities of implementing lazy loading, the good news is that there are many good libraries that can make implementation much easier for you. There is no need to roll your own code. It is easy to integrate a lazy loading library, even if you never really dig into the code to understand how it works.

Table 3-2 shows a list of some of the popular third-party libraries available. All of the links for these libraries are included in the end-of-chapter references.

Table 3-2. Android Lazy Loading Library Comparison

Class	Features	License and Copyright
Lazy Loader	A basic functional implementation. Implements disc and memory cache. Lightweight; no JAR file.	MIT Fedor Vlasov
Volley	From Google. Automatic HTTP stack selection, thread pools, disc and memory caching, and JSON support. Support from Google is not great. JAR file.	Apache 2.0 Google
Picasso	From Square. Image downloading and caching. Supports debug indicators. Support for all types of content resources. Distributed as a JAR file. Library size is about 120Kb.	Apache 2.0 Square
Google Shelves	Open source Google project that handles image lazy loading. Disc and memory caching, supports bitmap shadows and rounded images. Not easy to extract the relevant code.	Apache 2.0 Google
Universal Image Loader	Supports multiple views: *ListView*, *GridView*, *Gallery*. Image load progress. Based on Lazy Loader. Library is approximately 193KB.	Apache 2.0 Sergey Tarasevich
Fresco	From Facebook. Uses *Drawee* as image placeholders. Excellent documentation, including Chinese. Feature-rich, including image rotation and persistent MYSQL storage. Large library size.	BSD Facebook
Glide	Focus on smooth scrolling. Used in many open source projects. Very similar to Picasso, but with a bitmap format that results in lower memory consumption. Library size is large at about 430KB.	Apache/BSD Bumptech
Android Query	Feature-rich: aspect ratio, rounded corners, anchors, callbacks, zooming. Supports AJAX callbacks. Library size is about 100KB.	Apache 2.0 Android Query
Image Catcher Class	Released as part of the Google IO 2015 app. The Image catcher class uses an external library called Disk LRU Cache. Library size is only about 20KB.	Apache 2.0 Jake Wharton

As you can see, many Android image loading libraries are available. The good news is that they are all pretty similar in how they implement lazy loading.

You will look at the common architecture they share next and then you will implement a lazy loading project using some of the best features found in these libraries.

3.4   Lazy Loading Architecture

The key feature of all lazy loading implementations is the ability to download and cache images to the device disk cache (SD flash memory) and the memory cache (RAM memory).

When the users scroll up and down on the *ListView*, the images need to be retrieved and displayed in the *ImageView* holder while they are on screen and subsequently removed when they are scrolled off-screen.

Figure 3-1 shows a high-level lazy loading architecture.

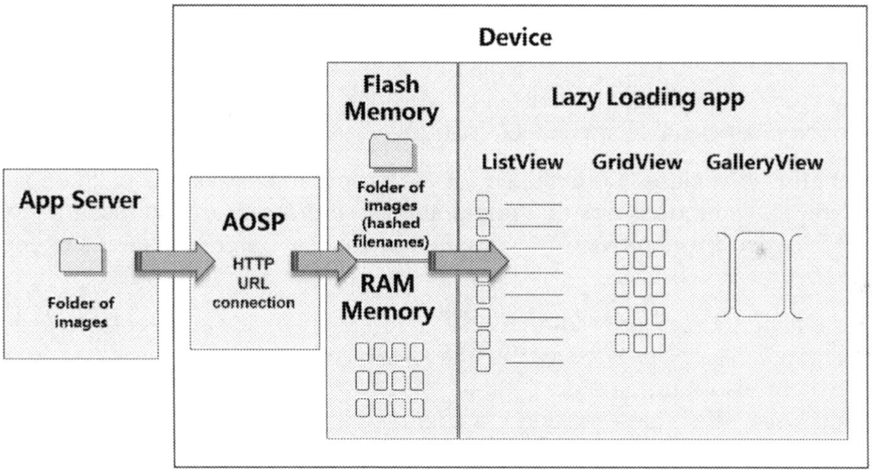

Figure 3-1. Lazy loading architecture

Some common characteristics for a lazy loading implementation are summarized below:

- ▨ An external app server contains the collection of images that will be initially loaded using HTTP.

- ▨ Each time an image is referenced by the app, there is a check to see whether it currently exists in disk cache or memory cache. If the image exists in one of the caches, it is loaded from cache.

- ▨ If the image does not exist in cache, the image is downloaded using HTTP, typically using a thread pool manager, which allows for multiple images to be downloaded simultaneously.

- Most of the lazy loading libraries support image downsampling. This allows for large images on the server to be reduced to a reasonable size for consumption by the app.

- After each image download has completed, the image is placed into disk and memory cache.

- The lazy loading code handles all of the disk and memory caching, as well as all view recycling when the user interacts with the UI. This helps to keep memory usage at a minimum, which is one of the key responsibilities of the lazy loading library.

- The memory cache is critical for a smooth user experience because it allows previously loaded images to be reloaded quickly.

- Some of the lazy loading libraries support advanced features such as touch-to-zoom, rounded corners, and debugging modes so you can see where images are being loaded from.

Memory Cache

The memory cache is important because it provides fast access to images. The tradeoff is that it also consumes valuable application memory.

The Android *LruCache* class is often used for the task of caching images. It keeps recently referenced images in a strong referenced *LinkedHashMap* and discards the least recently used (hence the acronym of LRU cache) members before the cache exceeds its designated size.

In older versions of Android, prior to Android 2.3 (API Level 9), it was popular to use a *SoftReference* or a *WeakReference* for the image caching. However, it is not recommended to use these methods today because the Java garbage collector is more aggressive with collecting soft/weak references, making the approach ineffective.

One of the key decisions in implementing the memory cache is choosing a suitable size for the *LruCache.*

According to the Android documentation, a number of factors should be taken into consideration:

- How memory intensive is the rest of your activity and/or application?

- How many images will be on-screen at once? How many need to be available to come on-screen?

- What is the screen size and density of the device?

- What resolutions are the images and how much memory will each take up?

- How frequently will the images be accessed?

In the chapter project you will set the memory cache at 25% of the device total memory. The code to accomplish this is shown next.

```
public class MemoryCache {
    private static final String TAG = "MemoryCache";
    private Map<String, Bitmap>
            cache=Collections.synchronizedMap(
            new LinkedHashMap<String, Bitmap>(10,1.5f,true));
    public MemoryCache() {
        //use 25% of available heap size
        setLimit(Runtime.getRuntime().maxMemory() / 4);
    }
}
```

This 25% decision is made based on the questions posed above. There is a total of 50 images and the average size of those images is about 70KB. No more than 5 images will be shown on the screen at one time, so 350KB will be the maximum RAM required to cache those images. Assuming most devices have 2MB available, 25% should give you plenty of overhead.

A cache that is too small is ineffective because it will result in excessive overhead. A cache that is too large can lead to out-of-memory exceptions because other applications and system services can become starved of the memory they require.

A memory cache speeds up access to recently viewed images. However, you can't always rely on images being available in the memory cache due to several reasons:

1. When users perform a fling option on a *ListView* or a *GridView*, it can result in a lot of images being loaded, which will result in the *LruCache* being filled up.

2. The application could be interrupted by another event, such as a phone call, and while your application is in the background, it could be destroyed.

3. The user may decide to place your app into the background by performing another operation on their device. When this occurs, the system may reclaim memory that had been allocated to your application.

For these reasons, a well-designed lazy load implementation needs to implement a disk cache as a fallback for the memory cache.

Disk Cache

A disk cache is needed for those cases when images are no longer available in a memory cache. Without the disk cache, you would need to go out to the network and perform another HTTP request to obtain the image.

Table 3-3 shows the approximate relative retrieve time required for images from the various sources.

Table 3-3. *Relative Lazy Load Retrieve Times*

Method	Approx. Retrieve Time (mSec.)
HTTP Network Request	300-1000
Device Disk Cache	100
Device Memory Cache	10

Because fetching images from a disk cache is relatively slow and these read operations are not time-deterministic, these operations should be performed in a background thread.

You will see in the Lazy Loading app that files stored in the disk cache are not exactly the same as the source files that were downloaded from the server. The files stored in the disk cache may be downsampled or compressed. This occurs when the original source files are determined to be too large based on a device-dependent setting you specify.

The filenames in the disk cache are also modified. If you inspect the files stored in the disk cache on your device, you will see unrecognizable filenames. These filenames are hash map keys that are generated from the original filenames.

You will examine the code that handles these transformations later in the Lazy Loading project.

3.5   Choosing a Library

Many of the lazy loading libraries are distributed as JAR files. Let's briefly discuss three such open source libraries available from the big players:

- Google Volley
- Square Picasso
- Facebook Fresco

These libraries are excellent choices if you are able to use libraries from these vendors. They are popular, very easy to integrate into your app, feature rich, well tested, and reasonably well supported (Picasso and Fresco more so than Volley).

Google Volley

Google originally announced the Volley library at Google I/O in 2013 in response to the trouble that many Android developers were having with networking and *AsyncTasks*. The Volley library has been popular.

To use Volley, follow these high-level steps:

1. Clone it on GitHub and build your own *volley.jar* file.

2. Include the *volley.jar* file as a library project within your Android project.

3. Use the classes such as *NetworkImageView*, *RequestQueue*, and *Request*.

One downside of Google Volley is that it is not easy to set up, is not well documented, and lacks support. However, it is popular, and once you have it set up, it is very simple to use. You simply add networking requests to a *RequestQueue* and Volley handles everything.

Volley provides an excellent way for you to transition away from *AsyncTasks* in your apps. The size of the *volley.jar* file is about 90KB.

Some of the key highlights of Google Volley:

▓ Volley has a custom view called *NetworkImageView* (subclassing *ImageView*) that makes it easy to load images. You can set the URL along with a default *ViewHolder*.

▓ Volley is a REST client that makes common networking tasks easy. It takes care of requesting, loading, caching, threading, and synchronization. You don't have to worry about async tasks or thread handling.

▓ Volley was designed for network operations that populate the UI. It is good for short operations, but not so good for large downloads, uploads, or streaming.

▓ Volley chooses the internal HTTP transport layer based on the device. It chooses *ApacheHttpClient* on Froyo and *HttpURLConnection* on Gingerbread and above. This is no longer such a critical benefit because so few devices are running Froyo and the *ApacheHttpClient* is being discontinued.

▓ Volley allows you to use external transports, such as *OKHttp*.

▓ Volley has built-in JSON to parse responses.

▓ Volley supports an extensive cancellation API, overcoming one of the pitfalls of implementing your own *AsyncTasks*.

Square Picasso

Square Inc. has a very nice lazy loading solution called Picasso. The library provides hassle-free image loading, disk and memory caching, and thread pools support.

To use Picasso in your apps, follow these high-level steps:

1. Download the JAR file from the Picasso site.

2. Install the JAR file into your IDE.

3. In Android Studio, you can add Picasso to the *build.gradle* file in the dependency section.

Once installed, lazy loading with the Picasso library can be accomplished with just one line of code.

```
Picasso.with(context).load("http://imagename.png").into(imageView);
```

Picasso is very easy to use and supports many advanced features. For example, loading a remote image into an *ImageView* while performing resizing, rotation, and supplying image placeholders during the download looks like this:

```
Picasso.with(this)
    .load("https://URL goes here")
    .resize(50,50)
    .into(imageView)
    .rotate(180)
    .placeholder(R.drawable.image_name)
    .error(R.drawable.image_name_error);
```

The key features of Picasso are the following:

- Supports image transformations so you can crop and resize images easily.

- Supports placeholder images with built-in retry (three times) before they are displayed.

- Includes a debug mode that displays flags on the corner of images. This allows you to see the image source such as network, disk, or memory.

- The Picasso library is distributed as a JAR file. The latest version is *picasso-2.5.2.jar*. The library size is 117KB.

- One of the key benefits of the Picasso library is that it supports all content sources: resources, assets, URLs, files, and content providers.

Facebook Fresco

Facebook introduced the open source Fresco library in March 2015 with the goal of allowing mobile devices to more efficiently manage images and eliminate out-of-memory crashes caused by the Java heap and the process of garbage collection.

According to Facebook, the Fresco library takes the existing libraries to a new level by using a new *Producer/Consumer* framework and a new type called *Drawee*. The Facebook approach is new and different. It is thus not as battle tested as the other libraries.

To use Fresco, follow these high-level steps:

1. In Android Studio or Gradle, just edit your *build.gradle* file to include the dependency for the latest version of *Fresco 0.9.0*.

2. In Eclipse, download the latest version of Fresco: *frescolib-v0.9.0.zip*. Then import the existing code into Android. Five projects should be added: *drawee*, *fbcore*, *fresco*, *imagepipeline*, and *imagepipeline-okhttp*.

Initializing Fresco is simple.

```
public void onCreate() {
    super.onCreate();
    Fresco.initialize(this);
}
```

You will need to add a custom name space in your XML as shown:

```
<LinearLayout
    xmlns:android="http://schemas.android.com/apk/res/android"
    xmlns:fresco="http://schemas.android.com/apk/res-auto"
    android:layout_height="match_parent"
    android:layout_width="match_parent">

    <com.facebook.drawee.view.SimpleDraweeView
        android:id="@+id/my_image_view"
        android:layout_width="130dp"
        android:layout_height="130dp"
        fresco:placeholderImage="@drawable/my_drawable" />
```

And finally, you can display images like this:

```
Uri uri = Uri.parse("https://path/fresco-logo.png");
SimpleDraweeView draweeView = (SimpleDraweeView) findViewById(R.id.my_image_view);
draweeView.setImageURI(uri);
```

One of the drawbacks of the Fresco library is that it is very large. Expect Fresco to add several MBs to your app's size. This is an order of magnitude larger than all the other lazy loading libraries.

Some of the key highlights of Facebook Fresco are as follows:

- Images are not stored in the Java heap, but instead in the *ashmem* heap. This is a memory region in Android that operates like the native heap, but has some additional system calls, including the ability to "unpin" the memory rather than freeing it.

- Progressive JPG images can be streamed, which means you don't have to wait for images to fully load before display.

- Images can be cropped at any point, not just in the center.

- JPG images can be resized natively.

- Supports GIF and WEBP animation.

If you do not wish to integrate one of these third-party libraries from the big vendors, the Universal Image Loader is an excellent alternative. It supports three different views: *ListView*, *GridView*, and *Gallery*.

In the Lazy Loading project, you will not use an external library. Instead, you will implement your own lazy loading class that implements memory and disk caching. You will see that this approach is very efficient as the entire project is only 45KB. Compare this with the popular lazy loading libraries discussed, which can be anywhere from 200KB up to more than 1MB in size.

3.6   Handling Image Assets

Working with images in Android can be tricky, especially if you are loading external images of unknown size. There are two important factors you need to consider:

- Image size
- Image aspect ratio

Attempting to load a large quantity of images can lead to out-of-memory exceptions, especially if your images sizes are large. When a user "flings" a *ListView*, this can result in dozens of image downloads.

If you have a deterministic set of images to be downloaded, you can ensure that they are properly compressed and sized for your Android app on the server. If you do not have this luxury, such as when you allow users to upload their own images or when you gather unknown images from the Internet, then you need to perform compression when you download to make sure you do not run into out-of-memory exceptions.

Images come in different aspect ratios. They are generally referred to as landscape or portrait. The special case is a square aspect ratio, which is less common. When lazy loading, it visually looks better in your layouts if you use a consistent aspect ratio for all the images. However, your image set is not always consistent, so you need to take this into consideration.

I will discuss some of the tools Android provides to compress images on the fly, and to display images consistently in your lazy load views if the aspect ratio of the images is mixed.

Size vs. Quality Tradeoff

In the Lazy Loading project you will be working with 50 images stored on a server. The original photos were of very high resolution.

Downloading such large images in a lazy load operation is certain to cause out-of-memory exceptions, even on the highest memory capacity devices available today. You need to prepare the images for the lazy load. Image editing programs, like Adobe's Photoshop, are able to perform batch resizing and compression operations on images. The key question is how large should your images be on your devices so they look sharp?

In the world of video, high definition is defined as 1920x1080 pixels (also known as full HD or 1080p). This has been an acceptable resolution for large television displays for many years now, and it certainly is acceptable for a high quality image display on any Android tablet or device.

Table 3-4 shows a summary of screen resolutions and image files sizes. The approximate file size depends on the image content and compression method used. Using JPG compression at a 60% setting is a good compromise.

Table 3-4. Image Resolution and Approximate File Sizes

Resolution	Description	Approx. File Size (KB)	Usage
1920x1080	Full HD	200	Full screen images on a tablet or Android TV
960x540	1/2 HD	75	High-quality image in an Android *Gallery*
480x270	1/4 HD	30	Acceptable thumbnail image for Android *ListView* or *GridView*

Note that the 1/2 HD and 1/4 HD files are only 75KB and 30KB, respectively. This is in the acceptable range for good lazy loading performance and will allow you to set your memory cache size at a small fraction of the device's available memory, assuming you don't have too many images. If you have thousands of images, then it would be best to have very small thumbnail images of 10KB or smaller.

You will see in the Lazy Loading project that images are stored at approximately 1/2 HD resolution on the server. Since you have a small number of images, you can store them in this relatively large size so that the quality will look good in the largest view, which is the *Gallery*.

If you require many more images, then you may wish to store multiple copies of the images in both high and low resolutions. The low resolution images could be used by the *GridView* and the *ListView*, and the higher resolution images could be used for the *Gallery*.

Image Downsampling

Most lazy loading implementations use some sort of downsampling when they process images downloaded from a server. This ensures that you don't try to process images that are too large for your views.

In the following code, the Android *BitmapFactory* class is used to decode the original file. This allows you to determine the actual height and width in pixels of the image. With this image size information you can generate a scaling factor by comparing these sizes to your required size. Once the scale factor is determined, you then perform another decode using the scale factor to obtain an image of suitable size for your lazy load views.

```
// Decoding the original file 'f'
    BitmapFactory.Options o = new BitmapFactory.Options();
    o.inJustDecodeBounds = true;
    FileInputStream stream1 = new FileInputStream(f);
    BitmapFactory.decodeStream(stream1,null,o);
    stream1.close();
// Find the correct scale factor based on the required width
    final int REQUIRED_WIDTH = 70;
    int width_tmp = o.outWidth, height_tmp = o.outHeight;
    int scale = 1;
    while (true) {
        if (width_tmp/2 < REQUIRED_WIDTH || height_tmp/2 < REQUIRED_WIDTH) break;
        width_tmp /= 2;
        height_tmp /= 2;
        scale *= 2;
    }
// Decode with scaling. The resulting bitmap will be scaled and
// can be applied to our ImageView holder in the ListView, GridView and Gallery
    BitmapFactory.Options o2 = new BitmapFactory.Options();
    o2.inSampleSize = scale;
    FileInputStream stream2 = new FileInputStream(f);
    Bitmap bitmap = BitmapFactory.decodeStream(stream2, null, o2);
    stream2.close();
```

The *BitmapFactory* class has two methods that you use to accomplish the downsampling.

- *decodeStream()*: This method allows you to decode the original image after it has been downloaded from the server or from local storage.

- *options()*: This method allows you to obtain image information using *.outWidth* and *.outHeight*. With this sizing information from the original image, you can calculate a scale factor. Using the scale factor, you can then use *.inSampleSize* to decode the image again. The resulting bitmap can be used safely for all of your lazy load views.

Aspect Ratio

The Lazy Loading project uses portrait images with a consistent size of 960 pixels high by 540 pixels wide. All of the pictures are stored on the server with this size. The aspect ratio of these pictures is thus 960 divided by 540, or 1.787.

When the images are lazy loaded, they will be downsampled to the size specified by the *REQUIRED_WIDTH* setting (shown in the previous code excerpt), while maintaining the aspect ratio. This code will be included in the *ImageLoader* class when you implement the project.

When the images are placed into their *ImageView* containers, they will be scaled according to the *scaleType* attribute.

The Android *scaleType* attribute provides several options to display images within the *ImageView* container. Table 3-5 shows the available options.

Table 3-5. Android scaleType Options

Scale Type	Description
Matrix	Scales the image using a supplied *Matrix* class. The *Matrix* class can be used to apply transformations, such as rotation.
fitXY	Scales the image to exactly fit inside the view. This does not maintain the aspect ratio and can result in images that appear distorted.
fitCenter	Scales the image to fit inside the view while maintaining the aspect ratio. At least one axis will exactly match the view and the result will be centered.
fitStart	Same as *fitCenter*, but the image will be aligned to the top of the view.
fitEnd	Same as *fitCenter*, but the image will be aligned to the bottom of the view.
center	Displays the image centered in the view with no scaling.
centerCrop	Scales the image so both dimensions are at least as large as the view, maintaining the aspect ratio, cropping any part of the image that exceeds the view. The image will not be distorted, but it will not be seen in its entirely.
centerInside	Scales the image to fit inside the view, while maintaining the aspect ratio. If the image is smaller than the view, this will produce the same result as *center*.

If you are displaying photos and wish to avoid scaling distortions, it is usually best to use the *center* or *fitCenter scaleTypes*. The following XML code shows how this might look for an *ImageView*:

```
<ImageView
    android:id="@+id/list_image"
    android:layout_width="wrap_content"
    android:layout_height="wrap_content"
    android:scaleType="fitCenter"
    android:padding="4dp"
    android:layout_margin="2dp"
    android:layout_gravity="center"/>
```

If you have mixed aspect ratios and you do not mind some cropping of your images when they are displayed in the lazy load view, *centerCrop* works well because it always produces a consistent sized image that looks good in a *ListView*.

3.7   Lazy Loading App

For the lazy loading implementation, let's define some simple requirements and then take a look at the available libraries to find the best approach.

1.   Lazy load 50 pictures stored on a server, configurable with a JSON file.

2.   Implement memory and disk caching.

3.   Support three switchable views including *ListView*, *GridView*, and *Gallery*.

4.   Keep the app as lightweight as possible.

Of course, all of the available libraries can meet the caching requirement. Only the Universal Image Loader has built-in support for switchable views, but at 200KB, it is not exactly lightweight.

In order to keep the app as lightweight as possible, you will implement your own memory caching and disk caching, and you will incorporate three switchable views.

If you require a lot of advanced features, such as zooming on images, rotation of images, and effects such as rounded corners or support for animated images, then it is probably better to choose one of the third-party libraries and not worry about rolling your own code.

Lazy Loading App Overview

Figure 3-2 shows a screenshot of the Lazy Loading app. The main layout contains an *ActionBar* on the top with a drop-down navigation, which is used to select the layout view. The default layout view is set to *ListView*. The main layout also contains two control buttons at the bottom as well as an Exit button, which may be positioned in the overflow area depending on device size. These buttons have the following functions:

- *ActionBar* drop-down navigation: Allows the user to select the view type for the lazy load. Default is *ListView*. *GridView* and *Gallery* can also be selected.

- Lazy Load button: When pressed, the device will check if the configuration file exists on the device. If not, it will be downloaded. A lazy load will then commence using the configuration file and the view type specified in the *ActionBar* drop-down navigation.

- Delete Files button: When pressed, all of the files, images, and the configuration file will be deleted from the local storage (disk cache) on the device. This function is not typically available in a lazy loading app, but it is included here to help you better understand how the app is working.

- Exit button: Exits the app by terminating the *MainActivity*. The button may appear in the overflow area depending on device width.

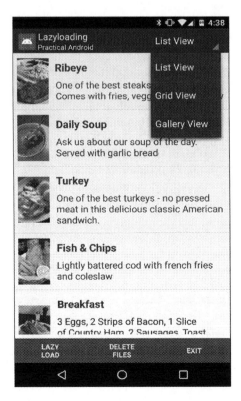

Figure 3-2. Sample lazy loading ListView

The Lazy Loading app meets each of the specified requirements. The app has a single activity, *MainActivity.java*, which connects to the server and downloads a JSON configuration file named *lazyloadconfig.txt*. This file specifies the images and their titles, and it includes a description for each image.

The image assets on the server have fixed image sizes to help you avoid the pitfalls of large images, which can lead to out-of-memory (OOM) exceptions.

The app supports three different Android views: *ListView*, *GridView*, and *Gallery.* Each view has its own adapter and layout, which is controlled by the *ActionBar* drop-down navigation setting.

The app has its own *ImageLoader* class, which implements the disk and memory caching. The app uses a background thread to perform the initial download of the JSON file. The app also uses a background thread when you delete files. The *ImageLoader* class uses a *ThreadPool* for downloading the individual images.

Using these approaches to implement the required functionality, the app size is minimized. The Lazy Loading app is only 43KB!

This is much smaller than if you used one of the open source libraries. I kept it simple because we did not require all of the features the third-party libraries provide. But you might; it just depends on your requirements and how you choose to meet those requirements.

Lazy Loading Project

Table 3-6 shows the layout of the Lazy Loading project.

Table 3-6. Lazy Loading Project Setup

Sources	Resources/layout	Res/
FileCache.java	activity_main_gallery.xml	values/arrays.xml
ImageLoader.java	activity_main_grid.xml	menu/actions.xml
MainActivity.java	activity_main_list.xml	
MemoryCache.java	gal_item.xml	
Utils.java	grid_item.xml	
	list_item.xml	

The main activity of the project is *MainActivity.java*. It handles all of the logic of the app including implementation of the three display views. Each of the view layouts is accomplished with an XML file for the main view (such as *activity_main_gallery.xml, activity_main_grid.xml,* and *activity_main_list.xml*). There are also XML files for the items in the three views: *list_item.xml, grid_item.xml,* and *gal_item.xml*.

The lazy loading class consists of three files: *ImageLoader.java* (which handles the main logic) and two subclasses called *MemoryCache.java* and *FileCache.java* (which handle the memory and disk caching).

Server Setup

The Lazy Loading app downloads image files from a web server. The following code shows the configuration URL for these assets. You can easily change these settings and rebuild the app if you want to use your own image repository.

```
// Server settings
private String serverFileBase = "http://www.yourserver.com/";
private String serverPicBase = "http://www.yourserver.com/image_directory/";
private String fileName = "lazyloadconfig.txt";
```

The configuration file name is also set in the app. The configuration file is stored in the *serverFileBase* directory and the images are stored in the *serverPicBase* directory.

The configuration file is a JSON text file that defines the list of pictures that will be displayed by the lazy load. The advantage of using the configuration file is that you can also include a title and description for each image. The app can then include these descriptors within the layouts.

The following example shows the layout of the JSON configuration file. It contains a title, a filename, and a description for each image that will be lazy loaded. The filename of the image needs to match an image that is stored in the *serverPicBase* directory on the web server. If it does not exist on the server, a blank or stub image will be displayed by the lazy load.

```
[
    [{"title":"your_image1_title"},{"filename":"1.jpg"},{"desc":"Your image1 description"}],
    [{"title":"your_image2_title"},{"filename":"2.jpg"},{"desc":"Your image2 description"}],
    [{"title":"your_image3_title"},{"filename":"3.jpg"},{"desc":"Your image3 description"}],
    [{"title":"your_image4_title"},{"filename":"4.jpg"},{"desc":"Your image4 description"}],
    [{"title":"your_image5_title"},{"filename":"5.jpg"},{"desc":"Your image5 description"}],
    [{"title":"your_image6_title"},{"filename":"6.jpg"},{"desc":"Your image6 description"}],
    [{"title":"your_image7_title"},{"filename":"7.jpg"},{"desc":"Your image7 description"}],
    [{"title":"your_image8_title"},{"filename":"8.jpg"},{"desc":"Your image8 description"}]
]
```

Note that when the JSON configuration file is first downloaded, it is stored locally on the device. This allows the app to work offline when there is no connectivity. The configuration file is only downloaded when it does not exist, so if you make changes to the configuration file, be sure to delete the local copy using the Delete Files button on the app. This will cause it to be downloaded again upon the next attempt, picking up the new changes.

MainActivity.java

The Lazy Loading Project supports three individual views: *ListView*, *GridView*, and *Gallery*. Each of the views is assigned a unique ID and adapter, as shown below. There are also three *ArrayLists* that will contain the URLs of the images, the titles of the images, and the descriptions of the image.

```
// IDs for the views
private static final int ID_LIST = 0;
private static final int ID_GRID = 1;
private static final int ID_GALL = 2;
```

```
// The current View ID: 0=List, 1=Grid, 2=Gallery
private int currentViewID;

// Views
private ListView list;
private Gallery gallery;
private GridView grid;

// Adapters
private LazyGridAdapter gridAdapter;
private LazyGallAdapter gallAdapter;
private LazyListAdapter listAdapter;

// Array Lists for the View Adapters
private static ArrayList<String> fetchURL = new ArrayList<String>();
private static ArrayList<String> imageTitle = new ArrayList<String>();
private static ArrayList<String> imageDesc = new ArrayList<String>();
```

The *onCreate* method of *MainActivity.java* is very straightforward. It checks for the existence of the disk cache folder and creates it if necessary. It clears each of the *ArrayLists*, and it also sets up the *ActionBar*, which contains the drop-down navigation choices that allow users to select a view. The default view is *ListView* and the corresponding *currentViewID* is set to 0. Note that the text labels for the three views are defined in the *res/values/arrays.xml* file.

```
@Override
public void onCreate(Bundle savedInstanceState) {
    super.onCreate(savedInstanceState);

    fileDir = new File(android.os.Environment.getExternalStorageDirectory(),"LazyloadImages");
    if (!fileDir.exists()) fileDir.mkdirs();

    // Setup the ActionBar and the Spinner in the ActionBar
    getActionBar().setDisplayShowTitleEnabled(true);
    getActionBar().setSubtitle("Android Software Development");
    getActionBar().setTitle("Lazyloading");

    Context context = getActionBar().getThemedContext();
    ArrayAdapter<CharSequence> listviews = ArrayAdapter.createFromResource(context, R.array.
                                  Views, android.R.layout.simple_spinner_item);
    listviews.setDropDownViewResource(android.R.layout.simple_spinner_dropdown_item);
    getActionBar().setNavigationMode(ActionBar.NAVIGATION_MODE_LIST);
    getActionBar().setListNavigationCallbacks(listviews, this);

    // Default to ListView
    currentViewID = 0;

    // Clear the ArrayLists
    fetchURL.clear();
    imageTitle.clear();
    imageDesc.clear();
}
```

To handle the drop-down navigation list, the *onNavigationItemSelected* method is implemented. When the user selects one of the items, the following code will execute to update *currentViewID* and then post the update to the UI thread handler so it can be displayed.

```
@Override
public boolean onNavigationItemSelected(int itemPosition, long itemId) {
    if (itemPosition == ID_LIST) {
        currentViewID = 0;
        mHandler.post(mUpdateResults);
    } else if (itemPosition == ID_GRID) {
        currentViewID = 1;
        mHandler.post(mUpdateResults);
    } else if (itemPosition == ID_GALL) {
        currentViewID = 2;
        mHandler.post(mUpdateResults);
    }
    return false;
}
```

There are three main buttons on the UI. These buttons are defined in *Res/menu/actions.xml* file.

The first button is the Lazy Load button. When pressed, this button performs the following functions:

- Creates a thread for network operations so you will not block the UI thread with a potentially long-running network operation.

- Checks to see if you have a local copy of the configuration file. If so, you will use it. If not, it will be downloaded and stored locally on the device.

- The configuration file is parsed as a JSON object and the contents are placed into three *ArrayLists*: *fetchURL*, *imageTitle*, and *imageDesc*. The *fetchURL ArrayList* will be used by the handler when it performs the lazy load.

- The handler is passed the *mUpdateResults* runnable if everything works as expected. This will cause the content view to be set based on the *currentViewID*.

- The handler is passed the *mNoConnection* runnable if something went wrong. Typically this would occur if network connectivity was not available.

The code to handle the Lazy Load button:

```
@Override
public boolean onOptionsItemSelected(MenuItem item) {
    if (item.getItemId() == R.id.load) {
        final ProgressDialog pd = ProgressDialog.show(MainActivity.this,"Loading",
                            "Loading file list and images...",true, false);
        new Thread(new Runnable(){
            public void run(){
                File masterFil = new File(fileDir, fileName);
```

```java
            if (masterFil.exists()) {
                try {
                    lazyLoadConfig = Utils.ReadLocalFile(masterFil);
                    masterAvail = true;
                } catch (IOException e) {
                }
            } else if (checkInternetConnection()) {
                lazyLoadConfig = Utils.DownloadText(serverFileBase + fileName);
                //save it to the local cache for later use
                File writeFile =new File(fileDir, fileName);
                BufferedWriter writer;
                try {
                    writer = new BufferedWriter(new OutputStreamWriter(new
                            FileOutputStream(writeFile, true), "UTF-8"));
                    writer.write(lazyLoadConfig);
                    writer.flush();
                    writer.close();
                    masterAvail = true;
                } catch (Exception e) {
                }
            } else {
                mHandler.post(mNoConnection);
            }
            // We have a masterfile.txt so set up the ArrayLists
            if (masterAvail) {
                // setup the fetchURL ArrayLists
                try {
                    configFileJson = new JSONArray(lazyLoadConfig);
                    for (int i=0; i<configFileJson.length(); i++) {
                        String fname =
                            jsonGetter2(configFileJson.getJSONArray(i),"filename").
                            toString();
                        fetchURL.add(fname);
                        String title =
                            jsonGetter2(configFileJson.getJSONArray(i),"title").
                            toString();
                        imageTitle.add(title);
                        String desc =
                            jsonGetter2(configFileJson.getJSONArray(i),"desc").toString();
                        imageDesc.add(desc);
                    }
                } catch (JSONException e) {
                    e.printStackTrace();
                }
                mHandler.post(mUpdateResults);
            } else {
                mHandler.post(mNoConnection);
            }
            pd.dismiss();
        }
    }).start();
    return(true);
}
```

The second button at the bottom of the main layout is the Delete Files button. This button allows the user to delete all of the images that have been cached on disk.

If you inspect the directory, you will see many files. The file names do not match the original file names stored on the server. This because the *ImageLoader* has created *HashMap* names for each of the files stored on the device.

The delete button also deletes the local copy of the configuration file, which resides in the same location. This will force the file to be redownloaded from the server the next time a lazy load is requested.

The Delete Files button code performs the following tasks:

- Shows a *ProgressDialog* while a background thread performs the work. This is done because deleting files can be a relatively long-running task, so the work is performed on a background thread while an indeterminate progress dialog is displayed.

- Deletes all the files stored on disk.

- Deletes the contents of the three *ArrayLists*.

- Updates the results on the UI thread.

The code to handle these functions looks like this:

```
if (item.getItemId() == R.id.delete) {
    // delete all the files on SD
    final ProgressDialog pd = ProgressDialog.show(MainActivity.this,"Deleting",
                              "Deleting files from device storage...",true, false);
    new Thread(new Runnable(){
        public void run(){
            switch (currentViewID) {
                case 0:
                listAdapter.imageLoader.fileCache.clear();
                break;
                case 1:
                gridAdapter.imageLoader.fileCache.clear();
                break;
                case 2:
                gallAdapter.imageLoader.fileCache.clear();
                break;
            }
            // delete all the images in the directory
            Utils.deleteDirectory(fileDir);
            // delete all items from the ArrayLists
            fetchURL.clear();
            imageTitle.clear();
            imageDesc.clear();
            // Update on the UI thread
            mHandler.post(mUpdateResults);
            pd.dismiss();
        }
    }).start();
    return(true);
}
```

The third button is the Exit button. It simply performs a *finish()* call on the *MainActivity*. This also triggers the *onDestroy()* method to be called, which will assist the Java garbage collection by resetting the views and their adapters to *null*.

```java
protected void onDestroy() {
    switch (currentViewID) {
    case 0:
        list.setOnItemClickListener(null);
        list.setAdapter(null);
        break;
    case 1:
        grid.setOnItemClickListener(null);
        grid.setAdapter(null);
        break;
    case 2:
        gallery.setOnItemClickListener(null);
        gallery.setAdapter(null);
        break;
    }
}
```

The *mUpdateResults* runnable, which gets posted back to the handler so the UI can be updated, checks the *currentViewID* and then displays the appropriate view. This is accomplished for each view by invoking the *setContentView* with the appropriate layout. The runnable also sets up the *onClickItem* for each of the items in the view. In this simple project, you just display a *Toast* message when any item is clicked.

In the following code, you pass the *fetchURL ArrayList* into each adapter. This *ArrayList* contains the image URLs that will be lazy loaded.

```java
final Runnable mUpdateResults = new Runnable() {
    public void run() {
        if (currentViewID == ID_LIST) {
            setContentView(R.layout.activity_main_list);
            list = (ListView) findViewById(R.id.list);
            listAdapter = new LazyListAdapter(MainActivity.this, R.layout.list_item,
                                    fetchURL, MainActivity.this);
            list.setAdapter(listAdapter);
            list.setOnItemClickListener(new OnItemClickListener() {
                public void onItemClick(AdapterView parent, View v, final int position, long id) {
                    Toast.makeText(MainActivity.this, "List item selected: " + position,
                            Toast.LENGTH_SHORT).show();
                }
            });
        } else if (currentViewID == ID_GRID) {
            setContentView(R.layout.activity_main_grid);
            grid = (GridView) findViewById(R.id.grid);
            gridAdapter = new LazyGridAdapter(MainActivity.this, R.layout.grid_item, fetchURL,
                                    MainActivity.this);
```

```
            grid.setAdapter(gridAdapter);
            int picHeight = Utils.getGridPicHeight(MainActivity.this);
            int picLength = (int) ((float)picHeight / 1.5);
            grid.setColumnWidth(picLength);
            grid.setOnItemClickListener(new OnItemClickListener() {
                public void onItemClick(AdapterView parent, View v, final int position, long id) {
                    Toast.makeText(MainActivity.this, "Grid item selected: " + position,
                            Toast.LENGTH_SHORT).show();
                }
            });
        } else if (currentViewID == ID_GALL) {
            setContentView(R.layout.activity_main_gallery);
            gallery = (Gallery) findViewById(R.id.gallery);
            gallAdapter = new LazyGallAdapter(MainActivity.this, R.layout.gal_item,
                                        fetchURL, MainActivity.this);
            gallery.setAdapter(gallAdapter);
            gallery.setOnItemClickListener(new OnItemClickListener() {
                public void onItemClick(AdapterView parent, View v, final int position, long id) {
                    Toast.makeText(MainActivity.this, "Gallery item selected: " + position,
                            Toast.LENGTH_SHORT).show();
                }
            });
        }
```

XML Layout Files

Each of the views has an XML file to define its layout. Table 3-7 shows the contents of these layout files. Within these files, attributes are specified for the high-level layout of the *ListView*, *GridView*, and *Gallery* views.

Table 3-7. XML Layouts for Three Lazy Loading Views

ListView

```
<LinearLayout
    android:layout_width="fill_parent"
    android:orientation="vertical"
    android:layout_height="wrap_content"
    android:layout_marginTop="0dip"
    android:layout_marginBottom="8dip">
    <ListView
        android:id="@+id/list"
        android:layout_height="0dip"
        android:layout_weight="1.0"
        android:layout_width="fill_parent"/>
</LinearLayout>
```

Gallery

```
<LinearLayout
    android:orientation="horizontal"
    android:layout_width="fill_parent"
    android:layout_height="fill_parent">
    <Gallery
        android:id="@+id/gallery"
        android:layout_width="fill_parent"
        android:layout_weight="1"
        android:spacing="1dip"
        android:layout_marginLeft="12dp"
        android:layout_marginRight="12dp"
        android:layout_height="match_parent"/>
</LinearLayout>
```

(continued)

Table 3-7. (*continued*)

GridView

```
<LinearLayout
    android:orientation="horizontal"
    android:layout_width="wrap_content"
    android:layout_height="fill_parent"
    android:layout_marginTop="2dip"
    android:layout_gravity="center"
    android:gravity="center">
    <GridView
        android:id="@+id/grid"
        android:layout_width="fill_parent"
        android:layout_height="fill_parent"
        android:numColumns="3"
        android:horizontalSpacing="4dp"
        android:verticalSpacing="4dp"
        android:stretchMode="spacingWidthUniform"/>
</LinearLayout>
```

The lower level item layouts for each of the views are contained in the *list_item.xml*, *grid_item.xml*, and *gal_item.xml* files. You can make adjustments to the files if you wish to change the way each of the individual items appears with the three views.

The controls for the widgets in each of the views is straightforward. Each of the widgets, *ListView*, *GridView*, and *Gallery*, are wrapped inside a *LinearLayout*. In order to fill the screen optimally, both the *ListView* and *Gallery* widgets use a *layout_weight="1"* attribute setting. The *GridView* widget sets the *numColumns="3"* attribute. If you wish to adjust the number of columns in your *GridView*, you can change this setting. You could alternatively set it programmatically.

ImageLoader.java

Since you are implementing your own lazy loading class rather than using of one of the third-party libraries, you need some code that will handle the image loading function, as well as the disk and memory caching. If you take a close look at the available open source libraries, you will see that, with the exception of the Facebook library, they all take a similar approach to implement these functions.

When you display images in Android, you normally assign a *bitmap* to an *imageView* using this approach:

```
ImageView img = (ImageView) findViewById(R.id.yourImageView);
img.setBackgroundResource(R.drawable.yourBitmapImage);
```

However, when lazy loading, you are going to let the *imageLoader* handle all of the image downloading, display, and caching for you.

Regardless of which of the three views the user has selected, you will invoke the *imageLoader* inside the adapter using the following line of code to populate the lazy loading images:

```
imageLoader.displayImage(imageURL, imageView);
```

The *displayImage* method found in the *ImageLoader* class takes two parameters:

- *imageURL*: The full URL of the image on the server. This will be used to download the image if necessary. It will also be used to generate a hash map name for storage and retrieval of the image in the disk cache.

- *imageView*: The location of the image in either the *ListView*, *GridView*, or *Gallery*. Upon retrieval of the image from memory, disk, or network download, the bitmap resource will be assigned to the *imageView*.

Partial code for the *ImageLoader.java* class is shown below, including the *DisplayImage* method. Note that *displayImage* first tries to retrieve the requested image from the memory cache. If available, it is assigned to the *ImageView* using *.setImageBitmap*. If the image is not available, it is queued for download and a blank stub image is assigned to the *ImageView* temporarily, while the download is processed.

If the download fails or the image cannot be retrieved, the stub image will remain indefinitely in the view.

```
public class ImageLoader {
    MemoryCache memoryCache = new MemoryCache();
    FileCache fileCache;
    private Map<ImageView, String> imageViews = Collections.synchronizedMap(
                                        new WeakHashMap<ImageView, String>());
    ExecutorService executorService;
    Handler handler = new Handler(); //handler to display images in UI thread

    public ImageLoader(Context context) {
        fileCache=new FileCache(context);
        executorService=Executors.newFixedThreadPool(5); // max number of worker threads
    }

    final int stub_id = R.drawable.blank150x225; // Define the stub image

    public void DisplayImage(String url, ImageView imageView) {
        imageViews.put(imageView, url);
        Bitmap bitmap = memoryCache.get(url);
        If (bitmap != null) imageView.setImageBitmap(bitmap);
        else {
            queuePhoto(url, imageView);
            imageView.setImageResource(stub_id);
        }
    }
}
```

```
...
private void queuePhoto(String url, ImageView imageView) {
// adds new image requests to the queue
...
private Bitmap getBitmap(String url) {
// code to make network requests using HttpURLConnection
...
private Bitmap decodeFile(File f){
// code using the BitmapFactory class to scale images automatically (downsampling)
...
public void clearCache() {
// code which clears all images from memory and disk cache
```

The hash file names for each of the images stored in the disk cache are derived from the hash map that is created by the Java *Collections.synchronizedMap* class as follows. The *WeakHashMap* is an implementation of *Map* with keys that are *WeakReferences*.

```
private Map<ImageView, String> imageViews = Collections.synchronizedMap(
                                new WeakHashMap<ImageView, String>());
```

When a user performs a fling motion on the UI, this could trigger many images to be retrieved. If network downloads are required, you need to manage all the background threads that may be created. The *executorService* is the best way to handle this. You assign a fixed thread pool of five threads using the *newFixedThreadPool* method.

```
executorService = Executors.newFixedThreadPool(5); // max number of worker threads
```

Given the small image sizes relative to device size, 5 is a reasonable number of simultaneous threads. If you have a much larger screen size, or much smaller images, you may want to increase this to 10 or even 20 threads. The *executorService* takes care of all the thread management for you.

MemoryCache.java

The memory cache class contains several public methods and one private method. The get and put methods are the main public methods used by *ImageLoader.java* to manage the bitmaps in the memory cache.

- *setLimit*: Allows the app to specify how much memory to reserve for the memory cache. The factors that should be considered for the cache limit were discussed earlier in the chapter.

- *get*: The main public method used by the *ImageLoader* to retrieve images from the memory cache.

- *put*: The main public method used by the *ImageLoader* to add new images to the memory cache.

    ▓   *checkSize*: An internal method used to manage the cache as items are added. The memory cache limit is set in the constructor method of *MemoryCache.java*. It is set at 25% of available memory.

    ▓   *clear*: Allows the app to clear the memory cache. This method is invoked when the user presses the Delete Files button on the app UI.

The main code for *MemoryCache.java* is shown next. The LRU cache is set up when the *LinkedHashMap* is defined. The map has *key/value pairs* consisting of the URL string and the bitmap image. It has the following three parameters:

    ▓   *Initial capacity*: Set to 10 buckets in the hash table. This will be automatically expanded as the hash table grows.

    ▓   *Load factor*: Set to .75. This value tells the system how full the table can be before the capacity is automatically increased up to the cache limit.

    ▓   *Boolean flag*: Specifies the ordering mode used by the cache. *True* indicates *access order*, which is needed for LRU. *False* indicates *insertion order*.

See the link in the references if you want to explore more about the *LinkedHashMap* used by the *MemoryCache*.

```java
// Note some of the exception handling has been removed in this excerpt for readability
public class MemoryCache {
    private Map<String, Bitmap> cache = Collections.synchronizedMap(
            new LinkedHashMap<String, Bitmap>(10, 0.75f, true));
    private long size = 0; //current allocated size
    private long limit = 2000000; //max memory in bytes
    public MemoryCache() {
        setLimit(Runtime.getRuntime().maxMemory()/4); // use 25% of available heap size
    }
    public void setLimit(long new_limit) {
        limit = new_limit;
    }
    public Bitmap get(String id) {
        if (!cache.containsKey(id)) return null;
        return cache.get(id);
    }
    public void put(String id, Bitmap bitmap) {
        if (cache.containsKey(id)) size -= getSizeInBytes(cache.get(id));
        cache.put(id, bitmap);
        size += getSizeInBytes(bitmap);
        checkSize();
    }
    private void checkSize() {
        if (size > limit) {
            Iterator<Entry<String, Bitmap>> iter=cache.entrySet().iterator();
            while(iter.hasNext()) {
                Entry<String, Bitmap> entry=iter.next();
                size-=getSizeInBytes(entry.getValue());
                iter.remove();
```

```
                if (size <= limit) break;
            }
        }
    }
    public void clear() {
        cache.clear();
        size=0;
    }
    long getSizeInBytes(Bitmap bitmap) {
        if (bitmap == null) return 0;
        return bitmap.getRowBytes() * bitmap.getHeight();
    }
}
```

FileCache.java

The file cache class is used by the *ImageLoader* to retrieve images from the disk cache. The following methods are implemented by *FileCache.java*:

- *getFile*: Retrieves a file from the disc cache based on the URL.

- *clear*: Deletes all of the files in the disc cache. The *FileCache.java* class is implemented as follows:

```
public class FileCache {
    private File cacheDir;
    public FileCache(Context context) {
        cacheDir = context.getCacheDir();
        if (!cacheDir.exists() cacheDir.mkdirs();
    }
    public File getFile(String url) {
        String filename=String.valueOf(url.hashCode());
        File f = new File(cacheDir, filename);
        return f;
    }
    public void clear(){
        File[] files=cacheDir.listFiles();
        If (files==null) return;
        For (File f:files) f.delete();
    }
}
```

Note that there is no method to put files into the disc cache. This happens automatically whenever an image needs to be downloaded over the network. The *ImageLoader* handles this work inside the *getBitmap()* method. When images are downloaded from the server, the call to *Utils.CopyStream* utility is where the bitmap is saved to the disk cache directory.

```
// Get image from web
URL imageUrl = new URL(url);
HttpURLConnection conn = (HttpURLConnection) imageUrl.openConnection();
conn.setConnectTimeout(connectTimeout);
conn.setReadTimeout(readTimeout);
```

```
conn.setInstanceFollowRedirects(true);
InputStream is = conn.getInputStream();
OutputStream os = new FileOutputStream(f);
Utils.copyStream(is, os);
os.close();
conn.disconnect();
bitmap = decodeFile(f);
```

Now that you have the *ImageLoader* class set up, all that remains is to set up adapters for each of the views.

Adapters

Within *MainActivity.java* you must implement an adapter for each of the lazy load views. Each of the three adapters handles the following actions:

- Implements *ViewHolders* for performance
- Calls the *ImageLoader* class to lazy load each of the images
- Inflates the view for each view type according to the item layout XML file for each view type
- Retrieves the title and description for each of the images from the *ArrayLists*

Lazy List Adapter

Figure 3-3 shows a close-up view of the *ListView* items. Each item contains a left-justified image together with left-justified text for the image title and image description. The layout is defined in *list_item.xml*.

Figure 3-3. *ListView item layout*

The *ListView* is set up for display on the UI in the *mUpdateResults* handler within *MainActivity.java.* The following code example implements the following steps:

- Sets up the content view
- Creates a local instance *list* of type *ListView*

⬛ Assigns the *LazyListAdapter* to *list* using the *setAdapter* method

⬛ Sets the *setOnItemClickListener* so that a pop-up can be displayed whenever the user clicks on one of the items in the list

```
setContentView(R.layout.activity_main_list);
list = (ListView) findViewById(R.id.list);
listAdapter = new LazyListAdapter(MainActivity.this, fetchURL, this);
list.setAdapter(listAdapter);
list.setOnItemClickListener(new OnItemClickListener() {
    public void onItemClick(AdapterView parent, View v, final int position, long id) {
        Toast.makeText(MainActivity.this, "List item: " + position, Toast.LENGTH_SHORT).show();
    }
});
```

The *LazyListAdapter* code is shown below. Each of the adapters extends *BaseAdapter* and implements a *ViewHolder* to optimize performance. The *getView* method does the work of displaying each of the items in the list. The image title and image description are obtained from the *ArrayLists* that were set up for them. A *LayoutParams* object named *params* is defined and it allows you to set the height and width of the image. The values in this example are derived from the device display size so that you have a proportional image size across different devices.

Images are displayed by invoking the *DisplayImage* method on the *ImageLoader* class. All three of the adapters use this approach.

```
private class LazyListAdapter extends BaseAdapter {
    private Activity activity;
    private ArrayList<String> data;
    private LayoutInflater inflater=null;
    public ImageLoader imageLoader;
    LinearLayout.LayoutParams params;

    public LazyListAdapter(Context context, ArrayList<String> d, Activity a) {
        super();
        imageLoader=new ImageLoader(context);
        this.data = d;
        inflater = (LayoutInflater) context.getSystemService(Context.LAYOUT_INFLATER_SERVICE);
        activity = a;
        data = d;
    }

    public int getCount() {
        return data.size();
    }
    public Object getItem(int position) {
        return position;
    }
    public long getItemId(int position) {
        return position;
    }
```

```
class ViewHolder {
    public ImageView image;
    public TextView title;
    public TextView desc;
}

public View getView(int position, View convertView, ViewGroup parent) {
    ViewHolder holder = null;
    // Inflate the view
    if (convertView == null) {
        convertView = inflater.inflate(R.layout.list_item, null);
        holder = new ViewHolder();
        holder.image = (ImageView) convertView.findViewById(R.id.list_image);
        holder.title = (TextView) convertView.findViewById(R.id.list_title);
        holder.desc = (TextView) convertView.findViewById(R.id.list_desc);
        convertView.setTag(holder);
    } else {
        holder = (ViewHolder) convertView.getTag();
    }

    String imageurl = data.get(position);
    holder.image.setTag(imageurl);

    int picHeight = gridPicHeight;
    int picLength = (int) ((float) picHeight / 1.5);

    params = new LinearLayout.LayoutParams(picLength,picHeight);
    params.gravity=Gravity.CENTER;
    params.height=picHeight;
    params.width=picLength;

    holder.image.setLayoutParams(params);
    holder.title.setText(imageTitle.get(position));
    holder.desc.setText(imageDesc.get(position));

    imageLoader.DisplayImage(serverPicBase + imageurl, holder.image);

    return convertView;
    }
}
```

Lazy Grid Adapter

Figure 3-4 shows the grid layout for the Lazy Loading app. The layout is a three-image-wide grid and includes a title below each of the images. In this layout, the description is not displayed.

Figure 3-4. *Lazy Loading app's sample GridView*

The setup is very similar to the *ListView*. In this case, you define a *GridView* object and set its adapter accordingly. Sometimes working with the *GridView* layout can be tricky. The key to achieving a proper layout is to set up the following attribute settings:

■ Assign the *setColumnWidth* attribute to the *GridView* programmatically as shown below. Set the column width equal to the image length.

■ Assign the *numColumns="3"* as shown in the *activity_main_grid.xml* file.

```
setContentView(R.layout.activity_main_grid);
grid = (GridView) findViewById(R.id.grid);
gridAdapter = new LazyGridAdapter(MainActivity.this, fetchURL, this);
grid.setAdapter(gridAdapter);
int picHeight = gridPicHeight;
int picLength = (int) ((float)picHeight / 1.5);
grid.setColumnWidth(picLength);
grid.setOnItemClickListener(new OnItemClickListener() {
public void onItemClick(AdapterView parent, View v, final int position, long id) {
    Toast.makeText(MainActivity.this, "Grid item: " + position, Toast.LENGTH_SHORT).show();
    }
});
```

The *LazyGridAdapter* follows the same structure as you saw in the *ListView* adapter. It uses a *ViewHolder* for performance and calls the *ImageLoader* to display the image.

```
private class LazyGridAdapter extends BaseAdapter {
    private Activity activity;
    private ArrayList<String> data;
    private LayoutInflater inflater=null;
    public ImageLoader imageLoader;
    LinearLayout.LayoutParams params;

    public LazyGridAdapter(Context context, ArrayList<String> d, Activity a) {
        super();
        imageLoader=new ImageLoader(context);
        this.data = d;
        inflater = (LayoutInflater) context.getSystemService(Context.LAYOUT_INFLATER_SERVICE);
        activity = a;
        data = d;
    }

    public int getCount() {
        return data.size();
    }
    public Object getItem(int position) {
        return position;
    }
    public long getItemId(int position) {
        return position;
    }
    class ViewHolder {
        public ImageView image;
        public TextView title;
    }
    public View getView(int position, View convertView, ViewGroup parent) {
        ViewHolder holder = null;
        // Inflate the view
        if (convertView == null) {
            convertView = inflater.inflate(R.layout.grid_item, null);
            holder = new ViewHolder();
            holder.image = (ImageView) convertView.findViewById(R.id.image);
            holder.title = (TextView) convertView.findViewById(R.id.imgTit);
            convertView.setTag(holder);
        } else {
            holder = (ViewHolder) convertView.getTag();
        }

        String imageurl = data.get(position);
        holder.image.setTag(imageurl);

        int picHeight = Utils.getGridPicHeight(activity);
        int picLength = (int) ((float)picHeight / 1.5);
```

```
        params = new LinearLayout.LayoutParams(picLength,picHeight);
        params.gravity=Gravity.CENTER;
        params.height=picHeight;
        params.width=picLength;

        holder.image.setLayoutParams(params);
        holder.title.setText(imageTitle.get(position));
        imageLoader.DisplayImage(serverPicBase + imageurl, holder.image);

        return convertView;
    }
}
```

Lazy Gallery Adapter

Figure 3-5 shows the gallery view. Note that the *Gallery* widget is deprecated as of Android 4.1 (API 16). While it can still be used, this is an indication that it could be altogether removed in future versions of Android. Some alternatives for the *Gallery* widget are shown in the references.

Figure 3-5. Lazy Loading app gallery view

In the *Gallery* view, you are displaying a large full screen image, along with a centered title below each image. As with the *GridView*, the description is not shown in this view.

The setup for the *Gallery* view in *MainActivity.java* is shown below. It is structurally the same as the *ListView*.

```
setContentView(R.layout.activity_main_gallery);
gallery = (Gallery) findViewById(R.id.gallery);
gallAdapter = new LazyGallAdapter(MainActivity.this, fetchURL, this);
gallery.setAdapter(gallAdapter);
gallery.setOnItemClickListener(new OnItemClickListener() {
    public void onItemClick(AdapterView parent, View v, final int position, long id) {
        Toast.makeText(MainActivity.this, "Gallery item: " + position, Toast.LENGTH_SHORT).
            show();
    }
});
```

The custom adapter for the *Gallery* view is called *LazyGallAdapter* and the code is shown below. Like the other adapters, it uses a *ViewHolder* for performance, sets the image size using *LayoutParams*, and displays the images using the *ImageLoader* class.

```
private class LazyGallAdapter extends BaseAdapter {
    private Activity activity;
    private ArrayList<String> data;
    private LayoutInflater inflater=null;
    public ImageLoader imageLoader;
    LinearLayout.LayoutParams params;

    public LazyGallAdapter(Context context, ArrayList<String> d, Activity a) {
        super();
        imageLoader=new ImageLoader(context);
        this.data = d;
        inflater = (LayoutInflater) context.getSystemService(Context.LAYOUT_INFLATER_SERVICE);
        activity = a;
        data = d;
    }

    public int getCount() {
        return data.size();
    }
    public Object getItem(int position) {
        return position;
    }
    public long getItemId(int position) {
        return position;
    }
    class ViewHolder {
        public ImageView image;
        public TextView title;
    }
```

```
public View getView(int position, View convertView, ViewGroup parent) {
    ViewHolder holder = null;
    // Inflate the view
    if (convertView == null) {
        convertView = inflater.inflate(R.layout.gal_item, null);
        holder = new ViewHolder();
        holder.image = (ImageView) convertView.findViewById(R.id.image);
        holder.title = (TextView) convertView.findViewById(R.id.imgCaption);
        convertView.setTag(holder);
    } else {
        holder = (ViewHolder) convertView.getTag();
    }

    String imageurl = data.get(position);
    holder.image.setTag(imageurl);

    int picHeight = Utils.getGallPicHeight(activity);
    int picLength = (int) ((float)picHeight / 1.5);

    params = new LinearLayout.LayoutParams(picLength,picHeight);

    holder.image.setLayoutParams(params);
    holder.title.setText(imageTitle.get(position));

    imageLoader.DisplayImage(serverPicBase + imageurl, holder.image);

    return convertView;
    }
}
```

3.8   References

Android and Java References

▨   Caching Bitmaps in Android: http://developer.android.com/training/
displaying-bitmaps/cache-bitmap.html

▨   Java Hash Map: http://docs.oracle.com/javase/6/docs/api/java/
util/HashMap.html

▨   Alternative for Gallery Widget, Horizontal Scroll View: http://developer.
android.com/reference/android/widget/HorizontalScrollView.html

▨   Alternative for Gallery Widget, View Pager: http://developer.android.
com/reference/android/support/v4/view/ ViewPager.html

Third-Party Lazy Loading Libraries

- LazyLoader - Fedor Vlasov: `https://github.com/thest1/LazyList`

- Google Volley Framework and Examples:
  `https://android.googlesource.com/platform/frameworks/volley`
  `https://github.com/ogrebgr/android_volley_examples`

- Square Picasso Library: `http://square.github.io/picasso/`
  `https://github.com/square/picasso`

- Google Shelves, Open Source Book Management App:
  `http://code.google.com/p/shelves/`

- Universal Image Loader (version 1.9.5.jar):
  `https://github.com/nostra13/Android-Universal-Image-Loader`

- Google Image Cacher Class as Part of the Google I/O App:

  `http://code.google.com/p/iosched/`

  `http://goo.gl/1TGHi`

  `https://github.com/google/iosched/tree/master/third_party/disklrucache`

- Facebook Fresco Image Management Library:
  `https://code.facebook.com/posts/366199913563917/introducing-fresco-a-new-image-library-for-android/`

  `http://frescolib.org/`

- Glide Image Management Library for Android: `https://github.com/bumptech/glide`

- Android Query Image Loading Library:
  `https://code.google.com/archive/p/android-query/wikis/ImageLoading.wiki`

  `https://github.com/androidquery/androidquery`

Chapter 4

Remote Crash Logs

4.1   Introduction

When creating and releasing Android apps, crashes are inevitable.

No matter how hard you try to prevent crashes, the nature of the mobile platform combined with the large number of unknown and untested devices will lead to undesired crashes.

Defining a test methodology is important so you can know when your app is ready to be shipped. Typically, you might only be able to test your apps on a few devices you own or have access to. A more robust test methodology would include testing on many devices, perhaps by making use of a third-party service. Unfortunately, regardless of the resources you apply to your testing phase, once the app is released, it is inevitably going to crash.

How you manage these crashes is critical to your app's longevity. Your users can tolerate a crash, but they expect to see it resolved in future updated releases. You need to know when crashes happen, and you need to have crash data so you can address the issue.

In this chapter, you will take a look at the popular remote crash logging options available in Android. You will implement an app that can crash upon request and will send a crash log including all pertinent information up to the server.

4.2   Chapter Project

The chapter contains the project shown in Table 4-1.

© Mark Wickham 2018

M. Wickham, *Practical Android*, https://doi.org/10.1007/978-1-4842-3333-7_4

Table 4-1. Chapter Projects

Title of Project	File Name	Description
Remote Crash Logging	*crashlog.zip*	This project displays a map and performs a location lookup to show the current device location. The map is implemented using the Open Street Map for Android library. The main view contains a button that will force a crash of the app. When the app crashes, a crash log will be sent up to the server using the ACRA (Application Crash Report for Android) library.

4.3   Remote Crash Log Solutions

Similar to lazy loading, remote crash logging is a must-have feature in your app, especially if you are releasing commercial apps. There is nothing worse than not knowing that your app is crashing and your customers are unhappy. You need to know when and why your app is crashing so you can fix the problem before your customers decide to uninstall your app. With remote crash logging, you will know immediately about any crashes that occur and you will have the data required to address the issue.

Table 4-2 shows some of the popular approaches for implementing remote crash logging in Android.

Table 4-2. Remote Crash Logs Approaches for Android

Library	Description	Link
Google Firebase Crash Reporting	Google's new integrated crash reporting platform. Helps you diagnose and fix problems in your app.	`https://firebase.google.com/docs/crash/`
Crittercism/ Apteligent	Mobile application performance management solution. Recently acquired by VMware.	`www.apteligent.com` `www.vmware.com`
BugSense/ Splunk Mint	App analytics platform. Collects crash, performance, and usage data from your app.	`https://mint.splunk.com/`
HockeyApp	Owned by Microsoft. Platform for mobile app developers that supports crash reporting. Open source SDKs for all mobile platforms.	`http://hockeyapp.net/features/crashreports/`
ACRA	App Crash Report for Android. Free open source. Interfaces to many back ends. Catches exceptions and retrieves lots of context data.	`http://acra.ch`
Crashlytics	Claims to be the most powerful and lightest. Now part of Fabric. Android and iOS support. Owned by Twitter.	`https://try.crashlytics.com`

There has been a lot of consolidation in the area of remote crash logging over the past several years. A lot of venture capital money has been raised in the areas of analytics and mobile app performance, and thus many of the entities who originally had libraries for remote crash logging have been rolled into larger platform offerings.

A brief summary of this activity:

- Google has integrated crash reporting into its Firebase platform.

- Crittercism and Apteligent merged and then were acquired by VMware.

- BugSense and Splunk merged and created a platform called Mint.

- Microsoft bought HockeyApp.

- Twitter bought Crashlytics and rolled in into its Fabric platform.

Each of the services offers a wide variety of features, often much more than just basic crash reporting. There's usually a free or basic service, and then you can scale up to a paid enterprise subscription package with higher services levels and features. If you decide to go with one of these vendors, check on pricing because some of the top tier packages can run up to $150 per month or more.

One of the exciting developments in crash reporting is that Google has recently integrated the function into its Firebase suite. Firebase crash reporting is free and is available for Android and iOS developers. This will undoubtedly shake up the crash reporting landscape. Firebase Crash Reporting contains a number of features, including

- Monitoring of fatal and non-fatal errors

- Collecting the data you need to diagnose problems

- Email alerts

- Integration with Firebase Analytics

- Free and easy to set up

To get started with Firebase Crash Reporting in your Android app, explore the Google information available at the link shown in Table 4-2.

ACRA, which stands for Application Crash Report for Android, has been around for quite some time. It is a free and open source library that is easy to integrate into your apps. You will use it in this chapter's sample project. It does not include all the analytics and performance features that exist in many of the libraries, but it does a fine job of basic remote crash logging.

A majority of the apps you are using today probably use one of the approaches listed above to implement remote crash logging.

How Crash Logging Works

Remote crash logging works by implementing a handler for uncaught exceptions. This Java feature allows you to take action when your app crashes due to an uncaught exception. The following code shows the basic outline for such a handler:

```
public class DefaultExceptionHandler implements UncaughtExceptionHandler{
    private UncaughtExceptionHandler mDefaultExceptionHandler;

    //constructor
    public DefaultExceptionHandler(UncaughtExceptionHandler pDefaultExceptionHandler)
    {
        mDefaultExceptionHandler= pDefaultExceptionHandler;
    }
    public void uncaughtException(Thread t, Throwable e) {
        //do some action like writing to file or upload somewhere

        //call original handler
        mStandardEH.uncaughtException(t, e);
    }
}
```

All of the third-party Android libraries use this same basic approach. They are able to capture app exceptions by implementing the Java *UncaughtExceptionHandler*. Using this approach, they are able to intercept the familiar app crash sequence and provide two key functions:

- Notify you of the crash, usually in a more stylish and friendly manner than the Android hard crash you are used to.

- Upload key context data to a server, so you can analyze the crash and hopefully provide a fix.

Once an exception is caught, the library usually provides several options for you, depending on how you would like to notify the user. Typically, at least the following crash notification options are available:

- Silent notification: When the app crashes, reports are automatically sent up to the server without notifying the user. A well-behaved app should allow users to opt-in or approve this transmission of data.

- Toast notification: When the app crashes, a toast notification is displayed for the user in place of the typical Android crash notification. The toast can display any text you wish to communicate. You will use this notification method in the sample project.

- Dialog notification: Upon app crash, the Android dialog is displayed. The contents can be customized, such as including a form that allows the user to submit additional information about the crash circumstances.

- Android notification bar: Upon crash, a notification is sent to the Android notification bar. This method is not commonly used. It has been deprecated in the ACRA library, but is still available if you wish to use it.

When a crash occurs, the library will perform system calls to obtain as much pertinent information as possible. The collected information is then uploaded to the server, preferably with the permission of the users, in order to help the developer understand and debug the crash. The most important data you shall see is the stack trace data.

4.4   App Crash Report for Android

The free open source ACRA library is a great way to get started with remote crash logging. At some point, you may decide you need analytics and performance monitoring for your apps. However, for basic remote crash reporting, ACRA does a fine job.

ACRA Overview

The latest version of ACRA is *acra-4.10.0.* Documentation for ACRA can be found at `http://acra.ch`. For source and downloads, visit the GitHub page at `https://github.com/ACRA/acra`.

If you are using Android Studio as your development environment, ACRA can be integrated into your Android project as a dependency with *Maven* or *Gradle*. For older development environments, the ACRA library (JAR or AAR file) can be downloaded and included directly into your project.

For Android Studio, Table 4-3 shows the dependencies that need to be included in your project to use ACRA.

Table 4-3. ACRA Build Integration

Maven	Gradle

```<dependency>```
    ```<groupId>ch.acra</groupId>```
    ```<artifactId>acra</artifactId>```
    ```<version>4.8.5</version>```
    ```<type>aar</type>```
```</dependency>```
	```dependencies {```
	    ```... your other dependencies ...```
	    ```compile 'ch.acra:acra:4.10.0'```
	```}```

The ACRA wiki page on GitHub contains a Getting Started page as well as an Advanced Usage page that provides everything you will need to know. Links are included in the chapter references.

Aside from notifying the user when a crash occurs, the most important task a remote crash log implementation needs to do is send relevant crash data up to the server.

Table 4-4 shows a list of the all the variables that are available in ACRA. In the chapter project, you will implement the app and server code required to send and receive all of these variables. These variables each contain valuable information about the device and the state of the system and running app at the time of the crash. The *STACK_TRACE* is the most important of the ACRA data fields.

Table 4-4. ACRA Available Data Fields

ANDROID_VERSION	DROPBOX	RADIOLOG
ANDROID_VERSION_CODE	DUMPSYS_MEMINFO	REPORT_ID
APP_VERSION_NAME	ENVIRONMENT	SETTINGS_GLOBAL
APPLICATION_LOG	EVENTSLOG	SETTINGS_SECURE
ANDROID_VERSION	DROPBOX	RADIOLOG
AVAILABLE_MEM_SIZE	FILE_PATH	SETTINGS_SYSTEM
BRAND	INITIAL_CONFIGURATION	SHARED_PREFERENCES
BUILD	INSTALLATION_ID	STACK_TRACE
BUILD_CONFIG	IS_SILENT	THREAD_DETAILS
CRASH_CONFIGURATION	LOGCAT	TOTAL_MEM_SIZE
CUSTOM_DATA	MEDIA_CODEC_LIST	USER_APP_START_DATE
DEVICE_FEATURES	PACKAGE_NAME	USER_COMMENT
DEVICE_ID	PHONE_MODEL	USER_CRASH_DATE
DISPLAY	PRODUCT	USER_EMAIL

ACRA is a lightweight solution. Integrating the library into your app only adds about 150KB to the size of your app. ACRA only provides crash data and does not provide any app analytics, nor does it help you capture information about Application Not Responding (ANR) errors within your app.

There are a couple of things to note when setting up your *manifest.xml* file. You will need to add the following permissions:

- *android.permission.INTERNET*
- *android.permission.READ_LOGS*

These permissions are required to access log data and send it up to the server. In the chapter project, additional permissions are required for the mapping functions you will incorporate into the app.

Lastly, in order to implement ACRA, you will need to set up the *MyApplication* class file, which I will cover in the chapter project.

4.5   ACRA Back-End Server

ACRA allows you to send reports to a back-end server of your choice. ACRA allows you to send reports to a server using several different methods, including the following:

- POST request to your own self-hosted script.

- Send reports by email.

- Send JSON-encoded crash variable content to your own self-hosted script.

- Implement your own sender.

- Use a variety of third-party senders and server back ends.

In the chapter project, you will implement your own self-hosted script to receive and store the crash data from the app.

The official backend for ACRA is Acralyzer. It was created and is maintained by the author of ACRA. It can be hosted on your own server. The only requirement for running Acralyzer is that you install *CouchDB* as the database engine. The good thing about Acralyzer is that it guarantees to display all of the possible data collected by ACRA.

If you do not wish to use Acralyzer and you also do not want to spend your time writing back-end code for managing your crash log files, there are a number of other back-end solutions that can simplify the task.

Because ACRA is open source, you are free to write your own back end and many people have. Table 4-5 shows a list of some of the ACRA back-end options available. For a complete list of back-end solutions, see the ACRA wiki page.

Table 4-5. ACRA Back-End Solutions

Back-End Solution	Description
Acralyzer	Official open source backend for ACRA.
BugSense	Commercial cross-platform analysis platform.
HockeyApp	Commercial cross-platform crash report collection solution from Microsoft.
Bugify	Commercial PHP bug and issue tracker.
Zubhium	Android platform dedicated to crash report management.
ACRAViz, Crash Reports Viewer, Crash Reports Dashboard, ACRA PHP Mailer, pacralyzer	PHP hosting solutions. There are many free open source ACRA PHP back ends.
Acracadabra, Jonny Crash	Ruby hosting solutions.
ACRA web.py, Django ACRA	Python hosting solutions.
Acra-reporter, sdimmick android crash reports	Google AppEngine hosting solutions.

Note that Google Forms and Google Docs are no longer supported as back ends for ACRA.

In the sample project, you will implement a self-hosted script to receive your crash log reports from the app. For the project, you will use PHP, but you can use the scripting language of your choice on the back-end server.

4.6   Open Street Map for Android

Although the main topic of this chapter is remote crash logging, you are going to need an app to crash. Rather than just implementing a trivial activity that crashes, let's try to do something more useful. That is where Open Street Map for Android (OSMdroid) comes in. I will cover all the code for implementing OSMdroid in this section.

OSMdroid's *MapView* is a replacement for the Android *MapView* class. The latest version of OSMdroid is version 5.6.5 and the download links for osmdroid-master are included in the chapter references.

Like the ACRA library, you can integrate OSMdroid into your project using the *Maven* or the *Gradle* build system if you are working in Android Studio.

If you wish to get a feel for the OSMdroid capabilities, you can download the sample app called OpenStreetMapViewer. This app demonstrates most of the capabilities of the library.

Like the *MapView* class, the OSMdroid library provides overlays for items that can be included on your maps. Figure 4-1 shows how the *compass*, *minimap*, *myLocation*, and *ScaleBar* can be overlayed onto any map. Similarly, you can also implement a list of markers if you have more than one location to highlight.

- *MyLocation* overlay: The default OSMdroid "person" icon will be displayed on the MapView in the center of the map to designate the current location of the device.

- *ScaleBar* overlay: The scale bar will appear centered at the top of the *MapView*. It will provide the numerical scale values that convey the zoom level information for the current view.

- *Minimap* overlay: The *minimap* overlay will display a small version of the entire map in the bottom right corner of the view.

- *Compass* overlay: The *compass* overlay is displayed in the upper left corner of the view. The compass will use the device sensors to display an indication of North direction.

Figure 4-1. Open Street Map overlays: compass, ScaleBar, MyLocation, and minimap

One of the nice things about using OSMdroid maps in your apps is that the library allows you to do some things that are not easily accomplished with the Android *MapView* class. Some advantages of using the OSMDroid *MapView* class are as follows:

- No third-party dependency is required because the OSMdroid *MapView* class is a replacement for Google's *MapView* class.

- Boundaries can be defined to restrict the scrolling of the map.

- Offline map tiles are supported. This allows your map to be functional even when connectivity is unavailable. The Android *MapView* class has made some progress in this area with the recent addition of offline tiles.

- Several tile sources are available. Figure 4-2 shows a summary of some of the tile sources you can use.

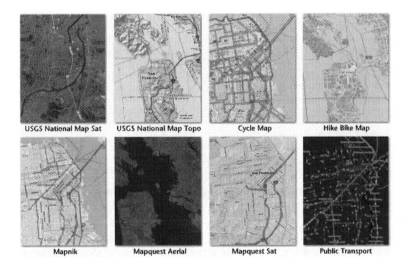

Figure 4-2. Open Street Maps for Android tile sources

- Custom tiles are supported. You can create your own tiles and store them locally or serve them over the network.

The code required to implement the map and overlays is straightforward and follows the Google Maps API closely. In order to use the library, the *MapView* and overlay objects can be created as shown below:

```
private MapView mMapView;
private IMapController mapController;
private ScaleBarOverlay mScaleBarOverlay;
private MyLocationNewOverlay mLocationOverlay;
private RotationGestureOverlay mRotationGestureOverlay;
private MinimapOverlay mMinimapOverlay;
```

```
mMapView = (MapView) findViewById(R.id.mapview);
mMapView.setBuiltInZoomControls(true);
mMapView.setMultiTouchControls(true);
mMapView.setClickable(false);
mMapView.setTileSource(TileSourceFactory.MAPQUESTOSM);
```

Note that the *setTileSource* method is used to specify the desired tile source for the map. One of the nice things about OSM is that you can adjust the tile source to your liking. Figure 4-2 shows some of the tile sources available for the library. (Note that some of the tile sources, such as MapQuest, are now requiring users to register before they can gain access to the tiles.)

Displaying a map requires a *MapView* control to be included in your layout. In the chapter project, the following XML is included within the main view to hold the *MapView* inside a *RelativeLayout*:

```
<RelativeLayout
    android:id="@+id/MapViewLayout"
    android:padding="0dip"
    android:layout_height="wrap_content"
    android:layout_width="fill_parent" >
    <org.osmdroid.views.MapView
        android:id="@+id/mapview"
        android:layout_width="match_parent"
        android:layout_height="match_parent" />
</RelativeLayout>
```

Centering the map at the current device location and setting a zoom level for the map is accomplished with the *mapController* object. For a more precise location, you can use the *LocationManager.GPS_PROVIDER*.

```
mapController = mMapView.getController();
LocationManager locationManager = (LocationManager) this.getSystemService(Context.LOCATION_
SERVICE);
String locationProvider = LocationManager.GPS_PROVIDER;
GeoPoint p1;
try {
    Location lastKnownLocation = locationManager.getLastKnownLocation(locationProvider);
    int lat = (int) (lastKnownLocation.getLatitude() * 1E6);
    int lng = (int) (lastKnownLocation.getLongitude() * 1E6);
    p1 = new GeoPoint(lat, lng);
    mapController.setCenter(p1);
} catch (SecurityException e) {
    // Let the user know there was a problem with GPS
}
mapController.setZoom(14);
```

Each of the overlays displayed in Figure 4-1 can be placed on any OSM map by including the following code:

```
this.mLocationOverlay = new MyLocationNewOverlay(new GpsMyLocationProvider(this), mMapView);
mMapView.getOverlays().add(this.mLocationOverlay);
mLocationOverlay.enableMyLocation();
```

```
mScaleBarOverlay = new ScaleBarOverlay(mMapView);
mScaleBarOverlay.setCentred(true);
mScaleBarOverlay.setScaleBarOffset(dm.widthPixels / 2, 10);
mMapView.getOverlays().add(this.mScaleBarOverlay);

mMinimapOverlay = new org.osmdroid.views.overlay.MinimapOverlay(this,
mMapView.getTileRequestCompleteHandler());
mMinimapOverlay.setWidth(dm.widthPixels / 5);
mMinimapOverlay.setHeight(dm.heightPixels / 5);
mMapView.getOverlays().add(this.mMinimapOverlay);

mCompassOverlay = new org.osmdroid.views.overlay.compass.CompassOverlay(this, mMapView);
mCompassOverlay.enableCompass();
mMapView.getOverlays().add(this.mCompassOverlay);
```

For more advanced features of OSMdroid, such as enabling rotation gestures, placing icons on maps with click listeners, or using your own tile sets, refer to the wiki page on GitHub.

While OSMdroid is not a line-for-line replacement for Google's *MapView*, it is very similar. If you find example code that uses Google's *MapView*, porting the code to the *OSMdroid* class will not be difficult.

4.7   Remote Crash Log App

To demonstrate remote crash logging with ACRA, you will implement a "crash feature" within an app that implements the Open Street Map (OSM) alternative to Google Maps to display the current location of the device on a map.

Remote Crash Log App Overview

Figure 4-3 shows a screenshot of the Remote Crash Log app. The main layout contains a *MapView* that fills the layout and two buttons centered at the bottom of the map:

- ▨ *Exit*: When pressed, the app will be terminated.

- ▨ *Crash*: When pressed, a crash will be triggered by executing code that causes an array out-of-bounds exception that is not caught by any exception handler.

Figure 4-3. Remote Crash Log app screenshot including overlays

Similar to Google Maps, the user is able to navigate the map by swiping in any direction, and zoom in or out by pressing the zoom controls, which appear upon any touch event.

Whenever the Crash button is pressed, an exception is generated and the app will crash. In the project, ACRA is configured to notify the user by displaying a toast notification while suppressing the standard Android crash message. Figure 4-4 shows how the crash notification is displayed after the Crash button is pressed.

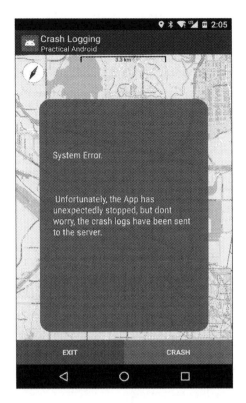

Figure 4-4. ACRA crash toast message

As with any toast message, the notification will be displayed for several seconds before the app is terminated and the crash log information is sent up to the server. The text of the toast notification is defined in the *res/layouts/strings.xml* file. The message content of the text box can be defined by setting the string variable as follows:

```
<string name="msg_crash_text">\n\n\n\nSystem Error.\n\n\n\n Unfortunately, the App has unexpectedly stopped, but dont worry, the crash logs have been sent to the server.\n\n\n\n\n\n\n\n</string>
```

In Figure 4-4, the extra line spacing before and after the text are created by including extra blank lines in the strings using the \n representation.

The message text is set up similarly if you configure ACRA for other notification modes including dialog notification or notification bar notification.

Remote Crash Log Project

Table 4-6 shows the layout of the crash log project. It is a relatively simple project and contains only two source files, a couple of layout files, and two libraries.

Table 4-6. Remote Crash Log Project Setup

Sources	Resources/	Res/libs
MainActivity.java	layout/main_layout.xml	acra-4.8.5.jar
MyApplication.java	values/strings.xml	classes.jar (*OSMdroid*)

The main activity of the project is *MainActivity.java*. It handles all of the logic of the app including implementation for the OSM map display.

There are two libraries included in the app: *acra-4.8.5.jar* is used to implement the remote crash logging function, while *classes.jar* handles the OSM mapping functionality.

AndroidManifest.xml

Within the manifest file, you need to do the following:

- ▓ The application element needs to point to your application class.

- ▓ Configure the application element. The *android:name* attribute must point to your application class.

- ▓ Define your *MainActivity* with *intent-filter*.

- ▓ Declare the INTERNET permission if you are sending other than by email.

- ▓ Declare the READ_LOGS permission, which is necessary for ACRA to access system logs.

```
<manifest xmlns:android="http://schemas.android.com/apk/res/android"
    package="com.wickham.android.crashlog"
    android:versionCode="1"
    android:versionName="1.0">
    <application
        android:icon="@drawable/ic_launcher"
        android:allowBackup="false"
        android:name="MyApplication"
        android:theme="@style/AppTheme"
        android:label="@string/app_name">
        <activity
            android:name="com.wickham.android.crashlog.MainActivity"
            android:label="@string/app_name"
            android:noHistory="true"
            android:uiOptions="splitActionBarWhenNarrow">
            <intent-filter>
                <action android:name="android.intent.action.MAIN"/>
                <category android:name="android.intent.category.LAUNCHER"/>
            </intent-filter>
        </activity>
    </application>
<uses-permission android:name="android.permission.INTERNET"/>
<uses-permission android:name="android.permission.READ_LOGS"/>
</manifest>
```

The application element in the manifest file will be defined next as you create a new application class.

MyApplication.java

For ACRA to work, you need to create an application class inside the package root. All of the ACRA configuration is done within this *MyApplication* class. It should extend *android.app. Application*. In the *MyApplication* class, you then define the *@ReportCrashes* variable. This is where you configure ACRA. The following elements will be defined:

- Custom report content, which is included within a *String Array*

- The ACRA notification mode, shown here as a *Toast*

- The HTTP sending details, including method and URL

The following code shows the complete code for *MyApplication.java*:

```
Package com.wickham.android.crashlog;

import org.acra.annotation.ReportsCrashes;
import org.acra.*;
import android.app.Application;

@ReportsCrashes(formKey = "",
                customReportContent = { ReportField.REPORT_ID,
                                        ReportField.APP_VERSION_CODE,
                                        ReportField.APP_VERSION_NAME,
                                        ReportField.PACKAGE_NAME,
                                        ReportField.PHONE_MODEL,
                                        ReportField.ANDROID_VERSION,
                                        ReportField.STACK_TRACE,
                                        ReportField.TOTAL_MEM_SIZE,
                                        ReportField.AVAILABLE_MEM_SIZE,
                                        ReportField.DISPLAY,
                                        ReportField.USER_APP_START_DATE,
                                        ReportField.USER_CRASH_DATE,
                                        ReportField.LOGCAT,
                                        ReportField.DEVICE_ID,
                                        ReportField.SHARED_PREFERENCES },

                formUri = "http://www.yourserver.com/crashed.php",
                httpMethod = org.acra.sender.HttpSender.Method.POST,
                mode = ReportingInteractionMode.TOAST,
                resToastText = R.string.msg_crash_text)
public class MyApplication extends Application {
    @Override
    public void onCreate() {
        ACRA.init(this);
        super.onCreate();
    }
}
```

The @ReportCrashes variable contains a number of name/value pairs that are used to configure ACRA:

- customReportContent: String array of all the data fields that will be reported. Refer to Table 4-4 for a complete list of fields available. The fields included will be referenced later in the server-side script so they can be retrieved and saved on the server. This example includes 15 of the fields, but you could include any of the items from Table 4-4.

- formURI: Specifies the URL of the receiving script on the server.

- httpMethod: Specifies the sending method to the receiving script.

- mode: Specifies the notification mode. For ACRA, this can be DIALOG, NOTIFICATION, SILENT, or TOAST.

- resToastText: Specifies the text message to be included in the notification.

MainActivity.java

The MainActivity will be used to implement the OSM map and its overlays. It will also allow you to force a crash that will be handled by ACRA through the MyApplication class.

The layout is specified in main_layout.xml. It includes a MapView nested inside a RelativeLayout wrapped in the main LinearLayout. See Listing 4-1.

Listing 4-1. main_layout.xml

```xml
<?xml version="1.0" encoding="utf-8"?>
<LinearLayout xmlns:android="http://schemas.android.com/apk/res/android"
    android:id="@+id/linearLayoutMain"
    android:layout_width="wrap_content"
    android:layout_height="wrap_content"
    android:orientation="vertical">
    <RelativeLayout
        android:id="@+id/MapViewLayout"
        android:padding="0dip"
        android:layout_height="wrap_content"
        android:layout_width="fill_parent" >
        <org.osmdroid.views.MapView
            android:id="@+id/mapview"
            android:layout_width="match_parent"
            android:layout_height="match_parent" />
    </RelativeLayout>
</LinearLayout>
```

Aside from the OSMdroid code, which was covered earlier in the chapter, the only other functionality handled by MainActivity are the two buttons placed at the bottom of the MapView. Those buttons are handled by the onCreateOptionsMenu.

```
@Override
public boolean onCreateOptionsMenu(Menu menu) {
    new MenuInflater(this).inflate(R.menu.actions, menu);
    return(super.onCreateOptionsMenu(menu));
}
@Override
public boolean onOptionsItemSelected(MenuItem item) {
    if (item.getItemId() == R.id.exit) {
        finish();
        return(true);
    }
    if (item.getItemId() == R.id.crash) {
        // simulate a crash right here, lets do an Index out of bounds condition ...
        String[] crashArray = new String[] {"one","two"};
        crashArray[2] = "oops";
        return(true);
    }
    return(super.onOptionsItemSelected(item));
}
```

The crash is accomplished by defining a string array with two members and then trying to reference a third member. That will certainly throw an *indexOutOfBoundsException*, which will be caught by ACRA and reported up to the server.

The labels for the two buttons are defined in the *actions.xml* file, shown in Listing 4-2.

Listing 4-2. actions.xml

```xml
<?xml version="1.0" encoding="utf-8"?>
<menu xmlns:android="http://schemas.android.com/apk/res/android">
  <item
    android:id="@+id/exit"
    android:showAsAction="always|withText"
    android:title="@string/exit"/>
  <item
    android:id="@+id/crash"
    android:showAsAction="always|withText"
    android:title="@string/crash"/>
</menu>
```

Once you have the app set up, all that remains is to choose and set up your ACRA back end.

PHP Self-Hosted Script

When ACRA intercepts a crash, it will POST the requested content to the server URL specified in the *MyApplication.java* class. All of the crash log data can then be received by the script using the PHP *$_POST* method.

On the server, you will create a PHP script called *Crashed.php* to perform the following functions:

- ▓ Calculate the current time on the server. This will be used to generate the filename for the crash data file.

- ▓ Open the file for writing in a subdirectory specified by the pathname stored in the variable *$FileLog*.

- ▓ Write out each of the ACRA variable names and contents onto a new line. This will be accomplished using the PHP *$_POST* environment variable to read the data passed by ACRA.

- ▓ Close the file.

Crashed.php

The following code shows the complete PHP file. In this example, you are creating a file in a directory on the server called */crashlogs*. The format of the filename is MMddhhmmss.txt, where MM=month, dd=day, hh=hour, mm=minute, ss=second.

```php
<?php
    $dt = new DateTime('now', new DateTimeZone('Asia/Hong_Kong'));
    // save the log to a filename with MMDDHHMMSS such as: "1123132456.txt"
    $orderday = substr($dt->format('Y-m-d H:i:s'),8,2);
    $ordermon = substr($dt->format('Y-m-d H:i:s'),5,2);
    $ordertim = substr($dt->format('Y-m-d H:i:s'),11,2) . substr($dt->format('Y-m-d H:i:s'),14,2)
                                                    . substr($dt->format('Y-m-d H:i:s'),17,2);
    $fname = $ordermon . $orderday . $ordertim . ".txt";
    $FileLog = $_SERVER['DOCUMENT_ROOT'] . "/crashlogs/" . $fname;
    $HandleLog = fopen($FileLog, 'a');

    fwrite($HandleLog, "REPORT_ID=" . $_POST['REPORT_ID'] . "\r\n");
    fwrite($HandleLog, "APP_VERSION_CODE=" . $_POST['APP_VERSION_CODE'] . "\r\n");
    fwrite($HandleLog, "APP_VERSION_NAME=" . $_POST['APP_VERSION_NAME'] . "\r\n");
    fwrite($HandleLog, "PACKAGE_NAME=" . $_POST['PACKAGE_NAME'] . "\r\n");
    fwrite($HandleLog, "PHONE_MODEL=" . $_POST['PHONE_MODEL'] . "\r\n");
    fwrite($HandleLog, "ANDROID_VERSION=" . $_POST['ANDROID_VERSION'] . "\r\n");
    fwrite($HandleLog, "STACK_TRACE=" . $_POST['STACK_TRACE'] . "\r\n");
    fwrite($HandleLog, "TOTAL_MEM_SIZE=" . $_POST['TOTAL_MEM_SIZE'] . "\r\n");
    fwrite($HandleLog, "AVAILABLE_MEM_SIZE=" . $_POST['AVAILABLE_MEM_SIZE'] . "\r\n");
    fwrite($HandleLog, "DISPLAY=" . $_POST['DISPLAY'] . "\r\n");
    fwrite($HandleLog, "USER_APP_START_DATE=" . $_POST['USER_APP_START_DATE'] . "\r\n");
    fwrite($HandleLog, "USER_CRASH_DATE=" . $_POST['USER_CRASH_DATE'] . "\r\n");
    fwrite($HandleLog, "LOGCAT=" . $_POST['LOGCAT'] . "\r\n");
    fwrite($HandleLog, "DEVICE_ID=" . $_POST['DEVICE_ID'] . "\r\n");
    fwrite($HandleLog, "SHARED_PREFERENCES=" . $_POST['SHARED_PREFERENCES'] . "\r\n");
    fclose($HandleLog);
    fclose($Handle);
?>
```

Assuming your app has connectivity, whenever the app crashes, a text file will be written on the server with the time-stamped filename into the directory specified by the *$FileLog* variable.

The following code shows what one of these files might look like. The STACK_TRACE variable is particularly useful. As you can see, it includes critical crash information such as the *ArrayIndexOutOfBounds* exception that caused your app to crash. This critical information will allow you to easily resolve the software defect that caused the crash. Note that the same 15 fields are included in the PHP file defined in the *MyAppliclation.java* class.

```
APP_VERSION_CODE=1
APP_VERSION_NAME=1.0
PACKAGE_NAME=com.wickham.android.crashlog
ANDROID_VERSION=4.3
STACK_TRACE=java.lang.ArrayIndexOutOfBoundsException: length=2; index=2
    at com.wickham.android.crashlog.MainActivity.onOptionsItemSelected(
    MainActivity.java:103)
    at android.app.Activity.onMenuItemSelected(Activity.java:2566)
    at com.android.internal.policy.impl.PhoneWindow.onMenuItemSelected(PhoneWindow.java:986)
    at com.android.internal.view.menu.MenuBuilder.dispatchMenuItemSelected
    (MenuBuilder.java:735)
    at com.android.internal.view.menu.MenuItemImpl.invoke(MenuItemImpl.java:152)
    at com.android.internal.view.menu.MenuBuilder.performItemAction(MenuBuilder.java:874)
    at com.android.internal.view.menu.ActionMenuView.invokeItem(ActionMenuView.java:547)
    at com.android.internal.view.menu.ActionMenuItemView.onClick (ActionMenuItemView.java:115)
    at android.view.View.performClick(View.java:4240)
    at android.view.View$PerformClick.run(View.java:17721)
    at android.os.Handler.handleCallback(Handler.java:730)
    at android.os.Handler.dispatchMessage(Handler.java:92)
    at android.os.Looper.loop(Looper.java:137)
    at android.app.ActivityThread.main(ActivityThread.java:5103)
    at java.lang.reflect.Method.invokeNative(Native Method)
    at java.lang.reflect.Method.invoke(Method.java:525)
    at com.android.internal.os.ZygoteInit$MethodAndArgsCaller.run(ZygoteInit.java:737)
    at com.android.internal.os.ZygoteInit.main(ZygoteInit.java:553)
    at dalvik.system.NativeStart.main(Native Method)

LOGCAT=10-01 12:07:36.465 D/OpenGLRenderer( 1653): Enabling debug mode 0
10-01 12:07:36.495 I/org.osmdroid.tileprovider.LRUMapTileCache( 1653): Tile cache increased . . .
10-01 12:07:36.515 D/dalvikvm( 1653): GC_FOR_ALLOC freed 19K, 3% free 10079K/10308K, . . .
10-01 12:07:36.535 D/dalvikvm( 1653): GC_FOR_ALLOC freed 38K, 3% free 10370K/10588K, . . .
10-01 12:07:36.555 D/dalvikvm( 1653): GC_FOR_ALLOC freed <1K, 2% free 10659K/10848K, . . .
```

If your app has a large number of users, you may find that managing all the crash log text files that are written to the server is not trivial. Rather than write out text files, you may wish to store these crash log files into a database or use one of the third-party back ends to manage the data.

Using a remote crash logging solution such as ACRA or another solution available from third-party vendors allows you to take control of your crashes. It is inevitable that your apps will crash, so when they do, you need to be aware of the situation and be able to provide fixes through app updates so future similar crashes can be avoided.

4.8   References

Android

▒ Obtain Device Location: `http://developer.android.com/guide/topics/location/strategies.html`

Google Firebase

▒ Firebase Crash Reporting: `https://firebase.google.com/docs/crash/`

OSMdroid

▒ Open Street Map for Android: `https://github.com/osmdroid/osmdroid`

Third Party

▒ ACRA (Application Crash Report for Android): `http://acra.ch`

▒ ACRA Back Ends: `https://github.com/ACRA/acra/wiki/Backends`

▒ ACRA Advanced Topics: `http://github.com/ACRA/acra/wiki/AdvancedUsage`

▒ Crittercism/Apteligent: `www.apteligent.com`

▒ Recently acquired by VMware, so possible future updates: `www.vmware.com/company/acquisitions/apteligent.html`

▒ Bug Sense/Splunk Mint: `https://mint.splunk.com/`

▒ HockeyApp: `http://hockeyapp.net/features/crashreports/`

▒ Crashlytics: `https://try.crashlytics.com`

Chapter 5

Uploading and Emailing

5.1 Introduction

Earlier in the book, I covered connectivity, including HTTP and image lazy loading, and then you learned how remote crash logs can be sent up to a server when your apps crash. While these patterns are extremely useful, some applications will have additional connectivity requirements, such as uploading files or sending emails.

In the Server Spinner project, you will implement a server-based spinner. The project will implement basic camera functionality to take a picture, which can then be uploaded to the server. As new pictures are uploaded to the server, the contents of the server spinner will be updated to include the newly uploaded images. The chapter will cover the back-end server setup to achieve this.

In the Emailing App project, you will learn how to send emails from your apps. Whether you are trying to gather feedback from your users or just send a message to an outside party, email is one of the simplest ways to accomplish a sharing functionality. The chapter project will cover three methods to send emails.

5.2 Chapter Projects

This chapter contains the projects shown in Table 5-1.

© Mark Wickham 2018
M. Wickham, *Practical Android*, https://doi.org/10.1007/978-1-4842-3333-7_5

Table 5-1. *Chapter Projects*

Title of Project	File Name	Description
Server Spinner	*ServerSpinner.zip*	The project implements a server-based version of the Android spinner widget. The server spinner contents are downloaded from the server. The contents of the spinner can be dynamically updated. The app demonstrates how to upload files. Pictures can be taken with the camera and then uploaded.
Emailing	*Emailing.zip*	If you wish to include email functionality within your apps, there are three different approaches that can be used. The Emailing project demonstrates how each of them can be implemented.

5.3   Overview

Android contains many widgets that can be used as user interface elements in your apps. The spinner widget is popular because it allows you to present multiple options for the user without taking up large amounts of precious screen real estate.

Figure 5-1 shows an example of a typical Android spinner widget.

Figure 5-1. *Android spinner widget*

A typical Android spinner loads the drop-down resource tags internally within the app. These tags are usually static string values that do not change. In the case of the Server Spinner app, the spinner content values will be dynamically downloaded from the server. The user will be able to take pictures using the smartphone camera and upload these pictures to the server. Each time a new picture is uploaded, it will become visible on the drop-down spinner, hence the term "server spinner."

The chapter also includes a project that implements email sending. Working with email within your apps has several advantages:

  ▓ Minimal server setup is required because most users already have email configurations.

▓ Email can contain almost any content, including attachments and diverse character sets.

▓ Email clients and the protocols they require are already present on almost every smartphone.

The chapter project will implement emailing using three different approaches:

▓ Intent service, which provides an interface to local device email clients

▓ Interface to an external mail server using the *JavaMail* API library

▓ Interface to an external mail server via a dedicated PHP script

5.4   Server Spinner: Server Setup

To implement the server spinner, you require some simple functionality on the server side. The following PHP scripts are required on the server:

▓ *return204.php*

▓ *listfiles-a.php*

▓ *deletefile.php*

▓ *uploadfile.php*

To determine if your server is reachable, you will implement the HTTP status code 204 check, which was covered in Chapter 2. See Listing 5-1 for the *return204.php* code.

Listing 5-1. return204.php

```php
<?php
http_response_code(204);
?>
```

The basic function to populate the spinner widget in the app is handled by a PHP script that lists out the files in a directory on the server. The script in Listing 5-2, *listfiles-a.php*, handles this task. The script needs to reside in the directory of the files you wish to list. Note that some files need to be excluded because you only want to list the image files. The *if* statement in the script handles the file exclusion by excluding specific filenames based on a pattern match.

Let's display the filenames in alphabetical order. This will make it easier to review the filenames when they appear in the spinner. The PHP *asort* function is used to accomplish the alphabetic sequencing.

Listing 5-2. listfiles-a.php

```php
<?php
$i = 0;
if ($handle = opendir('.')) {
    while (false !== ($file = readdir($handle))) {
        if ($file != "." &&
            $file != ".." &&
            $file != "listfiles-a.php" &&
            $file != "listfiles.php" &&
            $file != "phpfiles" &&
            $file != "deletefile.php" &&
            $file != "uploadfile.php" &&
            $file != "return204.php" &&
            $file != "deletefile.html" &&
            $file != "uploadfile.html") {
                $thelist = $thelist.$file." ";
                $files[$i] = $file;
                $i = $i + 1;
            }
    }
    closedir($handle);
}
// sort the files alphabetically
asort($files);
foreach ($files as $a) {echo $a." "; }
?>
```

The app allows users to delete items that appear in the server spinner. In order to accomplish this, you need to be able to delete the associated file on the server. The *deletefile.php* script handles this function.

From a security standpoint, deleting files on the server with a script can be potentially dangerous. Because of this, you add a layer of security by building a list of files that can be deleted, and then check if the requested file is contained in this list. Only when a match occurs can the file be deleted.

The script receives the filename of the file to be deleted. The PHP *str_replace* function is used to see if the requested file is contained in the list of acceptable files. A match occurs if the returned count is greater than zero. In this case, the PHP *unlink* function is used to delete the file. See Listing 5-3.

Listing 5-3. deletefile.php

```php
<?php
$file_to_delete = $_POST['inputfile'];
$full_file_path = "/yourserverpath/".$file_to_delete;
// build the list of files in the directory which can be deleted
$i = 0;
if ($handle = opendir('..')) {
    while (false !== ($file = readdir($handle))) {
```

```
        if ($file != "." &&
            $file != ".." &&
            $file != "phpfiles" &&
            $file != "listfiles-a.php" &&
            $file != "listfiles.php" &&
            $file != "uploader.php" &&
            $file != "deletefile.html" &&
            $file != "return204.php" &&
            $file != "uploadfile.html") {
                $files[$i] = $file;
                $i = $i + 1;
            }
    }
    closedir($handle);
}
// only allow the delete if the file is in the list of files in the directory
$check = str_replace($files, '****', $file_to_delete, $count);
if($count > 0) {
    if(unlink($base_directory.$file_to_delete)) echo "File Deleted.";
}
?>
```

The main point of the Server Spinner project is to demonstrate uploading of files. To receive a file on the server, you need another PHP script. The script in Listing 5-4 receives the name of the file to be uploaded and then handles the upload operation by calling the PHP *move_uploaded_file* function.

Listing 5-4. uploadfile.php

```
<?php
$fname = $_POST['filename'];
$target_path = "/yourserverpath/".$fname;
$upload_path = $_FILES['uploadedfile']['tmp_name'];
If (move_uploaded_file($upload_path, $target_path)) {
    echo "Moved";
} else {
    echo "Not Moved";
}
?>
```

These four scripts are required by and will be executed from the Android app.

It is a good idea to test your PHP scripts first, before implementing the Android app. You can write simple HTML pages to test the upload and delete operations. Examples of such HTML files (*uploadfile.html* and *deletefile.html*) can be found in the Server Spinner project assets along with the PHP files.

To use these test HTML files, you need to upload them to your server alongside the PHP scripts and then simply run these test HTML pages by pointing your browser at the URL.

5.5   Server Spinner App

With the PHP files tested and working on the server, you are now ready to implement the Android app.

Server Spinner App Overview

Figure 5-2 shows a screenshot of the Server Spinner app.

Figure 5-2. Server Spinner app screenshot

The Server Spinner app consists of the following buttons and text views:

- Sync button: Connects to the server and synchronizes the app content with the files currently stored on the server.

- Photo button: Allows the user to take a picture using the device camera. The picture will be uploaded to the server.

- Server Files button: The server spinner widget that shows the filenames of all the files stored on the server. The button text also shows the number of files currently stored on the server.

- Selected Picture text: Displays the name of the currently selected picture, as well as the file path of the picture on the server.

- Image: Displays an image of the currently selected picture.

- Delete button: When pressed, the currently selected picture will be deleted from the server. The server spinner widget will be updated accordingly.

- List of server files: Displays a list of all of the picture files currently stored on the server.

- Exit button: Exits the app.

The Sync, Delete, and Photo buttons interface with the PHP scripts described earlier to carry out their functions. The Sync button makes a call to *listfiles-a.php* to retrieve a list of the files on the server, which will be used to populate the server spinner. The Delete and Photo buttons make calls to *deletefile.php* and *uploadfile.php*, respectively, to accomplish their functions.

Server Spinner Project

Table 5-2 shows the layout of the Server Spinner project.

Table 5-2. Server Spinner Project Setup

Sources	Resources/	Res/libs
FileCache.java	activity_main.xml	
ImageLoader.java	newpic_name.xml	
MainActivity.java	photo_layout.xml	
MemoryCache.java		
Utils.java		

The project contains three Java sources files that you will recognize from the lazy loading project: *FileCache.java*, *ImageLoader.java*, and *MemoryCache.java* are used to handle the lazy loading of the image selected from the server spinner. I will not cover them again here.

MainActivity.java and *Utils.java* contain the key source code of the project and I will cover them next.

Working with the Camera

The purpose of the Server Spinner app is to demonstrate uploading of files to a server. In order to generate interesting content to upload, the app will allow the user to take photos using the device camera.

Working with the camera on Android devices is not trivial. Most of the problems arise from the huge variety of devices available. Each manufacturer enables different functionality depending on the physical camera hardware on the device.

In this project, you will stick with simple camera functions that should work on most devices.

Taking a photo with Android involves the following steps. The code is located in *MainActivity.java*.

- Set up a button that will be used to take the picture. This button will implement the *CameraClickHandler* class.

```
Button btnPhoto = (Button) findViewById(R.id.photo);
btnPhoto.setOnClickListener( new CameraClickHandler() );
```

- Set up the *CameraClickHandler*, which will start an activity using the *MediaStore.ACTION_IMAGE_CAPTURE* intent.

```
public class CameraClickHandler implements View.OnClickListener {
    public void onClick( View view ){
        File file = new File( path1 );
        Uri outputFileUri = Uri.fromFile( file );
        Intent intent = new Intent(android.provider.MediaStore.ACTION_IMAGE_CAPTURE );
        intent.putExtra( MediaStore.EXTRA_OUTPUT, outputFileUri );
        startActivityForResult( intent, 0 );
    }
}
```

- Implement the *onActivityResult* callback method to process the picture after it has been taken.

```
protected void onActivityResult(int requestCode, int resultCode, Intent data) {
    switch( resultCode ) {
        case 0:
            break;
        case -1:
            onPhotoTaken();
            break;
    }
}
```

- Process the picture, including uploading of the file, within the *onPhotoTaken* method.

The first three steps allow you to take a picture using the device camera by means of the Android *MediaStore.ACTION_IMAGE_CAPTURE* intent.

Once an image is captured, you can then process the image by using the *onPhotoTaken* method. In the Server Spinner project, you are going to perform the following functions inside the *onPhotoTaken* method:

- Display a dialog box so the user can accept and save the image.

- Process the image name that is entered so it excludes any special characters that do not work well inside a filename.

- Perform orientation and scaling operations using the *matrix* operator.

- Save a scaled-down bitmap image.

◼ Update the image in the app's *ImageView*.

◼ Update the server spinner with the new image filename.

◼ Upload the new image to the server.

The first step is accomplished using a dialog box. The dialog box allows you to accept a name for the picture that was just taken. It includes two buttons, CANCEL and SAVE, which allow the user to decide if they wish to proceed with the picture that was taken.

```
protected void onPhotoTaken() {
    pictureTaken = true;
    // pop up a dialog so we can get a name for the new pic and upload it
    final Dialog dialogName = new Dialog(MainActivity.this);
    dialogName.setContentView(R.layout.newpic_name);
    dialogName.setCancelable(true);
    dialogName.setCanceledOnTouchOutside(true);
    TextView picText=(TextView) dialogName.findViewById(R.id.newPicText);
    picText.setText(getString(R.string.new_pic_text1));
```

Figure 5-3 shows this dialog box. The XML layout file associated with the dialog box is *newpic_name.xml*.

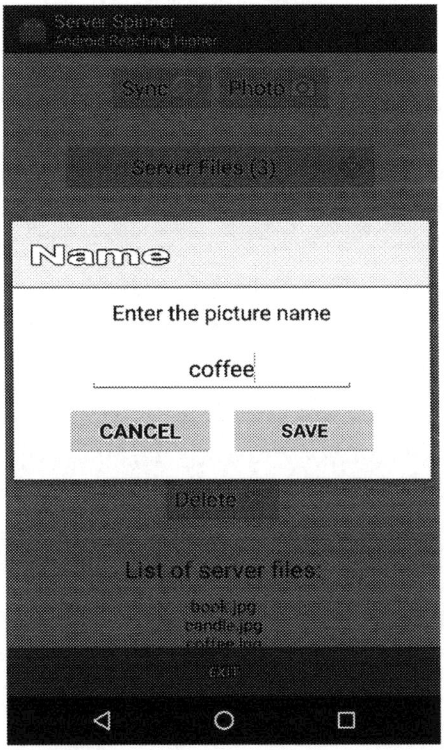

Figure 5-3. Dialog box: choosing a picture name

When the user presses the SAVE button in this dialog, the *setOnClickListener* code inside the *onPhotoTaken* method will be executed. This code handles all of the processing, including the uploading of the image, as follows:

```
picSave.setOnClickListener(new OnClickListener() {
    public void onClick(View v) {
        EditText nameET = (EditText) dialogName.findViewById(R.id.newPicEdit);
        String name = nameET.getText().toString();
        name = name.replaceAll("[^\\p{L}\\p{N}]", "");
        if (name.equalsIgnoreCase("")) name = "newpic";
        name = name.toLowerCase() + ".jpg";
        selectedPicName = name;

        //adjust for camera orientation
        Bitmap bitmapOrig = BitmapFactory.decodeFile( path1);
        int width = bitmapOrig.getWidth();
        int height = bitmapOrig.getHeight();
        // the following are reverse
        // we are going to rotate the image 90 due to portrait pics always used
        int newWidth = 150;
        int newHeight = 225;
        // calculate the scale
        float scaleWidth = ((float) newWidth) / width;
        float scaleHeight = ((float) newHeight) / height;
        // create a matrix for the manipulation
        Matrix matrix = new Matrix();
        // resize the bit map
        matrix.postScale(scaleWidth, scaleHeight);

        // save a scaled down Bitmap
        Bitmap resizedBitmap = Bitmap.createBitmap(bitmapOrig, 0, 0,
                                        width, height, matrix, true);
        File file2 = new File (path2 + selectedPicName);
        FileOutputStream out = new FileOutputStream(file2);
        resizedBitmap.compress(Bitmap.CompressFormat.JPEG, 100, out);
        out.flush();
        out.close();

        // update the picture
        ImageView img = (ImageView) findViewById(R.id.spinnerImg);
        img.setImageBitmap(resizedBitmap);

        // save new name
        TextView txt = (TextView) findViewById(R.id.selectedTitle);
        txt.setText(name);
        txt = (TextView) findViewById(R.id.selectedURL);
        txt.setText(serverPicBase + name);
        spinList.add(name);

        // upload the new picture to the server
        new fileUpload().execute();
        dialogName.dismiss();
    }
});
```

An *EditText* is used to accept the name of the image from the user. The *replaceAll* string function is used to remove unwanted characters. The file extension of .jpg is added to the entered name to create a valid filename for storing on the server.

The code also includes logic to adjust for camera orientation. You may find on certain devices that pictures are rotated unexpectedly. This can happen because camera hardware is sometimes mounted differently by the manufacturers depending on if the device is a tablet or phone. If you need to rotate pictures to correct for this behavior, you can use the *matrix* operator on the bitmap, as shown. The *matrix* operator is a very useful and powerful way to transform bitmap images.

You can also see in this code that the image is compressed and saved in JPG format using the bitmap *compress* function. In this example, the value is set at 100, which means no compression is performed. If you wish to reduce image file sizes, you can set the compression value to smaller values, such as 50, which would represent 50% compression.

Lastly, you can see the file is uploaded to the server by calling *fileUpload()*, which is shown next. The work is performed on a separate thread using *AsyncTask*. The actual file upload is performed first by calling *Utils.Uploader*. This utility is covered in the next section. After the upload completes, the server spinner is updated by making another network access to the *listFilesScript,* which returns a list of files on the server, which are then parsed to repopulate the server spinner.

```
private class fileUpload extends AsyncTask<Void, String, Void> {
    protected Void doInBackground(Void... unused) {
        // upload new picture to the server
        String postURL = uploadFilesScript;
        File file = new File(path2, selectedPicName);
        // upload the new picture
        Utils.Uploader(postURL, file, selectedPicName);
        // update the spinner and count
        fileList = Utils.DownloadText(listFilesScript);
        fileList = fileList.substring(0,fileList.length()-1);
        items = fileList.split(" ");
        spinList.clear();
        for(int i=0;i<items.length;i++) {
            spinList.add(i,items[i]);
        }
        mHandler.post(updateResults);
    }
}
```

MainActivity.java

At the top of *MainActivity.java*, the following five server path variables are defined. Adjust them to point at your own server. If you are running a local web server, you can simply use *localhost* for the top level URL.

```
private static String serverPath = "http://yourserver.com/return204.php";
private static String serverPicBase = "http://yourserver.com/";
private static String listFilesScript = "http://yourserver.com/listfiles-a.php"
private static String uploadFilesScript = "http://yourserver.com/uploadfile.php";
private static String deleteFileScript = "http://yourserver.com/deletefile.php";w
```

I covered all of the code required to handle taking a photo in the previous section. Now let's take a look at the remaining functionality of the app, including syncing with the server, uploading pictures, and deleting pictures from the server spinner.

Syncing with the Server

The server spinner widget itself is populated from the contents of an *ArrayList*, specifically *spinList* as defined in the following code:

```
ArrayList<String> spinList = new ArrayList<String>();
```

When the server spinner button is pressed, a drop-down list will appear, giving the user the opportunity to select a picture. When a picture is selected from the drop-down list, the picture will be loaded into the *ImageView* and the picture name will be loaded into the *TextView*.

The SYNC button performs the task of updating (syncing) the server spinner with the assets on the server. The button handler is implemented as follows:

```
// sync server button
Button btnSync = (Button) findViewById(R.id.sync);
btnSync.setOnClickListener(new View.OnClickListener() {
    public void onClick(View v) {
        clearPicture();
        sync();
    }
});
```

When the SYNC button is pressed, the current picture and picture name will be cleared. This is handled by a call to *clearPicture()*:

```
private void clearPicture() {
    // clear the selected image
    TextView tv = (TextView) findViewById(R.id.selectedTitle);
    tv.setText("---");
    ImageView img = (ImageView) findViewById(R.id.spinnerImg);
    img.setImageResource(R.drawable.nopic);
    tv = (TextView) findViewById(R.id.selectedURL);
    tv.setText("---");
}
```

The syncing is handled by the following code, which displays a progress dialog and then proceeds to download a file list from the server. This operation is handled on a background thread.

Server availability is confirmed using the HTTP status code 204 technique discussed in Chapter 2.

The *spinList ArrayList* is updated by parsing the file list that is returned from the server. A call to the *updateResults* handler updates the actual server spinner widget on the device.

```
public void sync() {
  // download the file list for the server spinner
  final ProgressDialog pd = ProgressDialog.show(MainActivity.this,"Syncing","Syncing file
  list from server...",true, false);
  new Thread(new Runnable() {
    public void run() {
    // see if we can ping the server first
    try {
      OkHttpClient httpClient = new OkHttpClient();
      Request request = new Request.Builder()
          .url(serverPath)
          .build();
      Response response = httpClient.newCall(request).execute();
      if ((response.code() == 200) || (response.code() == 204)) {
        Log.v("SYNC", "syncing");
        fileList = Utils.DownloadText(listFilesScript);
        fileList = fileList.substring(0,fileList.length()-1);
        items = fileList.split(" ");
        spinList.clear();
        for(int i=0;i<items.length;i++) {
          spinList.add(i,items[i]);
        }
        mHandler.post(updateResults);
      } else {
        Log.v("SYNC", "No Conn");
        mHandler.post(noConnection);
      }
    } catch (Exception e) {
      Log.v("SYNC", "Ex=" + e);
      mHandler.post(exceptionConnection);
    }
    pd.dismiss();
    }
  }).start();
}
```

Deleting an Item

Whenever a picture is selected, its name is stored in the following string variable:

```
private String selectedPicName;
```

Deleting an item from the server spinner can be accomplished by pressing the Delete button. When this happens, the currently selected picture will be deleted.

The Delete button handler is shown below. It performs calls to *clearPicture* followed by the *fileDelete* class.

```
// delete button
Button btnDel = (Button) findViewById(R.id.delete);
btnDel.setOnClickListener(new View.OnClickListener() {
    public void onClick(View v) {
        clearPicture();
        new fileDelete().execute();
    }
});
```

The *fileDelete* class performs the delete by passing the *selectedPicName* to the *deletefile. php* script on the server.

After the delete is completed, the server spinner is reloaded by again executing the *listfiles-a.php* script on the server and rebuilding the *spinList*.

```
private class fileDelete extends AsyncTask<Void, String, Void> {
    protected Void doInBackground(Void... unused) {
        // delete picture from server
        String postURL = deleteFileScript;

        if (spinList.contains(selectedPicName)) {
            Utils.Deleter(postURL, selectedPicName);
            // did the delete, so update the spinner and count
            fileList = Utils.DownloadText(listFilesScript);
            fileList = fileList.substring(0,fileList.length()-1);
            items = fileList.split(" ");
            spinList.clear();
            for(int i=0;i<items.length;i++) {
                spinList.add(i,items[i]);
            }
            mHandler.post(updateResults);
        }
    }
}
```

Utils.java

The *Utils.java* class contains two utilities that are called to perform the actual uploading and deleting of files on the server.

Uploading an Item

Uploader handles the uploading of image files taken by the camera. This class calls the *uploadfile.php* script on the server. Uploading files can be tricky, but we have a secret weapon that makes it much easier. You are going to use HTML multipart forms to pass the filename and the actual binary image up to the server. You will recall from Chapter 2 that the *DefaultHttpClient* stack has been deprecated, so we no longer have easy access to its sophisticated *MultipartEntity* method. Similarly problematic, multipart form support is not available for *HttpUrlConnection*. If you wish to extend the built-in *HttpUrlConnection* stack so it can handle files, the end-of-chapter links contain a reference showing how a file handling wrapper can be added.

Fortunately, there is an easier solution. The OkHttp stack can handle multipart forms using its *MultipartBody.Builder* class. *MultipartBody* allows you to simply specify the file name and the file contents using the *addFormDataPart* method. In the following example, the variable names match with those expected by the receiving PHP script on the server:

```
public static void Uploader(String postURL, File file, String fname) {
  try {
    OkHttpClient httpClient = new OkHttpClient();
    RequestBody requestBody = new MultipartBody.Builder()
        .setType(MultipartBody.FORM)
        .addFormDataPart("MAX_FILE_SIZE", "100000")
        .addFormDataPart("filename",fname)
        .addFormDataPart("uploadedfile", fname, RequestBody.create(MediaType.parse
        ("image/jpg"), file))
        .addFormDataPart("result", "my_image")
        .build();

    Request request = new Request.Builder()
        .header("Content-Type", "multipart/form-data; boundary=--32530126183148")
        .url(postURL)
        .post(requestBody)
        .build();
    Response response = httpClient.newCall(request).execute();
    if ((response.code() == 200) || (response.code() == 204)) {
        Log.v("UPLOAD", "Success: URL=" + postURL + " fname=" + fname + " file.length=" +
        file.length() + " response=" + response.code());
    } else {
      // Handle upload fail
      Log.v("UPLOAD", "Fail: URL=" + postURL + " fname=" + fname + " file.length=" +
      file.length() + " response=" + response.code());
    }
  } catch (Throwable e) {
    Log.v("EX", "ex=" + e);
  }
}
```

Similarly, the *Deleter* function also uses OkHttp's *MultipartBody.Builder* to pass the filename to be deleted up to the *deletefile.php* script on the server. The variable name of the file to be deleted is *inputfile*, which corresponds to the HTTP Post variable received by the *deletefile.php* script.

```
public static void Deleter(String delURL, String fname) {
  try {
    OkHttpClient httpClient = new OkHttpClient();
    RequestBody requestBody = new MultipartBody.Builder()
        .setType(MultipartBody.FORM)
        .addFormDataPart("inputfile",fname)
        .build();
    Request request = new Request.Builder()
        .header("Content-Type", "multipart/form-data; boundary=--32530126183148")
        .url(delURL)
        .post(requestBody)
        .build();
```

```
      Response response = httpClient.newCall(request).execute();
      if ((response.code() == 200) || (response.code() == 204)) {
          Log.v("DELETE", "Success: URL=" + delURL + " fname=" + fname + " response=" +
          response.code());
      } else {
          // Handle upload fail
          Log.v("DELETE", "Fail: URL=" + delURL + " fname=" + fname + " response=" +
          response.code());
      }
  } catch (Throwable e) {
      Log.v("EX", "ex=" + e);
  }
}
```

5.6   Mobile Email

Before smartphones existed, there was a lot of speculation about what would become
the "killer app" on a feature phone. Many people thought email would be that killer app.
Hindsight is 20/20, and it is pretty obvious now that the killer app turned out to be the app
itself! Nonetheless, email remains one of the most useful functions we carry out every day on
our mobile devices.

Initiating outbound emails is something we do regularly. We take it for granted. While
technically not complicated, it is fraught with pitfalls, largely because of the negative effect
caused by all of the spam email being generated.

It is estimated that 98% of all emails sent are spam. That is a staggering number. If you
have ever hosted your own email server, you will appreciate the gravity of the problem.
Fortunately, third-party email providers such as Google and Yahoo do a great job at shielding
us from the problem.

5.7   Mobile Email Approaches

When sending emails from Android, you need to interface with an email server to accomplish
the actual transmission of the email. The following approaches are commonly used:

   ▧   Use a web browser to access a web-based email interface.

   ▧   Use an email client already existing on the device to manage the
       sending.

   ▧   Use a third-party library to access a remote mail server.

   ▧   Interface directly to a mail server using a script.

Figure 5-4 shows a graphical view of the four approaches, including the protocols used to
reach the web server and email server.

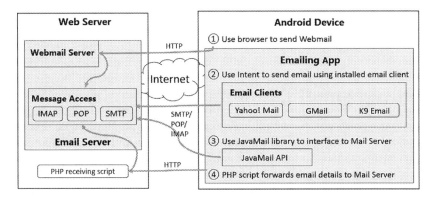

Figure 5-4. Android email approaches

The first approach involves connecting to the email server using the device browser. This approach is external to your own applications: useful, but not really of interest if you wish to include the functionality in your own apps. The remaining approaches can be implemented within your apps and I will discuss the implementation in detail. First, however, let's take a brief look at email protocols and email clients available for Android.

5.8   Email Protocols

A browser, using HTTP or HTTPS, can allow users to view and manage their email accounts. However, email clients, using specialized protocols, provide a more convenient access method on mobile devices.

Table 5-3 shows the common protocols and the specifications they rely on for sending and receiving emails.

Table 5-3. Email Protocols and Specifications

Protocol	Description
IMAP	Internet Message Access Protocol. Provides a method to access messages stored and possibly shared on a mail server. Permits client email apps to access remote messages as if they were stored locally. Transmitted over port 143 or 993 securely. Defined by RFC2060.
POP	Also referred to as POP3. Stands for Post Office Protocol version 3. It is a limited protocol for accessing a single mailbox. It is less capable than IMAP and is implemented by RFC1939. Typically transmitted over port 110 or 995 securely.
SMTP	Simple Mail Transfer Protocol. SMTP is widely used. It originated in 1982 and is defined by RFC821 and RFC822. It is used to transfer mail messages between hosts as well as to submit new messages to a host for delivery. Typically transmitted over port 25 or 465 securely.
MIME	Message Input Multibyte Encoding is the encoding standard used to describe the emails that are sent across the Internet. MIME is specified by RFC2046 and RFC2047. It is fully implemented by the *JavaMail* API you will use in the chapter project.

In order to effectively send or receive emails from your Android apps, you need to implement these popular mail protocols. Implementing these protocols from scratch would involve a high degree of effort. Implementing them by using a third-party library makes the task much simpler.

5.9   Android Email Clients

If you perform a quick search for email clients on the Android Play Store, you will see there are many options available. Some of the popular Android Email clients are shown in Table 5-4.

Table 5-4. Android Email Clients

Email Client	Description
Yahoo! Mail	Yahoo's popular email client.
Gmail	Google's popular email client. Tied to Google Play Services on Android devices.
K-9 Mail	Popular open source email client.
Boomerang	Startup company with Android email client and some other email plugins.
Boxer	Integrated suite of productivity apps incuding Android Email client.
Outlook	Microsoft's widely popular email client. Can be configured to use IMAP or POP3.

K-9 Mail is of particular note because it is an open source project. If you wish to implement your own email client, K-9 Mail is a great place to start. A link to the open source project is included in the chapter references.

5.10   Emailing App: AWS Server Setup

One of the methods you will implement to send emails involves calling a script on an external server to send out the email on behalf of your app. In the project, you will make use of Amazon Web Services (AWS) to set up the server.

On the server, you can choose from many of the popular server-side scripting languages, such as PHP, ASP, or Ruby. Listing 5-5 shows a PHP script that can send an email using the PHP *mail()* function. The PHP *mail()* function opens and closes an SMTP socket for each email that is sent.

Listing 5-5. sendemail.php

```php
<?php
    $name = $_POST['name'];
    $to = $_POST['to'];
    $from = $_POST['from'];
    $subject = $_POST['subject'];

    $message = "From: ".$name."\r\n";
    $message .= $_POST['message'];
    $headers = "From:" . $from;
    mail($to,$subject,$message,$headers);
?>
```

The *sendmail.*php script needs to be installed on the AWS instance to handle the PHP EMAIL functionality of the Emailing app. Setting up a simple server on AWS is a simple and effective way to send emails from Android without relying on third-party servers.

The easiest way to configure your AWS server is to install a LAMP web server, sometimes referred to as a LAMP stack on Amazon Linux. LAMP stands for Linux, Apache web server, MySQL database, and PHP scripting language, a reference to the four key packages needed to implement a public web server. The steps to installing LAMP on AWS are shown below. For further details, refer to the AWS link at the end of the chapter.

- Create an EC2 instance on AWS with public DNS. AWS has some affordable pricing plans for small virtual servers. New AWS users, depending on geographic region, are typically eligible for a free first year trial.

- Connect to your instance and update all packages.

  ```
  [ec2-user ~]$ sudo yum update -y
  ```

- Install Apache, MySQL, and PHP software packages.

  ```
  [ec2-user ~]$ sudo yum install -y httpd24 php70 mysql56-server php70-mysqlnd
  ```

- Start the Apache web server.

  ```
  [ec2-user ~]$ sudo service httpd start
  ```

- Use the *chkconfig* command to configure the web server to automatically start.

  ```
  [ec2-user ~]$ sudo chkconfig httpd on
  ```

- Add a security rule for the instance to allow HTTP traffic over port 80. Access the Amazon EC2 console at https://aws.amazon.com/console/

- Apache *httpd* serves file that are kept in the Apache document root, which can be found at */var/www/*.

- Install and configure FTP (File Transfer Protocol). You can use FTP to transfer the *sendmail.php* script discussed earlier. The Emailing app will make use of this script to send emails via AWS.

  ```
  [ec2-user ~]$ sudo yum install vsftpd
  ```

- Open the FTP ports on your instance in the AWS console, typically ports 20, 21, and 22.

▓   Edit the FTP config file and restart it.

```
## Use your favorite Linux editor to update the FTP configuration file
[ec2-user ~]$ sudo vi /etc/vsftpd/vsftpd.conf

## Make the following edits to the file ##
anonymous_enable=NO
pasv_enable=YES
pasv_min_port=1024
pasv_max_port=1048
pasv_address=<Public IP Address of your EC2 Instance>

## Restart
[ec2-user ~]$ sudo /etc/init.d/vsftpd restart
```

5.11   Emailing App

Like all good things in Android, there are multiple approaches for sending emails. Table 5-5 summarizes the approaches you will implement.

Table 5-5. *Emailing Approaches for Android*

Approach	Description
Android Intents	Intents provide a way to access functionality that is registered by other applications on your devices. Most smartphones have email apps, and their functionality can be accesses through their published Android Intents.
JavaMail API	A set of APIs from Oracle. The library is open source and can be used to connect to external email servers using email protocols such as SMTP, IMAP, or POP.
Script Interface to AWS	By implementing your own AWS-hosted PHP script, you can collect email content information from your users and then pass this information up to the server, which can deliver the email.

Each of these approaches has its merits and drawbacks.

Android Intents

Using Android Intents is the simplest of the approaches. It relies on the user having an email client installed on the device. This is likely, as most users have at least one email client. The user is able to choose which external email client will be used.

The main drawback of using Intents is that the user will be taken out of your app and into the email client app to complete the sending operation. The email fields can be prepopulated to minimize the time spent outside your app.

Figure 5-1 showed that special protocols are used to interface with mail servers. In order to interface directly with mail servers from your apps, you need to implement these protocols. The K-9 Mail open source project shows how this can be accomplished.

JavaMail API

However, there is an easier way: the JavaMail API.

The JavaMail API is a free open source library from Oracle. It can be included in your projects and makes interfacing to mail servers using the specialized protocols very simple. It is an extensive library that will let you implement nearly any email function that you require. Among its many features, the *JavaMail* API includes

- Platform-independent platform to build mail applications

- Protocol-independent platform to build mail applications

- Facilities for reading and sending emails

- Royalty-free implementation for SMTP, POP, and IMAP protocols

- Completely written in Java so it plays well with Android

The library is fairly lightweight, coming in at only 500KB. Thus, the JavaMail API is a good solution if you wish to implement email sending within your app without adding too much bloat, and without relying on Android Intents.

External AWS Interface

If you do not wish to add a library to your project, you can still send emails within your app by sending the required details up to the server for processing. This will require a receiving script on the server that can provide an interface to the mail server. In the chapter project, you will take a look at how to accomplish this by invoking a PHP script, *sendmail.php*, on a virtual server you configure using AWS.

The *sendmail.php* script relies on the server to have email sending capabilities. On the AWS LAMP server, this is handled by the open source *PHPMailer* class. The *PHPMailer* class is a full-featured email creation and transfer class used by many open source projects. Its source code is available on GitHub.

Emailing App Overview

Figure 5-5 shows a screenshot of the Emailing app. It allows users to specify each field for the outgoing email, including *From Address*, *To Address*, *Subject*, and *Body*. The app does not support attachments, but it could easily be extended using the *JavaMail API* method.

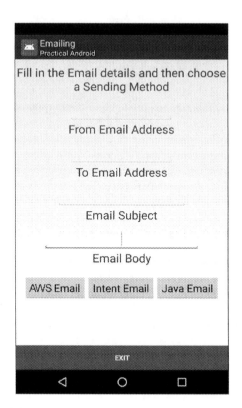

Figure 5-5. *Emailing app screenshot*

At the bottom of the layout are three buttons that allow the user to choose which sending method to use to send the email. In your app you probably don't need to implement all three methods; you can decide which one works best for your requirements.

Emailing Project

Table 5-6 shows the layout of the Emailing project.

Table 5-6. *Emailing Project Setup*

Sources	Resources/	Res/libs
MainActivity.java	layout/activity_main.xml	
GMailSender.java		
JSSEProvider.java		

The project contains three source files, and a single XML layout file. To set up JavaMail and OKHttp for your Android Studio project, include the following dependencies in your Build. Gradle file:

```
dependencies {
compile files('lib/javax.mail.jar')
compile files('lib/activation.jar')
compile 'com.squareup.okhttp3:okhttp:3.9.0'
}
```

The layout file contains the basic fields required to compose emails and the following buttons, which allow the user to select which emailing method to use when sending the email:

- AWS Email: Interfaces with a PHP script on an AWS server instance to send the email.

- Intent Email: Uses Android Intents to pass the message to an existing email client on the device.

- Java Email: Uses the JavaMail API to send outgoing emails.

The main source file is *MainActivity.java* and I will cover the key code next.

MainActivity.java

Configure the following variables according to your server and email settings. The *sendEmailScript* variable should point at your *sendmail.php* server script, which is called by the app when the user requests the server to send out the email.

The *emailAccount* and *emailPassword* variables are passed to the JavaMail API.

```
private static String sendEmailScript = "http://www.yourserver.com/sendemail.php";
private static String emailAccount = "your_email_account";
private static String emailPassword = "your_email_account_password";
```

Figure 5-6 shows a screenshot of the app with the email content fields populated. Each of these fields is represented by an *EditText* in the XML layout file. The *From Email Address* and the *To Email Address* each include the following *inputType* setting, which forces a valid email address to be entered:

```
android:inputType="textEmailAddress"
```

Figure 5-6. Composing an email

The content of these *EditText* boxes are consumed by the handlers for each of the buttons when they are pressed.

The easiest way to send an email from the app is by using the Android Intents. In the following code, you copy the completed fields from the *EditText* boxes, construct a URI using *StringBuilder*, and then start a new activity using *Intent.ACTION_SENDTO*:

```
// Intent button - Send email by using Android Intent
Button btnInt = (Button) findViewById(R.id.butIntent);
btnInt.setOnClickListener(new View.OnClickListener() {
  public void onClick(View v) {
      EditText fromET = (EditText) findViewById(R.id.box1);
      EditText toET = (EditText) findViewById(R.id.box2);
      EditText subjET = (EditText) findViewById(R.id.box3);
      EditText bodyET = (EditText) findViewById(R.id.box4);

      String emailFrom = fromET.getText().toString();
      String emailTo = toET.getText().toString();
      String emailSubj = subjET.getText().toString();
      String emailBody = bodyET.getText().toString();
      StringBuilder builder = new StringBuilder("mailto:" + Uri.encode(emailTo));
      if (emailSubj != null) {
          builder.append("?subject=" + Uri.encode(Uri.encode(emailSubj)));
```

```
        if (emailBody != null) {
            builder.append("&body=" + Uri.encode(Uri.encode(emailBody)));
        }
    }
    String uri = builder.toString();
    Intent intent = new Intent(Intent.ACTION_SENDTO, Uri.parse(uri));
    startActivity(intent);
  }
});
```

Figure 5-7 shows the layout that is generated when the user presses the Intent Email button.

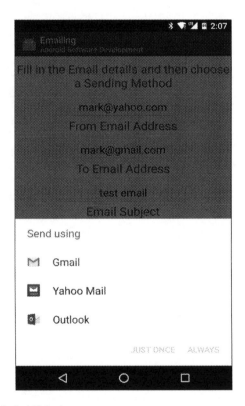

Figure 5-7. *Sending emails via Android Intent*

On the device shown, it provides the option for the user to send the email using any of the three email clients that were detected on the device, including, Yahoo, Gmail, and Outlook. The nice thing about the *ACTION_SENDTO* intent is that it is able to discriminate narrowly for email clients. It will exclude messaging clients such as Skype, Hangout, SMS, etc.

Sending email through the JavaMail API follows a similar approach. First, you copy the email details from the *EditText* fields. Then you create a *GMailSender* object, using the email user and password defined at the top of the *MainActivity.java*.

There is one difference. Note in the following code that you are performing these operations on a background thread and displaying progress via a *ProgressDialog*. This is required because sending the email is potentially a long-running network operation. You did not have to worry about this with the Intents approach because the client email app handled the sending of the email for you in the background.

```java
// JavaMail send button
Button btnJava = (Button) findViewById(R.id.butJava);
btnJava.setOnClickListener(new View.OnClickListener() {
    public void onClick(View v) {
        final ProgressDialog pd = ProgressDialog.show(MainActivity.this,
                                            "Sending",
                                            "Sending Gmail Java API Email...",
                                            true, false);
        new Thread(new Runnable(){
            public void run(){
                try {
                    EditText fromET = (EditText) findViewById(R.id.box1);
                    EditText toET = (EditText) findViewById(R.id.box2);
                    EditText subjET = (EditText) findViewById(R.id.box3);
                    EditText bodyET = (EditText) findViewById(R.id.box4);

                    String emailFrom = fromET.getText().toString();
                    String emailTo = toET.getText().toString();
                    String emailSubj = subjET.getText().toString();
                    String emailBody = bodyET.getText().toString();

                    GMailSender sender = new GMailSender(emailAccount, emailPassword);
                    sender.sendMail(emailSubj,
                                    emailBody,
                                    emailFrom,
                                    emailTo);
                } catch (Exception e) {
                    Log.e("SendMail", e.getMessage(), e);
                }
                pd.dismiss();
            }
        }).start();
    }
});
```

Figure 5-8 shows a screen capture of the *ProgressDialog* while the email is being sent by the JavaMail API. Once the email is successfully sent, the *ProgressDialog* box is dismissed.

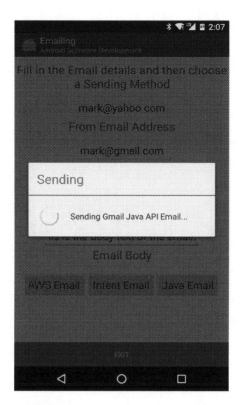

Figure 5-8. Sending email via the JavaMail API

The final email approach involves sending the email via script located on a remote AWS server. In this case, you also have a potential long-running network operation, so you include the *ProgressDialog* and background thread.

You are using *HttpClient* to send the email via the Post method. The *sendEmailScript* variable points to your server script. In this case, you are using an *ArrayList* of *Name/Value* pairs to store all of the email content from the layout *EditText* boxes. The following code shows the full implementation of the PHP Email button handler:

```
// AWS button
Button btnPHP = (Button) findViewById(R.id.butPhp);
btnPHP.setOnClickListener(new View.OnClickListener() {
  public void onClick(View v) {
    final ProgressDialog pd = ProgressDialog.show(MainActivity.this,"Sending","Sending AWS
    Email...",true, false);
    new Thread(new Runnable() {
      public void run() {
        try {
          EditText fromET = (EditText) findViewById(R.id.box1);
          EditText toET = (EditText) findViewById(R.id.box2);
          EditText subjET = (EditText) findViewById(R.id.box3);
          EditText bodyET = (EditText) findViewById(R.id.box4);
```

```
        String emailFrom = fromET.getText().toString();
        String emailTo = toET.getText().toString();
        String emailSubj = subjET.getText().toString();
        String emailBody = bodyET.getText().toString();

        OkHttpClient httpClient = new OkHttpClient();
        RequestBody formBody = new FormBody.Builder()
            .add("name", emailFrom)
            .add("to", emailTo)
            .add("from", emailFrom)
            .add("subject", emailSubj)
            .add("message", emailBody)
            .build();
        Request request = new Request.Builder()
            .url(sendEmailScript)
            .post(formBody)
            .build();
        Response response = httpClient.newCall(request).execute();
        }
      catch (Exception e) {
        e.printStackTrace();
      }
      pd.dismiss();
    }
  }).start();
  }
});
```

GMailSender.java

In addition to *MainActivity.java*, the project contains two additional source files, *GMailSender.java* and *JSSEProvider.java*.

The JavaMail API uses SMTP to send outgoing emails. In this case, the mail host needs to be defined in the *GMailSender.java* file, as shown in the following code. In this example, you are using GMail as the mail host. There is also a setting for the port number, so you can specify the unencrypted or encrypted port.

```
public class GMailSender extends javax.mail.Authenticator {
    private String mailhost = "smtp.gmail.com";
    private String user;
    private String password;
    private Session session;

    static {
        Security.addProvider(new com.wickham.android.emailing.JSSEProvider());
    }

    public GMailSender(String user, String password) {
        this.user = user;
        this.password = password;
```

```java
        Properties props = new Properties();
        props.setProperty("mail.transport.protocol", "smtp");
        props.setProperty("mail.host", mailhost);
        props.put("mail.smtp.auth", "true");
        props.put("mail.smtp.port", "465");
        props.put("mail.smtp.socketFactory.port", "465");
        props.put("mail.smtp.socketFactory.class",
                "javax.net.ssl.SSLSocketFactory");
        props.put("mail.smtp.socketFactory.fallback", "false");
        props.setProperty("mail.smtp.quitwait", "false");
        session = Session.getDefaultInstance(props, this);
    }

    protected PasswordAuthentication getPasswordAuthentication() {
        return new PasswordAuthentication(user, password);
}
```

JSSEProvider.java

When using the JavaMail API, the *JSSEProvider.java* class also needs to be included. This class does not need to be modified. This class is only required to handle the key manager and trust manager for TLS/SSL secure connections.

5.12   References

Uploading Files

- OkHttp Version 3: http://square.github.io/okhttp/3.x/okhttp/

- Posting a Multipart Request Using OkHttp: https://github.com/square/okhttp/wiki/Recipes

- Using the OkHttp3 MultipartBody.Builder: https://square.github.io/okhttp/3.x/okhttp/okhttp3/MultipartBody.Builder.html

- Extending HttpURLConnection for Multipart Form Support: https://stackoverflow.com/questions/34276466

Email

- JavaMail: https://javaee.github.io/javamail/

- JavaMail API FAQ (contains some very helpful information): https://javaee.github.io/javamail/FAQ

- K-9 Mail Open Source Project: https://github.com/k9mail/k-9

- POP/POP3: https://en.wikipedia.org/wiki/Post_Office_Protocol

- SMTP: https://en.wikipedia.org/wiki/Simple_Mail_Transfer_Protocol

- MIME: https://en.wikipedia.org/wiki/MIME

- IMAP: https://en.wikipedia.org/wiki/Internet_Message_Access_Protocol

- Installing LAMP on AWS: https://docs.aws.amazon.com/AWSEC2/latest/UserGuide/install-LAMP.html

Chapter 6

Push Messaging

6.1 Introduction

Push messaging is everywhere. You can see it used in almost all of the top apps today. If you take a look at your most frequently used apps, they tend to have a couple of things in common. They almost always provide a very useful service and they typically employ push messaging to deliver the service in a timely manner.

Push implementations are not the most high-profile, visible aspect of any app, but they are critical in ensuring that our devices receive that important update, notification, or content at precisely the right moment.

In this chapter, I will cover

- How push messaging works

- When it makes sense to use push messaging

- The different approaches for implementing push messaging

- The different technologies behind push messaging

- How to choose the right solution for your Android app

- Pros and cons of the push messaging approaches

- Implementation of two different Android push approaches:
  Google's Firebase Cloud Messaging, and open source push
  messaging with MQTT

© Mark Wickham 2018
M. Wickham, *Practical Android*, https://doi.org/10.1007/978-1-4842-3333-7_6

6.2   Chapter Projects

The projects shown in Table 6-1 will be presented in this chapter.

Table 6-1. Chapter Projects

Title of Project	File Name	Description
FCM Push Messaging	*FCMpush.zip*	Google Firebase Cloud Messaging implementation
MQTT Push Messaging	*MQTTpush.zip*	MQTT open source push implementation

6.3   Push Messaging Overview

Push messaging can be described as a permission-based mobile communications channel. It is described by one of the vendors as possibly the most powerful communication channel ever created—lofty praise for a technology that is not exactly new, but the rise of the smartphone has positioned push messaging as perhaps the most useful feature we can implement in our apps.

A quick scan of apps reveals the many use cases for push messaging. Notification of breaking news stories, airline flight status, sporting event scores, email notifications, stock market quotes and alerts, update notifications for apps, completion of long-running networking tasks, calendar event reminders, shopping alerts, social networking status changes, and travel notifications are just a few use cases.

There are several key characteristics of push messaging that make it so prominent in Android apps today:

- Push messaging is a powerful communication channel because there is no middle man to control the access. Think about the infrastructure required to broadcast a radio or television signal to a receiving device, or the expense required to distribute a message using print media. And, of course, these traditional channels do not provide a feedback path.

- The ongoing migration to Android smartphones provides us the opportunity to directly access a large captive audience. Over the past two decades, mobile device penetration rates in many developed markets have topped 1.0, indicating that each person has more than one device. Today, smartphone shipments are growing rapidly; it is estimated currently that over one billion Android smartphones are being actively used each month.

- Push messaging implementations on Android devices make use of the reliable service-based architecture. This software architecture is well suited for push message handling.

- Push messaging provides a near real-time delivery of messages. You will see that not all push technologies provide guaranteed delivery or quality of service (QoS) levels, but generally speaking, we can expect messages to be delivered to our devices in less than one second. The results are not deterministic and depend on network configurations.

- Push messaging saves battery life compared to the alternative of using polling to check a server periodically for new content. With a push messaging implementation, the application server knows exactly when a new message needs to be delivered and is able to deliver messages to the specific device.

- There are multiple methods that can be used to initiate or send push messages, which provides us with a lot of flexibility. We can use client SDKs to send messages from devices, restful APIs can be used to Post to a server URL, simple web-based consoles can be used, or most commonly, an application server can directly send out push messages when a condition is met.

Push Technologies

You saw earlier that implementing HTTP in Android is fairly straightforward. HTTP is the protocol that handles almost all Internet traffic. As useful as it is, HTTP was not designed with push messaging in mind. Yet HTTP is often abused as a substitute for push messaging for two primary reasons.

- HTTP is relatively easy to implement when compared to the specialized push messaging solutions.

- Push messaging requires a server. It is the server that maintains the record of registered devices to whom messages can be pushed. This added complexity can act as a barrier to entry for developers.

It is amazing how much push messaging functionality you can overload onto HTTP. Through a combination of versioning, synchronization, and polling the server, you can approximate the functionality of push messaging. However, if you take this approach, you will eventually discover that such solutions are no match for the simplicity, scalability, delivery times, and battery performance of implementing a proper push messaging solution.

Table 6-2 provides a summary of the push technologies I will cover in this chapter. The demo apps will implement push using Google Firebase Cloud Messaging and the open source technology MQTT.

Table 6-2. *Push Technology Overview*

Technology	Name	Description
HTTP	Hyper Text Transfer Protocol	Foundation of the Web. Can be used to provide push-like capabilities, but is not designed for this purpose.
FCM	Google Firebase Cloud Messaging	Previously called C2DM and then GCM. Used by many of the third-party push services. Google makes it easy.
AMQP	Advanced Message Queuing Protocol	Huge feature set and fine-grain control. No good library available for Android yet. Reliable, scalable, and interoperability for the enterprise. www.amqp.org
MQTT	Message Queue Telemetry Transport	Originally developed at IBM. Moved into the Open Source community. Has become a standard. Low footprint is ideal for the Internet of Things. www.mqtt.org
STOMP	Simple (Streaming)	Simple, lightweight, text-based. You can connect to a broker with a Telnet client. No queues or topics, you simply send to a destination. www.stomp.github.com

Google first introduced push messaging in 2012 with a new service called *Cloud to Device Messaging* (C2DM). In 2014, it evolved into what was known as *Google Cloud Messaging* (GCM) and in 2016 was further integrated into the Firebase suite and is now known as Firebase Cloud Messaging (FCM). FCM is a fully functional, feature rich, push messaging solution that Android developers can easily integrate into their apps. FCM is also used as the underlying transport by many third-party push service vendors. Figure 6-1 shows the timeline of Google's push messaging offerings.

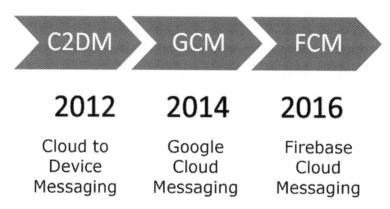

Figure 6-1. Google push messaging evolution

There are times when you may not be able to rely on the Google push messaging solution. I will discuss some of those situations later in the chapter. If your requirements dictate an alternative to Google's push solution, the open source Message Queue Telemetry Transport (MQTT) may be an option.

MQTT originated out of IBM and is now open source. It was originally developed to control remote telemetry equipment, but has now found a strong position within mobile devices and the Internet of Things (IoT) due to its low bandwidth requirements and light footprint. MQTT has completed standardization and has recently been gaining popularity in the Android and IoT communities.

Two additional push messaging protocols are worth mentioning: Advanced Message Queuing Protocol (AMQP) and Simple Text Orientated Message Protocol (STOMP). AMQP is widely used in banking, finance, and other industries that require a mission-critical push messaging solution. STOMP, as its names implies, is very simple. The protocol implements just a few basic messages and can handle binary messages by using UTF-8 encoding.

AMQP and STOMP implementations will not be presented in this chapter because Android libraries are not readily available. However, both AMQP and STOMP have open source and commercial Java clients and brokers that could be ported to Android. If you would like to further explore similarities and differences between MQTT and AMQP, the end-of-chapter links contain a helpful reference blog paper.

How Push Messaging Works

There are several push messaging solutions available to us as developers. Under the hood, they all rely on basically the same functionality and messaging flow. Push messaging achieves its magic by setting up and delivering messages to devices with three distinct phases:

- One-time registration of the device with the push provider, FCM in this case. ①

- One-time notification to the app server of the successful device registration. ② This includes storing the device ID into a database on the app server.

- The app server pushes the message(s) to the registered device(s). ③

Figure 6-2 shows a message ladder diagram indicating these three distinct phases: registration, notification, and delivery.

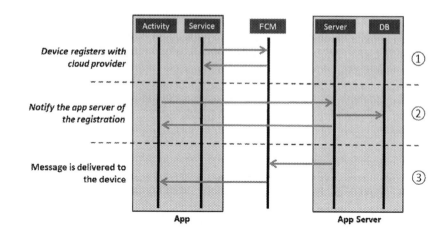

Figure 6-2. *Push messaging message ladder diagram of the three push phases: registration, notification, and delivery*

It is Important to highlight step ② where the registered device ID is stored in the database of the app server. This *pre-registering*, accomplished by steps ① and ②, allows the device to be directly identified whenever a message needs to be pushed down the magic of push.

Note that each push messaging provider has its own specific nomenclature to represent the device ID and the registration ID within these messages.

Choosing a Technology

When you require a push messaging solution for your app, you must decide on the technology and approach you are going to use. The approaches can be classified into the following categories:

- Third-Party Services
- Firebase Cloud Messaging
- Open Source Messaging Protocols

In addition to these approaches, the underlying messaging technology could include one or more of the protocols shown in Table 6-3.

Table 6-3. Push Messaging Protocols

Protocol	Description	Ports
XMPP	Extensible Messaging and Presence Protocol; used by many popular instant messaging services.	TCP or HTTP transport port 80 or 443 (secure)
MQTT	Message Queuing Telemetry Transport; great for mobile devices and the IoT.	TCP port 1883 or 8883 (secure)
HTTP	Hyper Text Transport Protocol; powers the Internet we all know and love.	TCP port 80 or 443 (secure)
AMQP	Advanced Message Queuing Protocol; high performance and robust feature set.	Frame-based binary protocol TCP port 5672

I will discuss more about FCM in the next section, but note that it can use either the HTTP or XMPP protocol.

Given this combination of approaches and implementation protocols, how do you choose the right implementation for your Android app? There are a few key questions that you need to answer to help you choose the correct implementation. Refer to Figure 6-3 for a logical representation of the decision process.

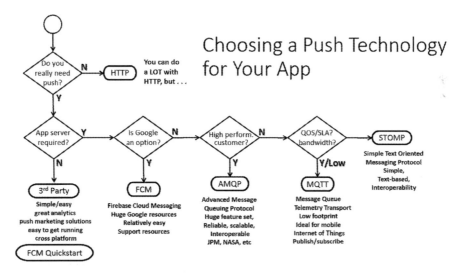

Figure 6-3. Choosing a push technology

One of the key considerations when choosing a push approach is whether or not you require an application server. Recall from Figure 6-2 that push messaging requires both an application server and a service provider. In your first project, you will be using Google's CM as the service provider. You will implement your own app server using some basic scripting on the server side. In the second project, you will use a publish/subscribe model and implement a server known as a broker.

6.4   Push Messaging Services

Third-party push messaging services are the easiest way to get started with push messaging in Android. These services allow you to get your app up and running quickly with a very small amount of effort.

They have become popular because they handle all of the application server setup. This is very advantageous as it allows you to focus on your app development and not worry about the back-end app server setup. It is worth noting that as Google has greatly enhanced its Firebase offering; the Google Firebase console can now provide many of the same features.

One potential drawback of using a third-party service is that you may have limited capabilities on the app server, especially if you need to implement complex logic to handle the pushing of messages to your registered subscriber base.

I will cover some of the popular third-party services in the next section.

Push Service Advantages

There are a number of advantages to using push services, and there are many vendors who provide them. The most important advantages are the following:

- Implementation is painless, so you are able to get your push messaging app up and running fast.

- You can create an account and configure the server back-end in just a few minutes.

- Almost all third-party push services provide a sample Android app which you can modify. You can have your own app up and running in only an hour or two.

- You don't need to spend time developing the server back end so you can focus on your Android apps.

- Cross-platform support is available. You can have a single provider support Android, IOS, or other platforms.

- It's not just limited to FCM transport on Android, although FCM is the only transport many of them use.

- It scales easily. They allow you to break the 1,000 device limit by handling the iterations automatically for you.

- Server bandwidth is available on demand. Most of the third-party push services allow you to start with a free trial account. Of course, as you add registered devices or functionality, costs can increase.

Note that pricing varies for each of the push services. Many of them are free to set up so you can test your app. However, as you begin to commercialize your app and scale your message volume, prices can become substantial.

Choosing a Push Service

There are a large number of third-party services available. Table 6-4 shows a summary of the popular push services. Most of them supply the needed developer resources (SDKs) to help you get push up and running in your Android app quickly.

Table 6-4. Push Messaging Third-Party Services

Name	Features	URL
Microsoft Azure	Microsoft cross-platform push solution	`www.microsoft.com`
Amazon Push Services	Excellent solution if you use Amazon App Store to distribute your apps	`www.amazon.com`
Push Whoosh	International language, remote APIs, uses FCM/API11	`www.pushwhoosh.com`
Urban Airship	Portland based, uses FCM, Analytics, Wallet	`www.urbanairship.com`
Xtify	New York based, IBM affiliated, global support, cross platforms	`www.xtify.com/pricing.html`
PushBots	Simple, cross platform, claims to be the price leader	`www.pushbots.com`
Parse Push	SaaS push service, cloud support, maximum back end flexibility	`www.parse.com/products/push`
Push.io	B2B push provider, billions served, ease of use, analytics	`http://push.io`
Quick Blox	Scalable, secure, 256-bit AES, reportedly offers good support	`http://quickblox.com/developers/Android`

These services have several key aspects in common, including

- They include a demonstration Android app you can download and tailor to get started quickly
- They have a website back end where you can set up and manage your account
- They include a push message control panel on the back-end website
- Many utilize FCM for the underlying transport mechanism

Services Setup Steps

The first step to incorporate a push service into your app is registration.

Registration is typically free and can be completed at the provider's website. Once you register, you will need to download the provider's Android .jar library file and the Android sample app project file.

The following are the generic steps you must complete to use a push service:

1. Set up your account on the provider's website. You will typically log into the provider's dashboard and define a new application project and configure your notification services. You will need to procure your FCM credentials from your Google Web Services dashboard.

2. Download the library .jar file, which you will need to import into your app.

3. Download the sample app from the provider.

4. Adjust and build your app using your package name and FCM credentials. This usually involves copying keys assigned to your application by the provider. See Figure 6-4 for examples of how this looks.

5. Launch the app on your device(s).

6. Set up the push service console.

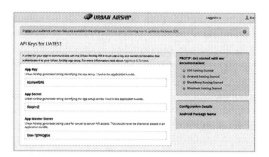

Figure 6-4. Setting up FCM credentials in a push service

With a minimal amount of effort, you will be able to implement push messaging into your app using a push service. This approach is ideal if you don't need to develop your own app server and you just need to be able to push out messages from an easy-to-use back end to some or all of your users.

6.5   Firebase Cloud Messaging

Firebase Cloud Messaging is now part of Google's Firebase Suite. All of the Firebase components are cross platform, which means they not only work on Android but also for iOS and the Web.

FCM is free to use. According to the official Firebase pricing page, the following additional Firebase features are also free:

- Analytics (covered in Chapter 4)
- App Indexing
- Authentication
- Dynamic Links
- Invites
- Notifications
- Crash Reporting (covered in Chapter 4)
- Remote Configuration

For a complete list of the latest Firebase library versions, refer to the "Available Libraries" section at `https://firebase.google.com/docs/android/setup`.

For Android developers, Google provides all the resources you need to implement your own push messaging solution with FCM including the client app and back-end server.

There is extensive support available on the Google and Android developer sites that covers the setup of FCM push messaging. Refer to the end-of-chapter links for a complete list of the most important FCM resources.

GCM/FCM Migration

Figure 6-1 showed how FCM evolved from GCM and is now the recommended replacement for GCM. Google has not deprecated GCM and it is not clear if and when they might do so. According to Google, they will continue to support the current version of GCM because they know a lot of developers are using GCM today, and they recognize that it takes time to update released client apps.

However, all the new client-side features will only be added to FCM. For this reason, it is recommended that developers use FCM for all new development, and begin the process of migrating existing GCM apps to FCM.

The good news is that because FCM relies on the underlying GCM engine, the differences between GCM and FCM are pretty minor. If you have an app that relies on GCM for push messaging, Google provides detailed instructions for migrating apps from GCM to FCM at `https://developers.google.com/cloud-messaging/android/android-migrate-fcm`.

FCM is easier to set up and implement due to a number of improvements:

- The *AndroidManifest.xml* file has been simplified by reducing the amount of permissions required. It no longer requires permissions for C2DM and WakeLock.

- The *AndroidManifest.xml* file no longer needs to include *GcmReceiver* because FCM handles this automatically.

- No library files (such as *gcm.jar*) need to be included in the project. For FCM, this is handled by the *build.gradle* files for Android Studio.

- The device registration message flow has been simplified with a new token management approach.

FCM Setup

Setting up an FCM project involves the following high-level steps. For more details, refer to the following links, which describe adding Firebase to your apps and setting up your FCM client app:

https://firebase.google.com/docs/android/setup

https://firebase.google.com/docs/cloud-messaging/android/client

A high-level summary of these steps is shown next.

Adding Firebase to Your Android Project

- Google FCM requires a device running Android 4.0 or newer and Google Play Services 11.4.2 or higher.

- FCM requires you to use Android Studio version 1.5 or higher.

- You will need the *applicationID* or *instanceID* from the *build.gradle* file in your Android project's module folder (typically *app/*). You will enter this ID in the Firebase console.

- Set up your project for FCM at the Firebase console at https://console.firebase.google.com. You have the choice to use the Firebase Assistant or you can manually add Firebase.

- To manually add Firebase, you can either import a Google project or create a new project. After you enter your app's package name, download the *google-services.json* file. You can download this file at any time; see the end-of-chapter links for details.

- Copy the *google-services.json* file into your projects *app/* folder.

Setting Up Your FCM Client App

▨ In Android Studio, add the FCM dependency to your gradle files:

Root-level *build.gradle* file:

```
buildscript {
    dependencies {
        classpath 'com.google.gms:google-services:3.1.1'
    }
}
```

App-level *build.gradle* file:

```
Dependencies {
    compile 'com.google.firebase:firebase-messaging:11.4.2'
}
```

▨ Add a service that extends *FirebaseMessagingService* to your *AndroidManifest.xml* file. This is needed if you want to use features beyond just receiving notifications.

```
<service
    android:name=".MyFirebaseMessagingService">
    <intent-filter>
        <action android:name="com.google.firebase.MESSAGING_EVENT"/>
    </intent-filter>
</service>
```

▨ Add a service that extends *FirebaseInstanceIdService* to your *AndroidManifest.xml* file. This is needed to handle creation, rotation, and updating or registration tokens.

```
<service
    android:name=".MyFirebaseInstanceIDService">
    <intent-filter>
        <action android:name="com.google.firebase.INSTANCE_ID_EVENT"/>
    </intent-filter>
</service>
```

▨ If FCM is critical to your app's function, be sure to set *minSDKVersion 8* or higher in the app's *build.gradle* to ensure it can only be installed on devices that support FCM.

▨ On initial startup of your app, FCM generates a registration token for the client app instance. You can retrieve and monitor the token with the following code:

```
@Override
public void onTokenRefresh() {
    // Get updated InstanceID token.
    String refreshedToken = FirebaseInstanceId.getInstance().getToken();
```

```
                    Log.d(TAG, "Refreshed token: " + refreshedToken);
                    // If you want to send messages to this application instance send the
                    // Instance ID token to your app server here ...
            }
```

Once the Firebase and FCM setup are completed, you are ready to push messages down to your device. You will see how to do this first with the FCM Quickstart app. Then you will move onto the fully functional FCM Android client app.

FCM Quickstart App

If you wish to introduce yourself to push messaging and would like to experiment with FCM, Google provides the Firebase Cloud Messaging Quickstart app to make it easy. The app is available on GitHub at https://github.com/firebase/quickstart-android/tree/master/messaging.

Figure 6-5 shows a snapshot and some highlights of the FCM Quickstart app.

Google's FCM Quickstart App

Firebase Cloud Messaging Quickstart, Available on Github:
https://github.com/firebase/quickstart-android/tree/
master/messaging

The App demonstrates registering an Android app for notifications and handling the receipt of messages through InstanceID and Tokens.

① Can be run on device or emulator.

② Use the Firebase console to send single messages.

③ Use the Firebase console to send a message to a topic.

④ For Topic messages, subscribe to the topic from the Device.

Figure 6-5. FCM Quickstart app

The app demonstrates registering an Android app for notifications and handling the receipt of messages through *InstanceID* and *Tokens*. The Quickstart app does not require an app server, and it will let you send downstream messages to your device from the Firebase console.

The FCM Quickstart app is a great way to get started, but what if you want advanced functionality, such as

- Sending downstream messages from your app,

- Sending topic messages with a publish/subscribe model,

- Sending to device groups, and

- Sending upstream messages?

To handle each of these advanced functions, you will need an application server. For the upcoming FCM project, you will implement your own app server on Amazon AWS.

FCM App

The FCM app presented in this chapter is a fully functional FCM push solution, adding the advanced capabilities of the app server that were not available for the Quickstart app. When you launch the FCM app, you will see the screen shown in Figure 6-6.

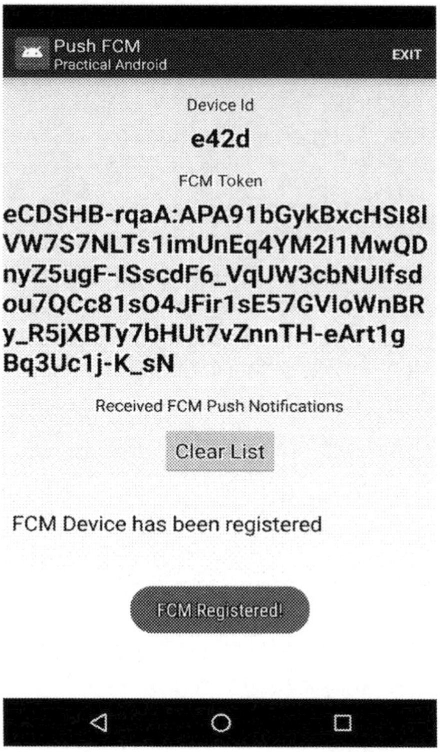

Figure 6-6. *FCM push messaging demo app registering the device and receiving messages*

Your device will automatically register with the FCM server. Recall that this was step ① in the push messaging ladder diagram. When the app receives the ID, it will register the device with your app server (recall step ② in the message flow). Now your device is ready to receive push messages.

Next, you will take a look at the code in the FCM project and how to set up your FCM application server. After implementation of the app server, you will be able to push messages down to registered devices from the app server, similar to the FCM Quickstart app used with the Google Firebase console.

FCM Project

Table 6-5 shows the overall file structure of the project.

Table 6-5. *FCM Push Project Structure*

Sources	Resources
MyFirebaseMessagingService.java MyFirebaseInstanceIDService.java	activity_main.xml
Global.java	
MainActivity.java	

The key aspects of each of the source files are summarized next.

AndroidManifest.xml

FCM greatly simplifies the *AndroidManifest.xml* file. You only need to define two services. The *MyFirebaseMessagingService* is required to handle messages. The *MyFirebaseInstanceIdService* is required to handle tokens. All of the cryptic *c2dm* references that were required for GCM are no longer required with FCM! A subset of the *AndroidManifest.xml* follows:

```
<service
    android:name=".MyFirebaseMessagingService">
    <intent-filter>
        <action android:name="com.google.firebase.MESSAGING_EVENT"/>
    </intent-filter>
</service>

<service
    android:name=".MyFirebaseInstanceIDService">
    <intent-filter>
        <action android:name="com.google.firebase.INSTANCE_ID_EVENT"/>
    </intent-filter>
</service>
```

The activity used in the app is defined in the manifest file, as shown below. The *MainActivity* runs when the app is launched. It obtains a unique ID for the device and then registers the device with FCM. Once registration is complete, the *MainActivity* receives incoming messages and displays them in a *ListView*.

```
<activity
    android:name="com.wickham.android.MainActivity"
    <intent-filter>
        <action android:name="android.intent.action.MAIN"/>
        <category android:name="android.intent.category.LAUNCHER"/>
    </intent-filter>
</activity>
<activity
    android:name="com.wickham.android.MainActivity"
</activity>
```

Global.java: Setting Up the FCM Credentials

Both the activity and the services used in the project will need references to your FCM credentials and URL interface to the app server. To centralize the access to the variables, the project will use a public *Global.java* class.

```java
public class Global {
  public static final String SERVER_URL = "http://www.your-server.com/register.php";
  public static final String EXTRA_MESSAGE = "Extra_Message";
  public static final String REGISTRATION_COMPLETE = "registrationComplete";
  public static final String PUSH_NOTIFICATION = "pushNotification";
  public static String DEVICE_NAME = "deviceName";
}
```

MainActivity.java

The *MainActivity.java* launches at startup and generates a unique id for the device. The unique *deviceID* is obtained with the following code.

```java
// Set a name for the device and truncate to last four characters
Global.DEVICE_NAME = Secure.getString(this.getContentResolver(), Secure.ANDROID_ID);
Global.DEVICE_NAME = Global.DEVICE_NAME.substring(Global.DEVICE_NAME.length()-4,
Global.DEVICE_NAME.length());
((TextView) findViewById(R.id.uniqueid)).setText(Global.DEVICE_NAME);
```

MainActivity.java next performs the following functions:

- Registers the device if it is not already registered.
- Sets up a broadcast receiver and listens for incoming messaging.
- Displays any new messages in a *ListView*. The *ListView* can be cleared by pressing the Clear List button.
- Displays a toast upon arrival of a new message

The broadcast receiver is implemented as follows. Whenever new messages are received by the broadcast receiver, the message payload is added to the *items ArrayList* and a Toast is also generated to notify the user.

```java
mRegistrationBroadcastReceiver = new BroadcastReceiver() {
  @Override
  public void onReceive(Context context, Intent intent) {
    // Check the intent type
    if (intent.getAction().equals(Global.REGISTRATION_COMPLETE)) {
      // FCM successfully registered
      Log.i (TAG, "Receiver=" + Global.REGISTRATION_COMPLETE);
      items.add(0, "FCM Device has been registered");
      incomingPushMsg.notifyDataSetChanged();
      Toast.makeText(getApplicationContext(), "FCM Registered!", Toast.LENGTH_LONG).show();
```

```
      // Display the token
      String token = FirebaseInstanceId.getInstance().getToken();
      ((TextView) findViewById(R.id.token)).setText(token);
      Log.i (TAG, "Refreshed Token");
    } else if (intent.getAction().equals(Global.PUSH_NOTIFICATION)) {
      // FCM message received
      Log.i (TAG, "Receiver=" + Global.PUSH_NOTIFICATION);
      //String newMessage = intent.getExtras().getString(Global.PUSH_NOTIFICATION);
      String newMessage = intent.getStringExtra(Global.EXTRA_MESSAGE);
      items.add(0, newMessage);
      incomingPushMsg.notifyDataSetChanged();
      Toast.makeText(getApplicationContext(), "New Message: " + newMessage,
      Toast.LENGTH_LONG).show();
    }
  }
};
```

MyFirebaseInstanceIDService

When implementing FCM, you need to include the *onTokenRefresh* method in the *MyFirebaseInstanceIDService.java*.

This small code block enables you to manage tokens. FCM has simplified registration with the *FirebaseInstanceID.getToken()* method.

```
public class MyFirebaseInstanceIDService extends FirebaseInstanceIdService {
  private static final String TAG = MyFirebaseInstanceIDService.class.getSimpleName();

  @Override
  public void onTokenRefresh() {
    super.onTokenRefresh();
    String refreshedToken = FirebaseInstanceId.getInstance().getToken();
    Log.i(TAG, "onTokenRefresh token=" + refreshedToken);
    // sending reg id to your server
    register(Global.DEVICE_NAME, refreshedToken);
  }

  private void register(String name, final String token) {
    Log.i(TAG, "Registering device with token=" + token);
    String serverUrl = Global.SERVER_URL;
    Map<String, String> params = new HashMap<String, String>();
    params.put("name", name);
    params.put("token", token);
    post(serverUrl, params);

    // Tell the UI we have been registered by FCM
    Intent registrationComplete = new Intent(Global.REGISTRATION_COMPLETE);
    registrationComplete.putExtra("token", token);
    registrationComplete.putExtra("name", name);
    LocalBroadcastManager.getInstance(this).sendBroadcast(registrationComplete);
  }
```

```java
private static void post(String endpoint, Map<String, String> params) {
  URL url;
  try {
    url = new URL(endpoint);
  } catch (MalformedURLException e) {
    throw new IllegalArgumentException("invalid url: " + endpoint);
  }
  StringBuilder bodyBuilder = new StringBuilder();
  Iterator<Map.Entry<String, String>> iterator = params.entrySet().iterator();
  // constructs the POST body using the parameters
  while (iterator.hasNext()) {
    Map.Entry<String, String> param = iterator.next();
    bodyBuilder.append(param.getKey()).append('=')
        .append(param.getValue());
    if (iterator.hasNext()) {
        bodyBuilder.append('&');
    }
  }
  String body = bodyBuilder.toString();
  Log.i(TAG, "Posting '" + body + "' to " + url);
  byte[] bytes = body.getBytes();
  HttpURLConnection conn = null;
  try {
    Log.i(TAG, "url=" + url);
    conn = (HttpURLConnection) url.openConnection();
    conn.setDoOutput(true);
    conn.setUseCaches(false);
    conn.setFixedLengthStreamingMode(bytes.length);
    conn.setRequestMethod("POST");
    conn.setRequestProperty("Content-Type","application/x-www-form-
    urlencoded;charset=UTF-8");
    // post the request
    OutputStream out = conn.getOutputStream();
    out.write(bytes);
    out.close();
    // handle the response
    int status = conn.getResponseCode();
    Log.i(TAG, "Status Code=" + status);
    if (status != 200) {
        // Handle failure
    }
  } catch (Exception e) {
    e.printStackTrace();
  } finally {
    if (conn != null) {
      conn.disconnect();
    }
  }
}
```

The code above is required to manage registration tokens because a token can change for a number of reasons, including

- The app deletes the Instance ID.
- The app is restored on a new device.
- The user uninstalls/reinstalls the app.
- The user clears the app's data.

The following single line of code shows how to obtain a FCM token. This token can then be sent up to your app server to manage your push subscribers.

```
String myToken = FirebaseInstanceId.getToken(); // You can send this token to your app server
```

MyFirebaseMessagingService.java

MyFirebaseMessagingService.java is the service that runs in the background and handles the messaging interface with Google FCM. The service implements the following important FCM method:

- *onMessage* is called whenever a message is received

The following code shows how the method is implemented in the FCM project. When a message is received, you create an Intent to display the message in the *ArrayList* on the Main Activity screen layout, and you then generate a notification for the user.

```
public class MyFirebaseMessagingService extends FirebaseMessagingService {

  private static final String TAG = MyFirebaseMessagingService.class.getSimpleName();

  @Override
  public void onMessageReceived(RemoteMessage remoteMessage) {
    String message = remoteMessage.getNotification().getBody();
    String data = remoteMessage.getData().toString();
    Log.i(TAG, "Message= " + message);

    if (remoteMessage.getNotification() != null) {
        Intent intent = new Intent(Global.PUSH_NOTIFICATION);
        intent.putExtra(Global.EXTRA_MESSAGE, message);
        LocalBroadcastManager.getInstance(this).sendBroadcast(intent);
    }
  }
}
```

Application Server Setup

In Chapter 5, you saw how to set up a server on AWS for sending emails from your Android app. For the FCM project, you will use a similar approach to set up an FCM application server. Other back-end technologies such as Ruby or ASP could just as easily be used. Google has many resources available to help you set up your application server; refer to *Server Setup* in the FCM links section of this chapter.

The process involves the following steps:

- Set up a publicly available LAMP server. You can use Amazon Web Services or other cloud-based providers. See the AWS LAMP server setup instructions in Chapter 5.

- Set up a MySQL database. You can use *PHPMyAdmin* or other managers. More about this later.

- Create a script on the server to store the tokens. You will use a MySQL database to store the registered users on the app server.

- Build a user interface. In the project you will use a simple HTML webpage with some basic JavaScript (*index.php*). You could make this much more sophisticated by leveraging popular content management systems (CMS) such as Joomla or Drupal.

- Add basic functions to the user interface so users can view registered devices and push messages to devices.

In order to complete the setup described above, you need to install several files on your app server. File Transfer Protocol (FTP) can be used to transfer these PHP files onto the app server.

If you are not familiar with PHP and AWS, do not be intimidated. The PHP scripts are only about a hundred lines of code, combined. Their purpose is to merely provide an interface to the Google FCM API and allow access to your app server database.

Next, let's review each of the required files that need to be installed on your AWS application server.

db_connect.php

This file contains a function that will connect to the database and store the registered devices. The database variables and GOOGLE_SERVER_KEY shown below must match the FCM project *Server Key* and MySQL database you will create.

```
public function connect() {
    define("DB_HOST", "localhost");
    define("DB_USER", "fcm_user1");
    define("DB_PASSWORD", "fcmuser1");
    define("DB_DATABASE", "fcm");
    $con = mysql_connect(DB_HOST, DB_USER, DB_PASSWORD);
    mysql_select_db(DB_DATABASE);
    return $con;
}
```

db_functions.php

This file contains two functions that will be used to store users into the database and to access all users currently registered. Function *storeUser* will insert a newly registered device into the database. Function *getAllUsers* is called by *index.php* and is used to display a list of all the users currently registered in the database.

FCM.php

This file contains the *send_notification* function. The function is called whenever you need to send a push notification down to a device. FCM requires you to send a push notification by calling the FCM Send API with a JSON-encoded message. The following *FCM.php* code handles this for you:

```php
<?php
class FCM {
  function __construct() {
  }
  public function send_notification($token, $message) {

    define("FIREBASE_API_KEY", "your-api-key");

    $url = 'https://fcm.googleapis.com/fcm/send';
    $fields = array(
      'to' => $token,
      'data' => $message,
    );
    $headers = array(
      'Authorization: key=' . FIREBASE_API_KEY,
      'Access-Control-Allow-Origin: *',
      'Content-Type: application/json'
    );

    $ch = curl_init();
    curl_setopt($ch, CURLOPT_URL, $url);
    curl_setopt($ch, CURLOPT_POST, true);
    curl_setopt($ch, CURLOPT_HTTPHEADER, $headers);
    curl_setopt($ch, CURLOPT_RETURNTRANSFER, true);
    curl_setopt($ch, CURLOPT_SSL_VERIFYPEER, false);
    curl_setopt($ch, CURLOPT_POSTFIELDS, json_encode($fields));
    $result = curl_exec($ch);
    if ($result === FALSE) {
        die('Curl failed: ' . curl_error($ch));
    }
    curl_close($ch);
    echo $result;
  }
}
?>
```

register.php

This script will serve as the interface with your Android app. Recall that you set up a reference to this file in the Android app's *Global.java* file. Whenever your app needs to register a new user on the application server, this script will be called. The code that stores the user in the database and sends the initial push notification is as follows:

```php
<?php
if (isset($_POST['name']) && isset($_POST['token'])) {
  $name = $_POST['name'];
  $token = $_POST['token'];

  include_once $_SERVER['DOCUMENT_ROOT'] . "/db_functions.php";
  include_once $_SERVER['DOCUMENT_ROOT'] . "/FCM.php";

  $db = new DB_Functions();
  $fcm = new FCM();

  $res = $db->storeUser($name, $token);
  $result = $fcm->send_notification($token, $name);
  echo $result;
}

fclose($handle);

?>
```

index.php

This is a simple HTML and JavaScript webpage that will display a list of your registered devices and also allow you to push a message down to any of the registered devices. Figure 6-7 shows a screenshot of the basic interface.

Although very crude, this simple webpage achieves some of the basic functions available on the Firebase console, which allows you to manage your devices or push down messages. Not quite as glamorous, but it gets the job done and it can easily be extended.

send_message.php

This simple script is used by *index.php* to send a push message to a registered device. This FCM example only allows you to push messages down to individual subscribers, but it would be very simple to modify *index.php* to call *send_message* within a loop to send messages to a group of devices or even to all of the registered devices on the application server. This type of group sending operation is sometimes referred to as "audiences" or "campaigns" when being set up on back-end push servers such as Firebase or Urban Airship.

Setting Up the Database

You will use a MySQL database on the application server to store the registered devices. There are different ways to set up this database depending on your choice for back-end technology. In a Linux/Windows PHP environment, *myPHPAdmin* is commonly used to create and manage the database and tables.

When you create your database and database user, make sure that the credentials match the variables that you set up in the *db_connect.php* file.

After the database is successfully created, you will need to create a table called *fcm_users*. This table will be used to store all of the devices that register with FCM and the application server. Refer to the sidebar for the SQL code to create this table.

MySQL Database Table Setup

After successful creation of your MySQL database, you will need to create an empty table to hold your registered devices. The table will have fields including *gcm_regid*, *name*, and *device_id*. Using *myPHPAdmin*, create the *gcm_users* table with the following SQL code:

```
CREATE TABLE IF NOT EXISTS `fcm_users` (
  `id` int(11) NOT NULL AUTO_INCREMENT,
  `fcm_token` text,
  `name` varchar(50) NOT NULL,
  `created_at` timestamp NOT NULL DEFAULT CURRENT_TIMESTAMP,
  PRIMARY KEY (`id`)
) ENGINE=InnoDB DEFAULT CHARSET=latin1 AUTO_INCREMENT=1 ;
```

After you execute this code, you can use the *myPHPAdmin* tool and you should see the empty *fcm_users* table that has been successfully created.

Pushing Down a Message

Now that you have your database set up, pointing your browser at the *index.php* script on your server will show you the currently registered devices on your application server, as shown in Figure 6-7.

Figure 6-7. FCM demo app pushing a message from the server to a registered device

The *index.php* file has some basic JavaScript and HTML code that allows it to display registered users and push individuals messages down to them.

Note that the *Name* and *DeviceID* for each registered are displayed. These were entered by the user when they first registered their device in *RegisterActivity.java*.

To send a push message down to any registered device, simply enter the message in the text box and press the Send button.

FCM Upstream Messaging

The FCM implementation presented in this chapter uses the *FCM Http Connection Server*. Upstream messaging works a bit differently and uses *Cloud Connection Server (CCS)* with XMPP protocol. Upstream messaging has a slightly different message flow. Figure 6-8 shows the key difference, highlighted in the oval box, when upstream messaging is used with CCS.

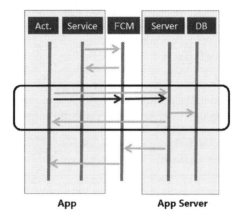

Figure 6-8. *FCM traditional model using HTTP (highlighted box light arrows) and FCM with upstream messaging using CCS (dark arrows)*

What does upstream messaging do for you? There are three main advantages:

* Upstream messaging provides a simplified API. There are only a few methods, so implementing your Android app will be less complex when you move to upstream messaging with CCS.

* Upstream messaging allows you to reuse upstream connections. Notice that with upstream messaging, your Android app only needs to send messages to FCM, and you do not need to send messages directly to your application server.

* Upstream messaging allows you to cancel notifications. This is very useful when you are using multiple devices. There is no easy way to do this when using the traditional FCM HTTP Connection Server. This valuable feature will likely drive the migration to upstream messaging in the future.

In the FCM project, you did not implement upstream messaging with XMPP. To see how to add this protocol and the enhanced features it provides, see the end-of-chapter links.

Topic Messaging

Another advanced FCM feature is topic messaging. Topic messaging allows your app server to send messages to devices that are subscribed to a specific topic. This functionality is based on the publish/subscribe model, which you will learn more about in the next part of this chapter.

In FCM, topic messaging supports unlimited subscriptions per app. Sending messages to topics is very similar to sending messages to individual devices. Check the Google resource pages to see how to send messages to topics using HTTP and XMPP. The main advantage of using topic messaging is that it is a more scalable push messaging model. You will explore this approach in detail with MQTT later in the chapter.

Considering FCM Alternatives

Firebase Cloud Messaging is the most popular push messaging implementation on Android today. Looking at the Android client app and the application server presented here, only a small amount of code was required to implement a complete push messaging solution.

However, there may be situations where using FCM is not the best option for your app. The following list includes some of those situations:

- You require guaranteed delivery of messages. Although FCM does not guarantee delivery of messages, it does allow some tracking of message delivery status on the FCM dashboard.

- Despite solid security with HTTPS, Google still knows who your registered users are and to which devices you are pushing messages. It is possible your clients don't wish to share this information with Google, even though the payload can be encrypted.

- You require a more scalable architecture such as a *publish/subscribe* model. Note that FCM has recently introduced *topic messaging*, which can provide a publish/subscribe architecture.

- FCM message size is limited to 4KB, messages are held up to four weeks, and queue data is pushed to the device when the app is running. These limits cannot be changed.

- FCM stores up to 100 messages if a device is offline. This limit cannot be adjusted. If you require greater offline storage, you will need a solution like MQTT where you have control over your own broker configuration.

- Up to 1,000 devices can be accessed per push request. This limitation can be overcome by sending multiple requests. Most of the third-party services using FCM handle this for you automatically, but it is something you need to handle yourself if you implement your own application server. Topic messaging is a good alternative.

- Depending on your requirements, a major drawback with FCM or third-party services based on FCM may be their lack of service-level agreement (SLA) or Quality of Service (QoS) features.

- Prior to Android SDK level 4.1, Google Cloud Messaging required a registered Google account. On newer devices, it requires the Google Services Framework (Android Play Store) to be present on the device. Keep in mind that Google Services Framework is not available on some devices, such as Kindle, etc.

- Google doesn't work (well enough) where you live due to server availability.

- With the FCM push solution, there is also no guarantee about the order of message delivery.

- You, or more importantly your client(s), require a completely in-house solution.

If you decide not to use FCM because of one or more of these reasons, there are some alternatives. If your application requires high performance or advanced features such as QoS, then MQTT or AMQP could be your best options. Both MQTT and AMQP allow for guaranteed delivery of messages. MQTT is ideal for mobile devices and the IoT.

You will implement MQTT on Android next.

6.6   Open Source Push Messaging with MQTT

MQTT is the acronym for the Message Queuing Telemetry Transport protocol. It was originally developed by IBM for telemetry applications. It has since been moved to open source world as an Eclipse project and version 3.1.1 of the protocol has completed standardization.

MQTT runs over TCP and works very well over low-bandwidth networks. The protocol is ideal for low power usage or connecting the IoT. The protocol was designed for low latency messaging over fragile networks, is battery efficient, and places the focus on sending messages rather than staying connected. The protocol was designed with a focus on minimal bytes flowing over the wire.

Applications that use MQTT send and receive messages by calling an MQTT library.

- The library acts like a mailbox, sending and receiving messages.

- The MQTT client library is small. It is also simple, with only five API calls.

- It is becoming more popular in the Android world, and stable Android libraries are freely available.

The protocol and library are totally abstracted and independent of the message content. The maximum message size is limited to 256MB; contrast this with the FCM limitations! However, the protocol was *not* designed for large data transfers. MQTT excels at high volume of small size messages, such as sensor data, stock quotes, game scores, or other typical push message content.

MQTT Introduction

MQTT uses a highly scalable publish/subscribe model. Not until Google recently added topic messaging to FCM was FCM able to match the scalability of MQTT.

MQTT messages are exchanged through a MQTT broker. MQTT clients can publish or subscribe to MQTT topics. Think of the publish/subscribe model as a hub-and-spoke model for messaging. Every client who wants to exchange MQTT messages needs to connect to the broker.

In the publish/subscribe model, a message is published once to a given topic, and every client who is subscribed to the topic will receive a copy of the message.

Figure 6-9 shows the typical publish/subscribe model. Always remember that MQTT clients can do both of the following:

- Publish messages to topics.

- Subscribe to topics for messages to be received.

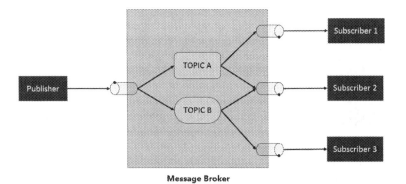

Figure 6-9. MQTT publish/subscribe model

One of the best things about using MQTT is that it supports three QoS levels. Table 6-6 shows how the MQTT QoS is similar to how FCM implementations perform.

Table 6-6. MQTT QoS Levels

QoS Level	MQTT QoS Level Description
0	Indicates that a message should be delivered at most once (zero or one times). The message will not be persisted to disk and will not be acknowledged across the network. This QoS is the fastest, but should only be used for messages that are not valuable. Note that if the server cannot process the message (for example, there is an authorization problem), then an exception will not be thrown. Also known as "fire and forget."
1	Indicates that a message should be delivered at least once (one or more times). The message can only be delivered safely if it can be persisted, so the application must supply a means of persistence using *MqttConnectOptions*. If a persistence mechanism is not specified, the message will not be delivered in the event of a client failure. The message will be acknowledged across the network. This is the default QoS.
2	Indicates that a message should be delivered once. The message will be persisted to disk and will be subject to a two-phase acknowledgement across the network. The message can only be delivered safely if it can be persisted, so the application must supply a means of persistence using *MqttConnectOptions*. If a persistence mechanism is not specified, the message will not be delivered in the event of a client failure.

MQTT App

Figure 6-10 shows a screenshot of the MQTT app. The project is a full-featured Android MQTT client that you can use as a foundation for your push messaging requirements.

Figure 6-10. MQTT demo app

The app is fairly straightforward and consists of a main activity and a background service. Upon launch, a unique *Device ID* is displayed. A simplified device *Target ID* is generated. This Target ID will be used to push messages down from the broker to the device.

The app also contains a horizontal linear layout with three control buttons which perform the following functions:

- Start Service starts the background MQTT service.
- Stop Service stops the background MQTT service.
- Clear List clears the list of received push messages from the *ArrayList*.

Below the control buttons, an *ArrayList* displays all of the push messages received. At the bottom of the screen is an additional button that will exit the app.

MQTT Project

Table 6-7 shows the high level architecture of the MQTT demo app.

Table 6-7. MQTT Project Structure

Source	Resources	Libraries
ConnectionLog.java	Main.xml	Paho-mqtt-client-1.0.1.jar
Global.java		Paho-mqtt-client-1.0.1-sources.jar
MqttService.java		
PushActivity.java		

PushActivity.java runs when you launch the app. It displays control buttons to start and stop the service, and to exit the app. It also displays a unique Device ID needed to push messages to the device from the broker, and also displays any received push messages from the broker in an *ArrayList*.

MqttService.java is the long-lived service that manages the MQTT connection with the broker.

Next, let's take a closer look at the key code inside the project, which includes a main activity, a service that implements the connection to the message broker, and a JAR library file.

MQTT Libraries for Android

There are currently two commonly used Android libraries for MQTT:

▓ *paho-mqtt-client-1.0.1.jar*

▓ *wmqtt.jar*

One of the advantages of MQTT over AMQP or STOMP is the availability of these well-tested libraries for Android. *Paho* is the Open Source Eclipse client library for Android. It is recommended because it is very stable and it implements version 3.1.1 of the protocol, which has been standardized.

In the MQTT project, both *paho-mqtt-client-1.0.1.jar* and *paho- mqtt-client-1.0.1-source.jar* are included. You can add the library to your Android Studio project by copying the files to the */libs* directory of your Android project, right-clicking the *.jar* file, and clicking "Add as a Library."

As mentioned in the introduction, the MQTT Android library is simple, with only five API calls.

▓ Connect: Connect to a MQTT broker.

▓ Publish: Publish a message to an MQTT topic.

▓ Subscribe: Subscribe to a topic.

▓ Unsubscribe: Unsubscribe from a topic.

▓ Disconnect: Disconnect from a MQTT broker.

You will see in *MqttService.java* how these methods are used to implement push messaging with MQTT.

Global.java

The *Globa.java* class is used to define some variables that will be used by the activity and the service in the Android MQTT client app.

Note that the *MQTT_BROKER* must point to the IP address of the MQTT broker, and *MQTT_PORT* is the port on which the broker is listening, typically 1883.

```java
public class Global {
    public static ArrayList<String> items = new ArrayList<String>();

    // MQTT params
    public static final String MQTT_URL_FORMAT = "tcp://%s:%d"; // URL Format
    public static final String MQTT_BROKER = "MQTT Broker URL";
    public static final int MQTT_PORT = 1883;
    public static final int MQTT_QOS_0 = 0; // QOS Level 0 (Delivery Once no confirmation)
    public static final int MQTT_QOS_1 = 1;  // QOS Level 1 (Delivery at least Once with conf)
    public static final int MQTT_QOS_2 = 2; // QOS Level 2 (Delivery only once with conf)
    public static final int MQTT_KEEP_ALIVE = 300000; // KeepAlive Interval in MS
    public static final String MQTT_KEEP_ALIVE_TOPIC_FORMAT = "%s/keepalive";
    public static final byte[] MQTT_KEEP_ALIVE_MESSAGE = { 0 }; // Keep Alive message to send
    public static final int MQTT_KEEP_ALIVE_QOS = MQTT_QOS_0; // Default Keep alive QOS
    public static final boolean MQTT_CLEAN_SESSION = true; // Start a clean session?
    // If the server is setup, we can use password access
    public static final String MQTT_USER = "mqttuser1";
    public static final char[] MQTT_PASSWORD = new char[]{'a','b','c','1','2','3'};
}
```

PushActivity.java

When the app is launched, *PushActivity.java* uses the following code to display a unique *DeviceID* and also generates a device *TargetID*, such as "adc7-982":

```java
mUniqueID = Secure.getString(this.getContentResolver(), Secure.ANDROID_ID);
((TextView) findViewById(R.id.uid_text)).setText(mUniqueID);

// set up our device ID with the "adc7-" + the last 3 chars of the uniqueID
mDeviceID = mClientID + "-" + mUniqueID.substring(mUniqueID.length()-3,
    mUniqueID.length());
((TextView) findViewById(R.id.target_text)).setText(mDeviceID);
```

The *DeviceID* will be used to push messages down to the device from the broker or server.

There is a function in the *PushActivity.java* called *pushItOut* that allows you to publish a message to a topic. The following code shows how this is accomplished. Once the *MqttClient* and *MqttTopic* and *MqttMessage* objects are set up, you simply call the *connect()*, *publish()*, and *disconnect()* methods to send the message.

```
private void pushItOut(final String top, final String msg) {
    // publish the message
    String url =
        String.format(Locale.US, Global.MQTT_URL_FORMAT, Global.MQTT_BROKER, Global.MQTT_PORT);
    mMemStore = new MemoryPersistence();
    mClient = new MqttClient(url,mUniqueID,mMemStore);

    // publish the msg to the topic
    MqttTopic mqttTopic = mClient.getTopic(top);
    MqttMessage message = new MqttMessage(msg.getBytes());
    message.setQos(Global.MQTT_QOS_2);
    mOpts = new MqttConnectOptions();
    mOpts.setCleanSession(Global.MQTT_CLEAN_SESSION);

    mClient.connect(mOpts);
    mqttTopic.publish(message);
    mClient.disconnect();
}
```

A *BroadcastReceiver* is used to communicate with the service. The key code is shown below. It handles starting and stopping of the service when buttons are pressed, as well as displaying of received messages via Toast.

```
BroadcastReceiver messageReceiver = new BroadcastReceiver() {
    public void onReceive(Context context, Intent intent) {
        String topic = "";
        String action = intent.getAction();
        If (action.equalsIgnoreCase(MqttService.NEW_MESSAGE)){
            Bundle extra = intent.getExtras();
            message = extra.getString("message");
            topic = extra.getString("topic");
            Toast.makeText(PushActivity.this, "A new message with topic="
            + topic + " hasarrived: " + message, Toast.LENGTH_LONG).show();
            incomingPushMsg.notifyDataSetChanged();
            list.scrollTo(0, 0);
        }
        if(action.equalsIgnoreCase(MqttService.STOP_SERVICE)){
                Button startButton =
                ((Button) findViewById(R.id.start_button));
            Button stopButton = ((Button) findViewById(R.id.stop_button));
            startButton.setEnabled(true);
            stopButton.setEnabled(false);
        }
        If (action.equalsIgnoreCase(MqttService.START_SERVICE)){
                Button startButton =
                ((Button) findViewById(R.id.start_button));
            Button stopButton = ((Button) findViewById(R.id.stop_button));
            startButton.setEnabled(false);
            stopButton.setEnabled(true);
        }
    }
};
```

MqttService.java

The key to the MQTT app lies in the implementation of a long-lived service that handles the MQTT protocol.

The service is started by *PushActivity.java* when the user presses the Start Service button. At this time, the service connects to the MQTT broker/server according to the connection parameters set at the top of the service.

```
private static final String MQTT_BROKER = "MQTT Broker URL";
// Broker URL or IP address
private static final int MQTT_PORT = 1883;
// broker port
```

When the service is started, the *connect()* method is called to establish the connection. The following is the key code to establish a MQTT connection with the broker:

```
mClient = new MqttClient(url,mDeviceId,mDataStore);

mClient.connect(mOpts);

// Subscribe to an initial topic, which is combination of client ID and device ID. String
initTopic = mDeviceId;

mClient.subscribe(initTopic, MQTT_QOS_0);

mClient.setCallback(MqttService.this);
mStarted = true; // Service is now connected

log("Successfully connected and subscribed starting keep alives");
startKeepAlives();
```

Note that you are specifying the *QOS level* and *the initTopic*, which is the *Device ID*, when you call the MQTT subscribe method.

At the end of the *connect()* code block, you should note the call to *startKeepAlives*. MQTT uses *keepAlive* messages to accomplish the long-lived TCP connection. A *keepAlive* message is published to the topic at the specified interval and with the specified QoS.

```
private static final int MQTT_KEEP_ALIVE = 60000;
// KeepAlive Interval in millisecs
private static final String     MQTT_KEEP_ALIVE_TOPIC_FORMAT = "%s/keepalive";
// Topic format for KeepAlives
private static final byte[] MQTT_KEEP_ALIVE_MESSAGE = { 0 };
// Keep Alive message to send
private static final int MQTT_KEEP_ALIVE_QOS = MQTT_QOS_0;
// Default Keepalive QOS

MqttMessage message = new MqttMessage(MQTT_KEEP_ALIVE_MESSAGE);
message.setQos(MQTT_KEEP_ALIVE_QOS);
return mKeepAliveTopic.publish(message);
```

When a message is received on a subscribed topic, the MQTT library will notify your service with a callback to *messageArrived*. The following code will receive the message, add it to the *Global.items ArrayList*, broadcast it back to *PushActivity.java* via Intent, and generate a notification for the user.

```
// Received Message from broker
@Override
public void messageArrived(MqttTopic topic, MqttMessage message) throws Exception {
    String msg = new String(message.getPayload());
    String top = new String(topic.getName());
    log("Topic=" + top + " Message=" + msg + " QoS=" + message.getQos());
    generateNotification(getApplicationContext(), msg);
    Global.items.add(0, msg);
    log("Got message=" + msg);
    Intent i = new Intent(NEW_MESSAGE);
    i.putExtra("message", msg);
    i.putExtra("topic", top);
    sendBroadcast(i);
}
```

ConnectionLog.java Logging and Debugging

In addition to the *PushActivity.java* and *MqttService.java* classes, this app also includes a *ConnectionLog.java* class.

This class logs debug messages to text files. The text files use a time-stamped file name and are stored as set by the following lines of code:

```
File logDir;
// Set the directory to save text files
logDir = new File(android.os.Environment.getExternalStorageDirectory(),"PushMQTT");
```

The log class can be seen used throughout the service to give you a running log of the underlying MQTT messaging activity:

```
if ((mClient == null) || (mClient.isConnected() == false)) {
    // quick sanity check - don't try and subscribe if we don't have a connection
    log("Connection error. No connection while trying to subscribe");
} else {
    log("Subscribing to: " + initTopic);
    mClient.subscribe(initTopic, MQTT_QOS_0);
}
```

This *ConnectionLog.*java class is a very important tool for debugging issues when you first are deploying MQTT and wish to make sure that everything is running properly.

MQTT Message Brokers

Because MQTT employs a publish/subscribe model, a message broker is required to send MQTT messages to the Android client. The Android client connects to the broker typically on TCP port 1883.

There are public brokers available that you can use for testing your MQTT Android app. You can also set up your own MQTT broker on Amazon Web Services (AWS). In the MQTT demo app, you are required to specify the URL of the MQTT broker.

There are several free and commercial MQTT broker packages that you can install on your server. The list below and Figure 6-11 show three of the most popular MQTT brokers. Setting up these brokers on a server is fairly straightforward. They are available in many back-end server technologies. I will cover installation of Mosquito on AWS in the next section.

- RSMB was one of the original MQTT brokers from IBM. It is not widely used but works well. Some vague language in the licensing terms needs to be considered if you wish to deploy RSMB commercially.

- HiveMQ is a popular commercial MQTT broker. It is a multi- protocol broker, which means that it can support many messaging protocols in addition to MQTT.

- Mosquito is a very popular broker because it is open source. It is easy to install and supports all of the latest features in the standardized protocol version 3.1.1. If you are looking at setting up your own MQTT broker to serve your Android client apps, Mosquito is an excellent choice.

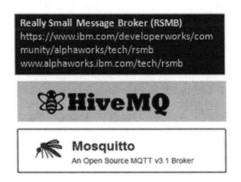

Figure 6-11. MQTT message brokers

MQTT Broker Setup for AWS

It is straightforward to set up an MQTT broker on Amazon AWS. The steps below summarize how to install the latest MQTT broker software on an AWS Linux instance:

- Create a new AWS Linux instance with a public DNS. This is similar to what you saw in Chapter 5; however, MQTT doesn't require the full LAMP setup. Of course, you can install the additional web server packages if you wish.

  ▓ Using the Security Group feature, adjust your server settings so that port
     1883 is open to incoming/outgoing MQTT messages. You can complete
     this by using a custom TCP rule for port 1883.

  ▓ Log into your Linux instance and add the CentOS mosquitto repository
     to YUM's list of repositories.

```
$ cd /etc/yum.repos.d
$ sudo wget http://download.opensuse.org/repositories/home:/oojah:/mqtt/CentOS_
CentOS-6/home:oojah:mqtt.repo
```

  ▓ Update your Amazon Linux Server.

```
$ sudo yum update
```

  ▓ Install Mosquito.

```
$ sudo yum install mosquitto
$ sudo yum install mosquitto-clients
```

  ▓ Start Mosquito.

```
$ sudo su
$ /usr/sbin/mosquitto -d -c /etc/mosquitto/mosquitto.conf > /var/log/mosquitto.log 2>&1
```

At this point, Mosquito should now be running on your server. Your Android client will be
able to connect to it, publish, and receive messages. In your Android client app, just include
the IP address of your AWS instance as the *MQTT_BROKER* URL.

Sending Messages with MQTT Web Clients

With MQTT, you can also use public servers with web socket clients to publish MQTT
messages. You can also deploy your own JavaScript web socket client to publish MQTT
messages. Open source packages are available. Two of the popular public web socket
clients are

  ▓ `www.hivemq.com/demos/websocket-client/`

  ▓ `iot.eclipse.org`

Figure 6-12 shows an example of the interface maintained by HiveMQ. These interfaces
typically have a two-step process to publish a message to your Android client.

  ▓ Connect phase: You need to specify the address of the MQTT broker
     you are using and press Connect.

  ▓ Publish phase: Enter the unique Device ID from the app on the web
     client to publish a message to a device. As soon as you publish the
     message, it will almost instantly appear on your Android device!

Figure 6-12. MQTT web client

MQTT Wrap Up

MQTT is a powerful, highly scalable alternative to FCM-based push messaging. You saw in the MQTT project how a small amount of code and a very lightweight library can bring the power of push messaging to your apps, while allowing you to retain total control of the infrastructure.

Sitting at the crossroads of Mobile and IoT, there is a lot of momentum behind MQTT. Many commercial apps are now using MQTT, including Facebook Messenger. MQTT is indeed a useful tool to have in your toolbox as you consider push implementations for your apps.

6.7   References

Firebase Cloud Messaging (FCM)

- Firebase Console: https://console.firebase.google.com/

- Google FCM Android Quickstart Demo App: https://github.com/firebase/quickstart-android/tree/master/messaging

- Add Firebase to Your App: https://firebase.google.com/docs/android/setup

- FCM Setup on Android: https://firebase.google.com/docs/cloud-messaging/android/client

- FCM Server Setup: https://firebase.google.com/docs/cloud-messaging/server

- FCM Receiving Messages on Android: https://firebase.google.com/docs/cloud-messaging/android/receive

- FCM Topic Messaging: https://firebase.google.com/docs/cloud-messaging/android/topic-messaging

- FCM Upstream Messaging: https://firebase.google.com/docs/cloud-messaging/android/upstream

▓ Migrating a GCM App to FCM: `https://developers.google.com/cloud-messaging/android/android-migrate-fcm`

▓ FCM Downloading the JSON config File: `https://support.google.com/firebase/answer/7015592`

MQTT Push Messaging

▓ MQTT Wiki on GitHub: `https://github.com/mqtt/mqtt.github.io/wiki`

▓ MQTT and Android: `https://github.com/mqtt/mqtt.github.io/wiki/mqtt_on_the_android_platform`

▓ MQTT Software: `https://github.com/mqtt/mqtt.github.io/wiki/software`

▓ MQTT Brokers: `https://github.com/mqtt/mqtt.github.io/wiki/brokers`

▓ MQTT Comparison to AMQP: `http://vasters.com/blog/From-MQTT-to-AMQP-and-back/`

▓ Implementing a Keep-Alive Service: `https://github.com/gipi/Android-keep-alive`

Chapter 7

Android Audio

7.1 Introduction

Android smartphones offer amazing audio capabilities.

Long before the modern smartphone existed, feature phones of the 1990s only had the capability to play and record audio using very low-quality codecs. This limitation was mainly due to the lack of device processing power and the limited bandwidth available on the networks at the time. Feature phones at the time did not have the bandwidth required to support high quality audio.

Two major advancements placed us on the path for what would become today's modern smartphones:

  ▦ *Advances in network technology*: Digital network protocols progressed from GSM to GPRS to UMTS and finally to today's LTE. These advancements represent the so-called 2G, 3G, and 4G generations which provided the increases in data bandwidth that would allow for much higher-quality audio codecs to be supported in mobile devices.

  ▦ *Advances in compression technology*: MP3 compression algorithms provide an acceptable balance between audio quality and file size. Personal music players were the first devices to adopt this technology, and it was only a matter of time for this technology to be merged into the mobile phone.

Table 7-1 shows a simplified version of the supported Android audio formats. There are many special rules and exceptions depending on device.

© Mark Wickham 2018
M. Wickham, *Practical Android*, https://doi.org/10.1007/978-1-4842-3333-7_7

Table 7-1. Supported Audio Formats

Codec	Encode	Decode	Details	File Type/Container
AAC	4.1+	Y	Mono/Stereo/5.0/5.1 up to 48khz sample	3GPP,MP4,ADTS AAC/.3gp,.mp4,.m4a,.aac,.ts
AMR NB/WB	Y	Y	5-12 kbps 12-24 kbps	3GPP/.3gp
FLAC	N	Y (3.1+)	Mono/Stereo/up to 44.1/48khz	FLAC/.flac
MP3	N	Y	Mono/Stereo/8-320kbps	MP3/.mp3
MIDI	N	Y	Support for ringtones	Type 0, 1/.mid, .ota, .imy
Vorbis	N	Y		OGG, Matroska/.ogg, .mkv
PCM	Y (4.1+)	Y	8-bit/16-bit Linear PCM rates to hardware limit	WAVE/.wav
Opus	N	Y (5.0+)		Matroska/.mkv

You care most about MP3, WAV (uncompressed), and AAC/MP4. Note that you can decode almost all of the codecs on any Android device, but if you want to encode, you have limited choices. You'll see how to implement encoding later in the chapter. Recall that AMR (Adaptive Multi-Rate) is the low quality codec (5-24 kbps) that is used for phone call audio.

Note: Y indicates encoding or decoding is available (all SDK versions) for a codec. N indicates encoding is not available for a codec.

This chapter will start with a quick review of audio basics, covering the Android audio APIs and codecs, which will help you to decide the best audio approach for your app.

The chapter will cover Android audio capabilities in the Android SDK (software development kit) and will not cover the Android NDK capabilities (native development kit). The primary addition the NDK provides is direct access to the OpenSL audio library. The SDK makes life much easier by providing APIs to handle the interface to this low-level library.

Android audio has come a long way. I will review the progress the platform has made and discuss the biggest remaining challenge for Android audio-latency. You will implement the Audio Buffer Size app to determine the latency of your devices.

You will implement the basic playing of audio assets using the high-level APIs such as *Media Recorder* and *Sound Pool*.

You will implement the common pattern of using a background service to play music while your app is free to perform its core functions in the foreground.

You will implement recording of uncompressed PCM audio using the internal smartphone microphone. You will then take a look at options for interfacing external microphones which can allow you to record professional quality audio directly from your Android devices.

You will explore the code required to accomplish basic audio effects processing and encoding of audio to compressed formats such as .mp3 and .mp4.

It is not always optimal to load up your app with audio samples. This is where audio synthesis comes into play. Pure Data and Csound are open source visual programming languages for sound synthesis and they run well on Android. You will implement Pure Data and take a look at Csound using the available libraries for each.

7.2   Chapter Projects

Table 7-2 shows the projects that will be presented in this chapter.

Table 7-2. Chapter Projects

Title of Project	File Name	Description
Audio Buffer Size +	*AudioBufferSize.zip*	Adaptation of Google's Audio Buffer Size app that shows optimal audio settings for your device and can estimate latency.
Playing Audio	*PlayingAudio.zip*	A configurable app that can play audio assets using the three Android audio-playing APIs.
Music Service	*MusicService.zip*	Demonstration of how to play music or sounds using a background service.
Recording Audio	*RecordingAudio.zip*	Demonstration of how to record audio and store the recording as PCM uncompressed .wav file.
Ringdroid +	*Ringdroid.zip*	Open source Google app that demonstrates how to handle all aspects of audio including recording and encoding into compressed formatted such as AAC (.mp4).
Pure Data Player	*PDplayer.zip*	A player app that can load Pure Data source files (.pd) and play them using the Pure Data audio synthesis engine.

Additionally, the third-party apps in Table 7-3 will be discussed.

Table 7-3. Third-Party Apps

App Name	Description
Splatency	App released by Superpowered, a vendor of low latency Android audio drivers, that can calculate the round trip audio latency of your device.
Circle of Fifths	Open source Pure Data app that demonstrates how to interface to the Pure Data library with a GUI. The app can play guitar chords using the Pure Data engine.
Csound6	Open source Csound app for Android that allows you to play Csound (.csd) files directly on your Android device using the Csound synthesis engine.

7.3   Audio Overview

Android audio is comprehensive. The platform gives you access to many advanced audio functions. As you have seen in many parts of Android, working with audio is a matter of mastering the classes and APIs that are available on the platform.

API and Class Summary

It can get confusing with all of the audio APIs and classes in Android. Let's break it down. Table 7-4 summarizes the classes and APIs for Android audio. As you can see, many of these APIs have been around since the beginning of Android with API of level 1. Others have been added into Android more recently.

Table 7-4. Android Audio APIs and Classes

Name	Description	API	Level
AudioTrack	Low-level API, not meant to be real time. Used in most audio apps. Manages and plays a single audio resource for Java applications. Streaming/decoding of PCM audio buffers to the audio sink for playback by "pushing" the data to the *AudioTrack* object. Supports .wav playback.	22	Low
AudioRecord	Manages the audio resources for Java applications to record audio from the hardware by "pulling" (reading) the data from the *AudioRecord* object. Can set rate, quality, encoding, channel config.	22	Low
AudioManager	*AudioManager* provides access to volume and ringer mode control.	1	
MediaPlayer	*MediaPlayer* class can be used to control playback of audio/video files and streams. Playback control of audio/video files and streams is managed as a state machine.	1	High
MediaRecorder	High-level API used to record audio and video. The recording control is based on a simple state machine. Does not support .wav or .mp3. Generally better to use Audio Record for more flexibility.	18	High
MediaStore	The media provider contains metadata for all available media on both internal and external storage devices.	1	
MediaFormat	*MediaFormat* is useful to read encoded files and every detail that is connected to the content. The format of the media data is specified as string/value pairs. Keys common to all audio/video formats.	16	

(continued)

Table 7-4. (*continued*)

Name	Description	API	Level
MediaCodec	*MediaCodec* class can be used to access low-level media codecs, such as encoder/decoder components. It is part of the Android low-level multimedia support infrastructure (normally used together with *MediaExtractor*, *MediaSync*, *MediaMixer*, *MediaCrypto*, *MediaDrm*, *Image*, *Surface*, and *AudioTrack*.)		Low
SoundPool	*SoundPool* uses the *MediaPlayer* service to decode the audio into a raw 16-bit PCM stream and play the sound with very low latency, helping the CPU decompression effort. Multiple audio streams at once.	8	High
AudioFormat	The *AudioFormat* class is used to access a number of audio formats and channel configuration constants that can be used in *AudioTrack* and *AudioRecord*.	8	
TextToSpeech	Synthesizes speech from text for immediate playback or to create a sound file. The constructor for the *TextToSpeech* class, using the default TTS engine.	4/21	
SpeechRecognition	This class provides access to the speech recognition service. The implementation of this API is likely to stream audio to remote servers to perform speech recognition.	8	
MediaExtractor	*MediaExtractor* facilitates extraction of demuxed, typically encoded, media data from a data source. Reads bytes from the encoded data whether it is an online stream, embedded resources, or local files.	16	

Pay particular attention to the "Level" column, which indicates if the particular API is a high- or low-level API. You will take a closer look at how to use these APIs in the projects that follow.

The high-level APIs *MediaPlayer*, *MediaRecorder*, and *SoundPool* are very useful and easy to use when you need to play and record audio without the need for low level controls. The low-level APIs *AudioTrack* and *AudioRecord* are excellent when you need low-level control over playing and recording audio. I will cover each of these APIs in greater detail in the projects that follow.

Note that I will not be covering the final three APIs listed, *TextToSpeech*, *SpeechRecognition*, and *MediaExtractor*, in this chapter. They are beyond the scope of this chapter, but keep in mind they are present in Android if you need these functionalities.

Choosing the Right API

As with most of the functions available on the Android platform, there is almost always more than one way to accomplish a given task. Audio is no exception. Figure 7-1 shows the various classes and APIs you can employ to accomplish common audio tasks.

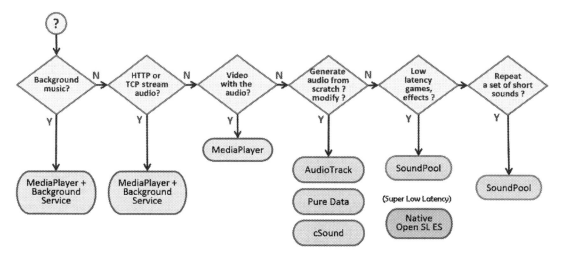

Figure 7-1. Android audio decision flowchart

Choose the approach that best matches your needs. You will see most of these approaches implemented in the example projects.

7.4   Latency

No discussion on audio would be complete without talking about latency. Audio latency has been one of the most annoying issues on the entire platform, as you shall see.

Audio performance on Android is device dependent; however, it is safe to say that we Android developers are second-class citizens when it comes to audio latency on our mobile platform. Android audio latency has seen improvements but still lags other platforms. The most recent significant improvements include

- OpenSL supported was added on Android 2.3+.

- USB Audio is included in Android 5.0+ (API 21), but is not yet supported by most devices.

Table 7-5 must be the most depressing chart in this book. It shows that, aside from a special group of Samsung devices, all Android devices suffer from roundtrip audio latencies of more than 35ms. Most musicians would agree that we require about 10ms to 15ms latency for professional audio.

Table 7-5. Android Device Latency Summary Data (Source: Supowered splatency.apk, subset of data)

Device	OS	Latency (ms)	Sample rate (Hz)	Buffer Size
iPad Air (first) + USB audio	iOS	6	48,000	64
iPhone 4s	iOS	7	48,000	64
iPhone 5s	iOS	7	48,000	64
iPhone 6 Plus	iOS	9	48,000	64
iPad Air (first)	iOS	10	48,000	64
iPad mini 2	iOS	11	48,000	64
Google Pixel XL	Android 8.1.0	11	48,000	96
Google Pixel XL	Android 7.1	26	48,000	192
Sony Experia	Android 7.1	28	48,000	192
Htc Nexus 9	Android 7.1.2	13-29	48,000	128
Motorola Nexus 6	Android 7.0	11-32	48,000	192
Samsung SM-G Pro Audio SDK	Android 5.0	15	48,000	240
Samsung Galaxy S5	Android 6.0.1	23-72	48,000	240
Samsung Note 4 Pro Audio SDK	Android 5.0.1	24	48,000	240
Google Pixel	Android 7.1.1	28	48,000	192
LGE Nexus 5	Android 6.0	35-72	48,000	240
Htc Nexus 9 + USB audio	Android 5.0.1	35	48,000	256
Samsung Galaxy Nexus	Android 5.1	40	44,100	144
Samsung Nexus 10	Android 5.1.1	43	44,100	256
Huawei Nexus 6P	Android 6.0	44	48,000	192

In summary, almost every iOS device ever produced has better audio latency than every Android device ever produced. Think about that statement; it is quite astonishing. It is not because we are running Linux. Many Linux platforms, such as Chromebooks and Macbooks, have excellent audio latency performance. I will break down the Android latency contributors in the next section.

Note that the new Google Pixel devices and Samsung devices are the lowest latency Android devices. Why is that? Samsung released the Samsung Pro Audio SDK for many of their high-end phones and tablets. How did they implement it? They ported an open source low-level audio interconnect library called JACK to Android. By using the Samsung Pro Audio SDK, developers are able to bypass the Android APIs that contribute to latency, thus overcoming this deficiency.

In the case of the new Google Pixel devices, Google has relied on the latest Android 8.0 release along with the increased CPU performance of the device to reduce the buffer size from 192 bytes to 96 bytes. For the first time, the Google Pixel XL is approaching the 10ms latency barrier.

How does this dismal audio latency performance affect us as Android developers? Monetizing audio apps has greatly lagged on Android. According to App Annie, audio app downloads are No. 5 on iOS in terms of popularity and No. 3 in terms of revenues, only trailing the games and social media app categories. On Android, the audio category does not even register in the top 10.

If you want to write a professional low-latency audio app on Android at this time, you basically have three choices:

1. Target your professional audio app for Samsung devices with the Samsung Pro Audio SDK or the latest Google Pixel XL.

2. Use a proprietary third-party audio driver such as the one available from Extreamsd at `www.extreamsd.com/index.php/2015-07-22-12-01-14/usb-audio-driver`.

3. Wait for USB audio to become fully supported in future versions of Android. USB audio first appeared in Android 5.0 (API 21), but has not yet been widely supported by any device manufacturers.

Latency Breakdown

Let's review some definitions for the different types of audio-related latency.

- *Output Latency*: The time from when you press a button or piano key until you hear the sound. As suggested before, concert pianists are not going to be happy if this latency is much greater than 10ms.

- *Control Input Latency*: Display reaction time.

- *Application Latency*: Everything that happens in the app layer.

- *Audio System Latency*: Everything that happens in the system layer.

Figure 7-2 shows a breakdown of the latency contributors on the Android platform. Audio enters through the microphone, makes the roundtrip through the stack, and then exits through the speaker.

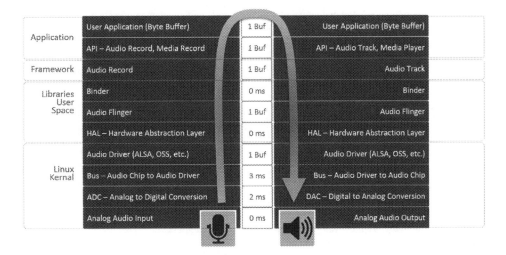

Figure 7-2. Android roundtrip latency

The timings in the center column of the diagram represent the latency contributions. Recall that we have to pass through the stack twice. Generally, the hardware processes things pretty quickly and has a minimal impact on latency. Most of the low-level layers only contribute a few milliseconds to the overall latency. The HAL (Hardware Abstraction Layer) is provided by the device manufacturer as the interface to the Android libraries and framework where the more significant latency contributions occur.

Notice that at many of the higher levels in the latency roundtrip, we are processing buffers of audio, and it turns out that the audio buffer size is a key contributor to device latency. Notice in the rightmost column of Table 7-5 the buffer size for Android devices is much larger than for iOS devices, which always have a buffer size of just 64 samples. The buffer size for most Android devices is 240 samples. This directly correlates to higher latency.

To fully understand why this is, it is important to understand a few key terms and how they are related.

- *Byte Buffers*: When we process digital audio (PCM) on Android, we process byte buffers, which are 16-bit integers.

- *Audio Buffer Size*: The number of samples in the PCM audio buffer. This is determined by the device manufactured. You will see in the Audio Buffer Size app how to determine this on your device.

- *Sample Rate*: The rate at which the system processes audio. For Android devices processing PCM audio, this is either 44,100 Hz or 48,000 Hz (samples per second). The Audio Buffer Size app will also allow you to see how this is set for your device.

- *Sample*: When you record or play audio, you may have stereo or mono source audio. A stereo source will have a left and a right channel for each sample, whereas mono audio will just have a single channel for each sample. Note that we could have up to five or even seven channels of audio data per sample if we were using surround sound encoding.

When we process audio in Android using the low-level APIs such as *AudioRecord* and *AudioTrack*, we are processing *byte buffers* and the audio buffer size is the key contributor to a device latency.

For example, if we are processing audio with an audio buffer size of 240 samples and a sample rate of 48,000 Hz:

Time to process 1 sample = 1 / 48000 = .0208 milliseconds * 240 samples = 5 milliseconds

Thus, each time we need to process the audio buffer in the Android stack, we incur additional 5 ms of latency. This adds up quickly, especially when we consider the necessary roundtrip.

The most important guidelines for minimizing audio latency in Android are

- Match up your app's audio buffer size with the device setting. You will see how to detect audio buffer size in the next project.

- Match up your app's sample rate with the device setting. You will see how to detect sample rate in the next project.

- Minimize the number of times you process audio buffers at your application level. There is not much you can do about the latency added in the API, framework, and libraries layers if you choose to use the low-level APIs such as *AudioRecord* and *AudioTrack*.

Audio Buffer Size App

Despite the latency issue, Android audio has come a long way. To help developers understand the capabilities of their devices, Google introduced the open source Audio Buffer Size app some time ago. It is now part of the AOSP (Android Open Source Project).

Figure 7-3 shows the Audio Buffer Size app. I added a "+" to its icon to distinguish it from the original Google project. This app allows you to determine your device buffer size and sample rate. After launching and starting by pressing the button, it first reads the settings from the platform and then performs some calculations to derive them.

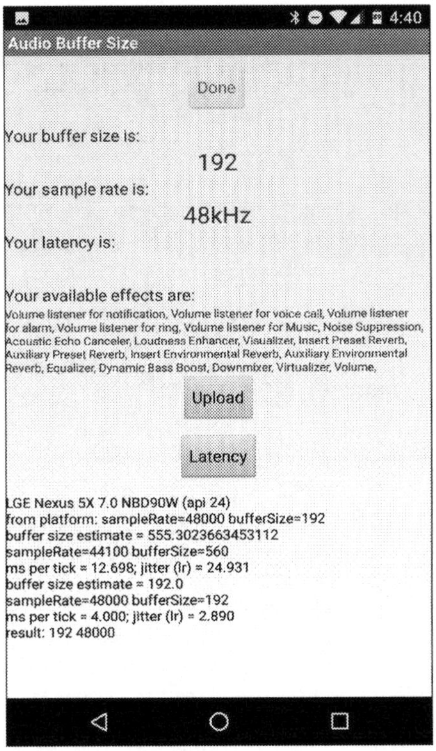

Figure 7-3. Audio Buffer Size + app

The app reports back your buffer size and sample rate.

This app includes two additional features not available in the original version of the app:

- A simple latency test
- A device effects query

After the initial test is completed, you can run the latency test by pressing the button. The latency calculated is an output latency test and you will look at the code next.

The device effects query is a simple API call and you will also take a look at this code.

Audio Buffer Size Project

Audio on Android is device dependent. If you need to know what your device capability is, you can use the Audio Buffer Size app. See Table 7-6 for the project structure.

Table 7-6. Audio Buffer Size Project Structure

Sources	Resources/layout	Libraries
AudioBufferSize.java	main.xml	

All of the work is performed in the single activity called *AudioBufferSize.java*. After you run the buffer size and sample rate calculation, you will have the opportunity to run a latency test I added.

An Upload button uploads the buffer size and sample rate to an application server that Google has apparently used to maintain a list of results for all devices. This is similar to how the splatency.apk has recorded latency for thousands of Android devices, discussed earlier.

Device Effects Query

You will see that the app populates a field titled "Your supported affects are:". I added this device effects query to the app, and it is accomplished with the following code:

```
Sring list;
Descriptor[] effects =
    AudioEffect.queryEffects();
    for (final Descriptor
        effect : effects) {
            list = list + effect.name.toString() + ", ";
        }
```

Most devices support at least ten built-in audio effects. I will discuss more about these built-in audio effects and how you can use them later in the chapter.

Measuring Latency

There are a few ways to measure audio latency in Android:

1. Connect an oscilloscope to your smartphone. This is not very practical.

2. Use an external microphone to record the sound of pressing a button, which plays a tone. The recorded waveform can be used to determine the time between the tap sound and the subsequent tone (output latency).

3. Use a custom app such as the modified Audio Buffer Size app or a third-party app such as splatency.apk from Supowered.

The third method is the most practical and I added this feature to the Audio Buffer Size app. It provides a simple test of output latency. You will be measuring the time it takes for a sound to be played after a button is pressed.

Once the app completes its initial calculations and returns your buffer size and sample rate, you will be able to press the latency button to perform the latency test. The test can be repeated as many times as you wish.

Let's take a look at the key code to perform the latency test. Don't worry about the code for *GenerateTone* for now; you will review this code in the next app.

```java
final Button latencyButton = (Button) findViewById(R.id.latencyButton);
latencyButton.setOnClickListener(new OnClickListener() {
    public void onClick(View v) {
        mLatencyStartTime = getCurrentTime();
        latencyButton.setEnabled(false);

        // Do the latency calculation, play a 440 hz sound for 250 msec
        AudioTrack sound = generateTone(440, 250);
        sound.setNotificationMarkerPosition(count /2); // Listen for the end of the sample

        sound.setPlaybackPositionUpdateListener(new OnPlaybackPositionUpdateListener() {
            public void onPeriodicNotification(AudioTrack sound) { }
            public void onMarkerReached(AudioTrack sound) {
                // The sound has finished playing, so record the time
                mLatencyStopTime = getCurrentTime();
                diff = mLatencyStopTime - mLatencyStartTime;
                // Update the latency result
                TextView lat = (TextView)findViewById(R.id.latency);
                lat.setText(diff + " ms");
                latencyButton.setEnabled(true);
                logUI("Latency test result= " + diff + " ms");
            }
        });
        sound.play();
    }
});
```

As you can see in this code, when the *latencyButton* gets pressed, a sound begins to play. Not shown in the code is the *generateTone* routine, which, in addition to playing the tone, also records a *mLatencyStartTime*.

You are using an *AudioTrack* object called *sound* to play the tone. On the *sound* object, you are setting two important methods:

- *sound.setNotificationMarkerPosition*
- *sound.setPlaybackPositionUpdateListener*

The first method tells *AudioTrack* to notify you when the end of the sound is reached because you are providing a parameter of *count/2*, which is the total number of samples since the tone has left and right channels.

The second method contains the code that is executed when the marker is reached. It calculates *mLatencyStopTime*. The difference between the start and stop times is the latency, and the result is populated back to the main view for the user to see.

The latency results on average should be about half the round trip latency because this code is measuring output latency (the time difference between when the button is pressed and the sound is heard).

Repeating the test multiple times can give you an idea of the standard deviation or variance in your latency results. You will notice that you can get widely varying results depending on the state of your device at the time of the test. Remember: Android and Linux are not real-time operating systems, which means these results are not deterministic and can vary.

7.5   Playing Audio

If you want to play audio in your Android apps, there are three APIs to choose from. You need to choose the approach that best matches your needs. Table 7-7 shows a summary of the APIs.

Table 7-7. *Android Audio APIs for Playing Sounds*

API	Description
MediaPlayer	Streams and decodes in real time for local or remote files Good for long clips and applications such as background music. More CPU and resource intensive. Relatively long initialization time. *MediaPlayer* is a state machine!
SoundPool	Good for short audio effects or clips. Stored uncompressed in memory, 1MB limit. Clips must be fully loaded before playing. Supports volume and speed control, looping, simultaneous sounds, priorities.
AudioTrack	Lowest-level audio API on Android. Provides a channel you can configure. Push and pull byte data to the channel. Configure rate, samples, audio format, etc. You can decode audio in unsupported formats

In summary, *MediaPlayer* is the good general-purpose class to play a file, *SoundPool* is well suited for short audio effects, and *AudioTrack* lets you get into the low-level audio configurations.

OPEN SL ES was included in Android starting at version 2.3. You are not going to work directly at the native level and call OPEN SL ES in the chapter projects, but keep it in mind when you are using the low-level APIs such as *AudioTrack* and *AudioRecord*. These APIs make use of OPEN SL ES.

Playing Audio App

Figure 7-4 shows the inspiration for the Playing Audio app. It is the Novation Launchpad. This is a popular device used by musicians and DJs to play music. It is technically considered a USB controller and does not actually produce any sounds itself, but I used its functional layout and style to inspire our Android app.

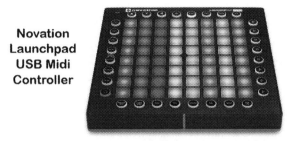

Novation
Launchpad
USB Midi
Controller

Figure 7-4. Novation Launchpad, inspiration for the Play Audio app

There are several requirements for this app:

- A responsive platform to play sounds.

- The ability to use any of the three APIs to play those sounds.

- A way to easily add more sounds without having to change the code.

- A way to easily adjust how sounds are played so we can experiment with the APIs.

- A color-coded grid similar to the many buttons on the Launchpad in which different colors represent the different APIs that can be used to play sounds.

Figure 7-5 shows a snapshot of the Playing Audio app.

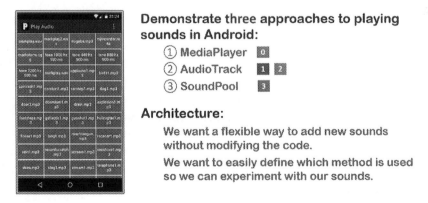

Figure 7-5. Playing Audio App

Note that you are using a *GridView* in the app and distinct colors represent the different playing methods for the various sounds. I will cover the code required to achieve this in the next section.

Playing Audio Project

The project structure is shown in Table 7-8. All of the code is included in *MainActivity.java*. There is a single .xml file for the main view and another .xml file for the *array_list_items*. However, the *GridView* is built dynamically from the audio resources, so there is no need to make any edits to the .xml files.

Table 7-8. Playing Audio Project Structure

Sources	Resources/layout	Resources/raw
MainActivity.java	activity_main.xml	birds1.mp3
	array_list_item.xml	dog1.mp3
		laugh.mp3
		markplay2.wav
		markstorm.ogg
		mjwcondsr.m4a
		soundfile.txt

Note that audio resources for the app are stored within the project in the *Resources/raw* directory. The app could be easily modified so that these resources are loaded from the device SD card or even remotely loaded from the Internet.

Note there is a special file in *Resources/raw* called *soundfile.txt*. This is the configuration file for app and I will discuss it next.

JSON Configuration

In this app, you will use JSON to configure the app. This will allow you to achieve a flexible and expandable architecture.

There are four sound types that can be used to play sounds in the app. This could easily be expanded to include more. Three of the types relate directly to the APIs previously discussed, and an additional fourth type is a special case type (*SoundType* = 2) that plays tones.

Table 7-9 shows how the *soundType* object will be defined. Note that type 2 allows the setting of a parameter as additional information for that type.

Table 7-9. Playing App Sound Types

Sound Type	API	Parameter
0	*MediaPlayer*	None
1	*SoundPool*	None
2	Generate Tone using *AudioTrack*	Frequency in Hz
3	*AudioTrack*	None

The JSON configuration file for the project is stored locally on the device in the following location:

Resources/raw/soundfile.txt

It is stored in the same location as the sound files that will be played by the app.
The following code shows what the JSON file *soundfile.txt* might look like:

```
[
  [ {"name":"markplay.wav"},        {"resID":"markplay"},   {"soundType":0}, {"param1":0} ],
  [ {"name":"markplay2.wav"},       {"resID":"markplay2"},  {"soundType":0}, {"param1":0} ],
  [ {"name":"nogabe.mp3"},          {"resID":"nogabe"},     {"soundType":0}, {"param1":0} ],
  [ {"name":"mjwcondsr.m4a"},       {"resID":"mjwcondsr"},  {"soundType":0}, {"param1":0} ],
  [ {"name":"markstorm.ogg"},       {"resID":"markstorm"},  {"soundType":0}, {"param1":0} ],
  [ {"name":"tone 1000 hz 500 ms"}, {"resID":""},           {"soundType":2}, {"param1":1000} ],
  [ {"name":"tone 440 hz 500 ms"},  {"resID":""},           {"soundType":2}, {"param1":440} ],
  [ {"name":"stream1.mp3"},         {"resID":"stream1"},    {"soundType":1}, {"param1":0} ],
  [ {"name":"telephone1.mp3"},      {"resID":"telephone1"}, {"soundType":1}, {"param1":0} ],
  [ {"name":"thunder1.mp3"},        {"resID":"thunder1"},   {"soundType":1}, {"param1":0} ],
  [ {"name":"train1.mp3"},          {"resID":"train1"},     {"soundType":1}, {"param1":0} ],
  [ {"name":"wind1.mp3"},           {"resID":"wind1"},      {"soundType":1}, {"param1":0} ],
  [ {"name":"windchimes.mp3"},      {"resID":"windchimes"}, {"soundType":1}, {"param1":0} ]
]
```

Within the JSON array, you can see subarrays that each contain four objects with key:value pairs of data.

Each array in the JSON file represents a sound that can be played and includes the following four objects:

▩ *name*: The name of the sounds that appears on the button in the *GridView*

▩ *resourceID*: The resource ID of the sound, which is stored internally in the app

▩ *soundType*: The sound type as defined earlier

▩ *parameter*: A parameter that can be used to further specify how the sound is played

Note that JSON file or the audio resources could be stored externally or even lazy loaded. In this project they reside internal to the app.

Once the JSON file is loaded and parsed, a *GridView* and *GridAdapter* are used to display the sounds for the user.

The *GridView* and *GridAdapter* are defined with the following code:

```
gridview = (GridView) findViewById(R.id.gridView1);
gridAdapter = new GridAdapter(MainActivity.this, R.layout.array_list_item, buttonName);
gridview.setAdapter(gridAdapter);
```

I won't show the entire *GridAdapter* code here, but you can easily look it up in the project. It is a standard *GridAdapter* and it sets the title of each button based on the *name* field and the color of each button based on the *soundType* field.

Next, let's look at the code to play sounds using each of the APIs.

You will use a *case* statement based on the *soundType* to determine which API to use. First, you will look at the high-level APIs *MediaPlayer* and *SoundPool,* followed by the low-level API *AudioTrack.*

Playing Audio with the MediaPlayer

MediaPlayer has a lot of functionality and yet it is pretty simple to just play simple sounds. In this app, it will be used to play all sounds with *soundType* = 0.

Once you generate your audio *URI* from the *resourceID*, you just start the *MediaPlayer*.

The code is shown below. Notice that it is a simple process to invoke the *.setDataSource,* *.prepare*, and *.start* methods on the *MediaPlayer* object.

```
switch (type) {
    case 0:
        // Release any resources from previous MediaPlayer
        if (mp != null) mp.release();
        mp = new MediaPlayer();
        Uri u = Uri.parse("android.resource://com.wickham.android.playaudio/" + resid);
        mp.setDataSource(MainActivity.this, u);
        mp.prepare();
        mp.start();
        break;
```

Playing Sounds with SoundPool

Recall that *SoundPool* is ideal when you need to play short sounds. *SoundPool* will be used when *soundType* = 1.

Setup for *SoundPool* is a little more involved than with *MediaPlayer* because you have to load your sound, which can take a bit of time, so you use a listener to know when it is ready.

Once loaded, the *onLoadComplete* method will be triggered and you can then use the *.play* method to play the sound.

Notice the extra control you get on Priority, Volume, Repeat, and Frequency. This is one of the advantages for *SoundPool*. See the following key code:

```
private void playSoundPool(int soundID) {
    int MAX_STREAMS = 20;
    int REPEAT = 0;
    SoundPool soundPool = new SoundPool(MAX_STREAMS, AudioManager.STREAM_MUSIC, REPEAT);
    soundPool.setOnLoadCompleteListener(new OnLoadCompleteListener() {
```

```
    @Override
    public void onLoadComplete(SoundPool soundPool, int soundId, int status) {
        int priority = 0;
        int repeat = 0;
        float rate = 1.f; // Frequency Rate can be from .5 to 2.0
        // Set volume
        AudioManager mgr = (AudioManager)getSystemService(Context.AUDIO_SERVICE);
        float streamVolumeCurrent =
            mgr.getStreamVolume(AudioManager.STREAM_MUSIC);
        float streamVolumeMax =
            mgr.getStreamMaxVolume(AudioManager.STREAM_MUSIC);
        float volume = streamVolumeCurrent / streamVolumeMax;
        // Play it
        soundPool.play(soundId, volume, volume, priority, repeat, rate);
    }
});
soundPool.load(this, soundID, 1);
}
```

Playing Audio with AudioTrack

AudioTrack is the low-level API for playing audio. In this project, it will be used to play sounds when *soundType* = 2.

The *PlaySound* function shown below uses *AudioTrack* to play the sound with *soundID*. Notice that *AudioTrack* is run on a thread.

Inside the thread, the first thing you do is set up the sample rate and buffer size parameters. Remember to match the buffer size and sample rate for your device. In the code below, the buffer size is automatically calculated using the *.getMinBufferSize* method, while the sample rate is specified directly as 44,100 Hz.

You then invoke the *.play* method on the object and then invoke the *.write* method on the *AudioTrack* object to copy the raw PCM audio data to the object.

You can see this is a much lower level approach to producing audio. But, this ability to directly read and write buffers to the audio hardware gives you a lot of power including the ability to encode and decode.

```
private void playSound(final int soundID) {
    playingThread = new Thread(new Runnable() {
        public void run() {
            int minBufferSize = AudioTrack.getMinBufferSize(44100, STEREO, PCM_16BIT);
            AudioTrack audioTrack = new AudioTrack(STREAM, 44100, STEREO, PCM_16, BUFSZ, STREAM);
            audioTrack.play();

            int i = 0;
            int bufferSize = 512;
            byte [] buffer = new byte[bufferSize];
            InputStream inputStream = getResources().openRawResource(soundID);
            while((i = inputStream.read(buffer)) != -1) audioTrack.write(buffer, 0, i);
                inputStream.close();
```

```
            }
        },"AudioRecorder Thread");
    playingThread.start();
}
```

Generating a Tone with AudioTrack

To emphasize the power of using the *AudioTrack* low-level API, you will implement a tone generator using *AudioTrack*.

GenerateTone is used to handle *soundType* = 3 in the app. When it is called, you determine the frequency in Hz of the tone from the JSON parameter.

In the code below, you load up the raw PCM data with sin wave values using the *math.sin* function. Of course that produces a tone. Why do you load up [i + 0] and [i + 1] into the byte array? The duplicate sample makes up the left and right audio channels. You are producing a stereo sound, even though it won't sound like stereo because the exact same tone is produced in each channel.

```
private AudioTrack generateTone(double freqHz, int durationMs) {
    int count = (int)(44100.0 * 2.0 * (durationMs / 1000.0)) & ~1;
    short[] samples = new short[count];
    for(int i = 0; i < count; i += 2){
        short sample = (short)(Math.sin(2 * Math.PI * i / (44100.0 / freqHz)) * 0x7FFF);
        samples[i + 0] = sample;
        samples[i + 1] = sample;
    }
    AudioTrack track = new AudioTrack(AudioManager.STREAM_MUSIC, 44100,
    AudioFormat.CHANNEL_OUT_STEREO, AudioFormat.ENCODING_PCM_16BIT,
    count * (Short.SIZE / 8), AudioTrack.MODE_STATIC);
    track.write(samples, 0, count);
    return track;
}
```

This gives you an idea of what you can do with low-level control of the PCM data that can be used to produce audio using *AudioTrack*.

Experiment with the Playing Audio App

The Playing Audio app is an excellent way to experiment with audio assets and see which API is best suited for playing your audio assets.

For example, you may have an .mp3 song that has a very long duration. What happens if you try to play it using *SoundPool*? You will see that it is truncated after only a few seconds of playing. This is due to the *SoundPool* limitations with file size.

What happens if you try to play .mp3 files with *AudioTrack*? You will see this leads to unhandled exceptions, as *AudioTrack* only works with raw PCM data.

Play around and experiment by configuring your JSON file to play your audio assets using the different APIs

7.6   Playing Audio with a Background Service

For playing background music in your apps, the background service is the best architecture. This architecture allows you to play long-running music tracks in the background while performing other more critical operations in the foreground.

Music Service App

Figure 7-6 show a screenshot of the Background Service app.

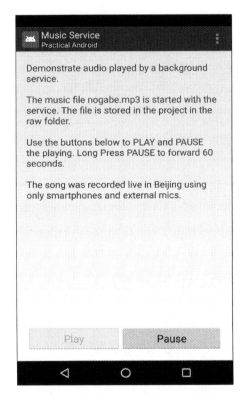

Figure 7-6. Background Service app

The Music Service app plays the track *nogabe.mp3* in the background. The song file is stored locally in the */Resources/raw* folder. The length of the song is approximately five minutes. I will discuss more about this interesting recording later.

Once the app is launched, the song will begin to play. You can see there are some very basic controls available, including Play and Pause buttons.

There is also an undocumented feature that allows you to skip forward in the track. The skip forward can be accomplished by long-pressing the Pause button. Each time you long-press the Pause button, the track will skip forward 30 seconds. This type of function is often implemented by providing a *SeekBar* with seek forward and seek backward buttons to move the position within the track.

Music Service Project

Table 7-10 shows the structure of the Music Service project.

Table 7-10. Music Service Project Structure

Sources	Resources/layout	Resources/raw
MainActivity.java	activity_main.xml	nogabe.mp3
MusicService.java		

The project contains an activity *MainActivity.java*, and a service *MusicService.java*.

You need to register your service in the *manifest.xml* file, so be sure to include the following code in your manifest file:

```
<application
    <service
        android:name="com.wickham.android.musicservice.MusicService"
        android:label="Music Service"
        android:enabled="true">
    </service>
```

MainActivity.java

Within the activity, three steps are required to interface with the service that will be running in the background.

1. Bind the service to the activity.

2. Start and connect to the service.

3. Control the service from the activity.

The following code shows how the three steps are accomplished:

```
// Bind the Service
bindService(new Intent(this,MusicService.class), Scon,Context.BIND_AUTO_CREATE);

// Connect to Service
public void onServiceConnected(ComponentName name, IBinder binder) {
    mServ = ((MusicService.ServiceBinder)binder).getServiceInstance();}

// Start the service
Intent music = new Intent();
music.setClass(this,MusicService.class);
startService(music);

// Controlling the service
mServ.resumeMusic();
mServ.pauseMusic();
```

The services *.resumeMusic* and *.pauseMusic* methods are used within the activity to control the playing of the song by the service when the corresponding buttons are pressed.

MusicService.java

Once you have the service defined in the *manifest.xml*, implementing the service is fairly straightforward.

Inside the service, you use *MediaPlayer* to play the song. It is the best choice for playing long audio files in a background service. Using *MediaPlayer*, you just need to create the object and specify the song you wish to play. Notice that there are a couple of extra methods you are using to set looping and volume controls.

The key source code follows, which shows how to set up a service for background playing with *MediaPlayer:*

```
public class MusicService extends Service implements MediaPlayer.OnErrorListener{
    private final IBinder mBinder = new ServiceBinder();
    MediaPlayer mPlayer;
    private int length = 0;

    public MusicService() { }
    public class ServiceBinder extends Binder {
        public MusicService getServiceInstance() {
            return MusicService.this;
        }
    }
    @Override
    public IBinder onBind(Intent arg0){return mBinder;}

    @Override
    public void onCreate () {
        super.onCreate();
        mPlayer = MediaPlayer.create(this, R.raw.nogabe);
        mPlayer.setOnErrorListener(this);
        mPlayer.setLooping(false);
        mPlayer.setVolume(100,100);
        mPlayer.setOnErrorListener(new OnErrorListener() {
            public boolean onError(MediaPlayer mp, int what, int extra) {
                onError(mPlayer, what, extra);
                return true;
            }
        });
    }
}
```

With the service bound to the activity, you are free to control the playing of the song at any point during the lifecycle of the activity.

Note that in this project you have specified the song to be played inside the service, but this could easily be adjusted so that you can pass a song ID into the service and play any song. This is how most music player apps are structured.

7.7   Recording Audio

Similar to playing sounds in Android, you can use the Android APIs to record audio. You will implement the Recording Audio app to learn how this can be accomplished. In the project, you will use the *AudioRecord* low-level API to record uncompressed PCM audio data and store the results to a .wav file.

Recording Audio App

Figure 7-7 shows the Recording Audio app. The main layout reports the buffer size and sample rate determined by querying the device.

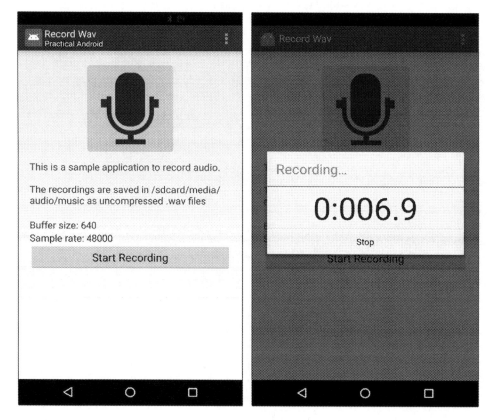

Figure 7-7. Record Audio app

In the project, you will record audio from the built-in mic and save the uncompressed file as a .wav. Recordings are saved onto the SD card as .wav files to *sdcard/media/audio/music/*.

There is a single button that begins the audio recording when pressed. When the app is recording audio, a dialog box is shown and it displays accumulated recording time. The dialog box includes a Stop button, which will stop the recording.

When recordings are stopped, an additional dialog box is shown, which allows the user to enter the filename of the recording that will be saved.

Recording Audio Project

Table 7-11 shows the structure of the project.

Table 7-11. Recording Audio Project Structure

Source	Resources/layout	Libraries
RecordWavActivity.java	activity_main.xml	
FileSaveDialog.java	file_save.xml	
	record_audio.xml	

The main code is found within *RecordWavActivity.java*. The main layout file is *activity_main.xml*. There are no external libraries used. The code for the file saving dialog box is handled in *FileSaveDialog.java*.

RecordWavActivity.java

In the app, you are going to be recording 16-bit PCM audio. The settings are defined in the beginning of the app, including the location where the recorded files will be saved:

```
private static final int    RECORDER_BPP = 16;
private static final String AUDIO_RECORDER_FILE_EXT_WAV = ".wav";
private static final String AUDIO_RECORDER_FOLDER = "media/audio/music";
private static final String AUDIO_RECORDER_TEMP_FILE = "record_temp.raw";
private static int          RECORDER_SAMPLERATE; // Samplerate is derived from the platform
private static final int    RECORDER_CHANNELS = AudioFormat.CHANNEL_IN_STEREO;
private static final int    RECORDER_AUDIO_ENCODING = AudioFormat.ENCODING_PCM_16BIT;
```

The app automatically sets buffer size and sample rate using the following code, which you saw in the Audio Buffer Size app:

```
// Get the buffer size from the platform
bufferSize = AudioRecord.getMinBufferSize(8000,
                        AudioFormat.CHANNEL_CONFIGURATION_MONO,
                        AudioFormat.ENCODING_PCM_16BIT);
// Get the sample rate from the platform
AudioManager audioManager = (AudioManager) this.getSystemService(Context.AUDIO_SERVICE);
String sr = audioManager.getProperty(AudioManager.PROPERTY_OUTPUT_SAMPLE_RATE); RECORDER_
SAMPLERATE = Integer.parseInt(sr);
```

Within the main recording loop you will use the *AudioRecord* API to record audio to a temporary file. The *AudioRecord* object is set up as follows:

```
private AudioRecord recorder = null;
recorder = new AudioRecord(MediaRecorder.AudioSource.MIC,
    RECORDER_SAMPLERATE,
    RECORDER_CHANNELS,
    RECORDER_AUDIO_ENCODING,
    bufferSize);
```

When the user presses the Start Recording button, a main recording loop will be activated. Inside the main recording loop, you will be copying byte buffers from the *AudioRecord* object into a temporary file.

A few key points about the recording audio main loop:

▨   *WriteAudioDataToFile* is where the magic happens!

▨   You use a Boolean flag called *isRecording* to show that recording has started and remains in progress.

▨   You read from the *AudioRecord* Object into a byte buffer

▨   After each buffer is read, you then write data out to the temporary file until the user presses the STOP RECORDING button.

▨   The Recording progress counter is updated periodically so the user can see the recording is in progress.

The main loop for recording PCM audio is as follows:

```java
private void writeAudioDataToFile() {
    byte data[] = new byte[bufferSize];
    String filename = getTempFilename();
    FileOutputStream os = null;
    os = new FileOutputStream(filename);
    int read = 0;
    float elapsedSamples = 0;
    if (null != os) {
        while(isRecording) {
            read = recorder.read(data, 0, bufferSize);
            elapsedSamples = elapsedSamples + bufferSize / 4; // Left and Right channels
            if (AudioRecord.ERROR_INVALID_OPERATION != read) {
                os.write(data);
            }
            long now = getCurrentTime();
            if (now - mRecordingLastUpdateTime > 100) { // Update the recording clock 1/10 sec
                mRecordingTime = elapsedSamples / RECORDER_SAMPLERATE;
                runOnUiThread(new Runnable() {
                    public void run() {
                        int min = (int)(mRecordingTime/60);
                        float sec = (float)(mRecordingTime - 60 * min);
                        mTimerTextView.setText(String.format("%d:%05.1f", min, sec));
                    }
                });
                mRecordingLastUpdateTime = now;
            }
        }
    }
    os.close();
}
```

After the recording is stopped, the user is then given a dialog where a filename can be entered. Once entered, the recorded file will be written out in .wav format. This operation will be performed on a background thread.

The .wav file contains a header and the body. Since you are working with raw PCM data, you do not have to worry about encoding for this operation.

The code below, *mSaveSoundFileThread*, shows how you accomplish saving the .wav file which is comprised of the following components:

- Read in the temporary file, which was saved in the recording loop. The temporary filename is *inFilename.*

- Write out the .wav file header according to the .wav specification. The .wav file header is always 44 bytes, as shown in the next example.

- Write out the audio data, which is comprised of all the samples stored in the temporary file.

- Delete the temporary file.

```
mSaveSoundFileThread = new Thread() {
    public void run() {
        try {
            FileInputStream in = null;
            FileOutputStream out = null;
            long totalAudioLen = 0;
            long totalDataLen = totalAudioLen + 36;
            long longSampleRate = RECORDER_SAMPLERATE;
            int channels = 2;
            long byteRate = RECORDER_BPP * RECORDER_SAMPLERATE * channels / 8;
            byte[] data = new byte[bufferSize];
            in = new FileInputStream(inFilename); // Read from the tmpfile

            // And save the output file (.wav)
            out = new FileOutputStream(outFilename);
            totalAudioLen = in.getChannel().size();
            totalDataLen = totalAudioLen + 36;

            // First the header
            WriteWaveFileHeader(out, totalAudioLen, totalDataLen,
                            longSampleRate, channels, byteRate);

            // Followed by the audio samples
            while(in.read(data) != -1) {
                out.write(data);
            }
            in.close();
            out.close();
            deleteTempFile(); // Clean up the tmp file since we wrote out the wav file
        }
    }
};
mSaveSoundFileThread.start();
```

Every audio file has a format header. The .wav file header is 44 bytes. If you ever have a problem with audio apps and only 44 bytes are written, then you know the header was written but not the actual audio samples. For details of all the fields, please refer to the specification link as shown in the chapter references.

The following code excerpt shows how the .wav header is set up:

```java
private void WriteWaveFileHeader(
    FileOutputStream out, long totalALen, long totalDataLen, long longSampleRate,
    int channels,long byteRate) throws IOException {
        byte[] header = new byte[44];
        header[0] = 'R'; // RIFF/WAVE header
        header[1] = 'I';
        header[2] = 'F';
        header[3] = 'F';
        header[4] = (byte) (totalDataLen & 0xff);
        header[5] = (byte) ((totalDataLen >> 8) & 0xff);
        header[6] = (byte) ((totalDataLen >> 16) & 0xff);
        header[7] = (byte) ((totalDataLen >> 24) & 0xff);
        header[8] = 'W';
        header[9] = 'A';
        header[10] = 'V';
        header[11] = 'E';
        header[12] = 'f'; // 'fmt ' chunk
        header[13] = 'm';
        header[14] = 't';
        . . .
        header[34] = RECORDER_BPP; // bits per sample
        header[35] = 0;
        header[36] = 'd';
        header[37] = 'a';
        header[38] = 't';
        header[39] = 'a';
        header[40] = (byte) (totalAudioLen & 0xff);
        header[41] = (byte) ((totalAudioLen >> 8) & 0xff);
        header[42] = (byte) ((totalAudioLen >> 16) & 0xff);
        header[43] = (byte) ((totalAudioLen >> 24) & 0xff);
        out.write(header, 0, 44);
}
```

The resulting .wav file can be played by any audio application across platform that supports the .wav standard. Keep in mind that .wav files can be quite large, especially with 16-bit samples and sample rates of 44 kbps or 48 kbps. Encoding can help you reduce the size of audio files by using compressed formats. You will look at this later in the chapter.

Interfacing External Microphones

Even though you have recorded the .wav files as uncompressed audio, they still often don't sound that great. Why is that? The poor audio quality is due to the limitations of the internal microphone on the smartphone.

Adding external microphones could eliminate the following shortcomings of the mobile device's microphone:

■ Device microphones are not designed for high fidelity. Manufacturers do not have the space or wish to incur the cost of integrating high-quality microphones into smartphones.

■ Low-cost device microphones are not able to discriminate. They just amplify and capture everything, and lack the ability to separate the sounds you really want to record from all of the background noise.

Interfacing a professional mic to our smartphones by connecting them to an external pre-amp can dramatically improve recordings. There are a number of third-party products available. Figure 7-8 shows the iRig Pre, which works well on Android devices.

Figure 7-8. Interfacing professional microphones

These devices allow us to connect professional microphones with three-pin XLR connections to our devices using the audio jack. Most of the interfaces support dynamic microphones, which are typically used for live performances, as well as condenser microphones, which are typically used for studio recording. Condenser microphones require 48-volt phantom power and this can be supplied by devices like the iRig Pre because they have a 9-volt battery that is used to generate the phantom power for condenser microphones.

To illustrate the difference in audio quality between internal and external microphone, I produced a set of four recordings. Each recording was made with the recording audio app I previously covered. The recordings were stored as .wav files and each was recorded in the same noisy environment (a noisy Starbucks in Beijing!).

The following four microphones were used in the recording test:

■ Internal smartphone microphone

■ Senheiser omni-directional condenser microphone (a high-end microphone that requires 48-volt phantom power and has a wide pickup pattern)

■ Senheiser shotgun condenser microphone (a high-end microphone that has a very narrow pickup pattern and is often used on a boom pole in film production)

■ Shure SM-58 dynamic microphone (inexpensive industry standard for live performance vocals)

You can listen to the recordings in the file *mic-compare.mp3*. Figure 7-9 shows how the audio waveforms look when imported into a digital audio workstation (DAW) and analyzed.

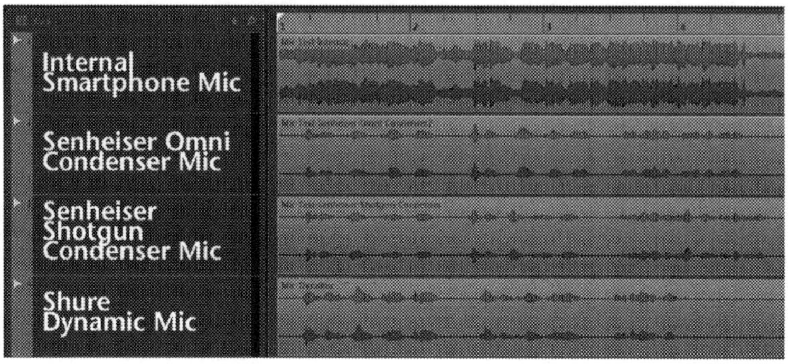

Figure 7-9. Microphone comparison

Notice in the waveforms how the smartphone internal mic records *everything* with *high* gain. Compare the signal-to-noise ratios and notice how *clean* the external mics are because they have the ability to discriminate.

When I covered the Music Service Project, recall that the track *Nogabe.mp3* was played in the background. I recorded this track in Beijing using only smartphones with external microphone interfaces.

Figure 7-10 shows the setup for this four-track recording.

Figure 7-10. Multitrack recording with smartphones

I mixed the four individual .wav file recordings in Cubase, but you can use any digital audio workstation software to complete the final mix. Simply import each .wav file, align them, and add some basic effects processing (you will see how to do this with Android in the next section).

This is a powerful capability that Android enables for us. In the past, we needed expensive dedicated multi-track recording equipment, but today, inexpensive smartphones with the availability of external interfaces makes the live recording process much more economical.

7.8   Advanced Audio

You have seen how to play and record audio in Android using the high-level and low-level APIs. Now let's take a look at processing audio by adding effects and encoding audio, which is necessary if you wish to save audio in compressed audio formats such as .mp3 and .mp4.

Built-in Audio Effects

Built-in audio effects make it easy to apply audio effects in Android. Recall in the Audio Buffer Size app you displayed built-in supported effects on the device. The built-in effects query was accomplished with the following code:

```
Sring list;
Descriptor[] effects = AudioEffect.queryEffects();
for (final Descriptor effect : effects) {
    list = list + effect.name.toString() + ", ";
}
```

This function returns a list of supported effects on the device. Different devices support different built-in effects. My Nexus device supports 12 effects:

- Loudness Enhancer
- Insert Preset Reverb
- Virtualizer
- Acoustic Echo Canceler
- Visualizer
- Dynamic Bass Boost
- Auxiliary Preset Reverb
- Insert Preset Reverb
- Insert Environmental Reverb
- Volume
- Equalizer
- Auxiliary Environmental Reverb

Most devices include all of these effects or a large subset of these effects. Refer to the Android documentation for a description of each effect. The built-in effects can be attached to any *MediaPlayer* or *AudioTrack* object and typically require two parameters: *Priority* and *AudioSessionID*.

The following code demonstrates how to attach a *PresetReverb* effect. Note that there are several presets available. The presets make it easy to achieve a desired effect. In the code below, I am using the *.PRESET_LARGEHALL* preset.

The chosen effect needs to be attached to an AudioTrack object, as is the case for each of the following examples.

```
PresetReverb mReverb = new PresetReverb(1, mAudioTrack.getAudioSessionId());
mReverb.setPreset(PresetReverb.PRESET_LARGEHALL);
mReverb.setEnabled(true);
mAudioTrack.attachAuxEffect(mReverb.getId());
mAudioTrack.setAuxEffectSendLevel(1.0f);
```

The following code shows how to add the *BassBoost* effect. You can specify the strength of the bass boost.

```
BassBoost bassBoost = new BassBoost(1,mAudioTrack.getAudioSessionId());
bassBoost.setEnabled(true);
BassBoost.Settings bassBoostSettingTemp = bassBoost.getProperties();
BassBoost.Settings bassBoostSetting = new BassBoost.Settings(bassBoostSettingTemp.
toString());
bassBoostSetting.strength=2000;
bassBoost.setProperties(bassBoostSetting);
mAudioTrack.attachAuxEffect(bassBoost.getId());
```

The following code shows how to add the *EnvironmentalReverb* effect. It allows for finer control than you saw with the *PresetReverb* effect. *EnvironmentalReverb* accepts a number of parameters, including *ReverbLevel*, *DecayTime*, and *Diffusion*.

```
EnvironmentalReverb reverb = new EnvironmentalReverb(1,0);
mAudioTrack.attachAuxEffect(reverb.getId());
reverb.setDiffusion((short) 1000);
reverb.setReverbLevel((short) 1000);
reverb.setDecayTime(10000);
reverb.setDensity((short) 1000);
mAudioTrack.setAuxEffectSendLevel(1.0f);
reverb.setEnabled(true);
```

You can see in these examples that all of the built-in effects work in a similar manner. After setting up the object, you just need to *attach* the effect to your audio object, set the level, and make sure the effect is *enabled*.

Encoding

When you record audio using *AudioRecord* in Android, you get uncompressed PCM. You saw this in the main recording loop in the Record Audio project. How do you get .mp3 or .mp4 or other compressed audio data? The answer is encoding.

In Android, *codecs* encode audio data to compressed formats. Codecs operate on three kinds of data: compressed, raw audio, and raw video. All three can be processed using *byte buffers*, although typically for video we would use a *surface*.

Raw audio buffers contain entire frames of PCM audio data, which is one sample for each channel in channel order. Each sample is a 16-bit signed integer in native byte order.

Ringdroid App

Ringdroid is a Google open source project that is an excellent example of how to architect encoding into an Android audio app. The link to the latest version of Ringdroid can be found in the chapter references.

The main purpose of Ringdroid is to let you record your own ringtones, hence the name. But I will use it to explain encoding, which it performs very well. Ringdroid needs to encode ringtones because saving them as uncompressed .wav files would not be feasible since the files would be too large.

Note that Ringdroid also has a very useful debugging method called *DumpSamples*. If you want to see what the raw PCM data looks like, you can use this method to dump out a CSV file of your audio samples, which you can then read using Excel or a spreadsheet program of your choice.

When you launch the Ringdroid app, you will see that many audio files on your device are detected, including

- Ringtones
- Notifications
- Alarms
- Music

A content manager is used to manage the four audio types. I will not cover the content manager or assigning ringtones. If you are interested in how this is accomplished, just refer to the code because it is pretty straightforward.

The app also has some good examples of setting up a surface view and drawing the audio waveform.

Setting up a Codec

Ringdroid has a class called *SoundFile.java*. Inside this class is a good example of audio encoding. It consists of two steps:

- Setting up a codec
- A main encoding loop

The following code excerpt shows how to set up a codec in Android using the *MediaCodec* API. It requires setting up input and output byte buffers, setting the bitrate, number of channels, and *mimeType*.

Notice that in this example you are specifying to encode to AAC/mp4. Table 7-1 listed the available encoding formats supported by Android. The bit rate of 64 kbps per channel provides a stereo bitrate of 128 kbps, which is pretty good quality for music.

```java
public void WriteFile(File outputFile, float startTime, float endTime) throws java.
io.IOException {
    int startOffset = (int)(startTime * mSampleRate) * 2 * mChannels;
    int numSamples = (int)((endTime - startTime) * mSampleRate);
    int numChannels = (mChannels == 1) ? 2 : mChannels;

    String mimeType = "audio/mp4a-latm";
    int bitrate = 64000 * numChannels; // for good quality: 64kbps per channel.

    MediaCodec codec = MediaCodec.createEncoderByType(mimeType);
    MediaFormat format = MediaFormat.createAudioFormat(mimeType, mSampleRate, numChannels);
    format.setInteger(MediaFormat.KEY_BIT_RATE, bitrate);
    codec.configure(format, null, null, MediaCodec.CONFIGURE_FLAG_ENCODE);
    codec.start();

    // Get an estimation of the encoded data based on the bitrate. Add 10% to it.
    int estimatedEncodedSize = (int)((endTime - startTime) * (bitrate / 8) * 1.1);
    ByteBuffer encodedBytes = ByteBuffer.allocate(estimatedEncodedSize);
    ByteBuffer[] inputBuffers = codec.getInputBuffers();
    ByteBuffer[] outputBuffers = codec.getOutputBuffers();
    MediaCodec.BufferInfo info = new MediaCodec.BufferInfo();
```

After this code is completed, the codec is *defined* and *started*, and you have a *MediaCodec info* object that will be used by the encoding main loop to accomplish the encoding.

Encoding Main Loop

Once you have the codec set up, you need to implement the encoding main loop. Note the following:

- You retrieve byte buffers from *mDecodedBytes*.

- You queue those bytes to the codec where the encoding work will be performed.

- You retrieve encoded bytes from the codec and place them into *encodedBytes*.

This process continues while you have bytes to process.

```java
ByteBuffer encodedBytes = ByteBuffer.allocate(estimatedEncodedSize);
ByteBuffer[] inputBuffers = codec.getInputBuffers();
ByteBuffer[] outputBuffers = codec.getOutputBuffers();
ByteBuffer[] = new byte[frame_size * numChannels * 2];
byte[] encodedSamples = null;
```

```
while (true) {
    // Feed the samples to the encoder.
    int inputBufferIndex = codec.dequeueInputBuffer(100);
    if (!done_reading && inputBufferIndex >= 0) {
        inputBuffers[inputBufferIndex].clear();
        mDecodedBytes.get(buffer, 0, bufferSize);
        inputBuffers[inputBufferIndex].put(buffer);
        presentation_time = (long) (((num_frames++) * frame_size * 1e6) / mSampleRate);
        codec.queueInputBuffer(inputBufferIndex, 0, buffer.length, presentation_time, 0);
    }
    // Get the encoded samples from the encoder.
    int outputBufferIndex = codec.dequeueOutputBuffer(info, 100);
    if (outputBufferIndex >= 0 && info.size > 0 && info.presentationTimeUs >=0) {
        outputBuffers[outputBufferIndex].get(encodedSamples, 0, info.size);
        outputBuffers[outputBufferIndex].clear();
        codec.releaseOutputBuffer(outputBufferIndex, false);
        encodedBytes.put(encodedSamples, 0, info.size);
    }
}

int encoded_size = encodedBytes.position();
encodedBytes.rewind();
codec.stop();
codec.release();
codec = null;
```

The Android *MediaCodec* API greatly simplifies audio encoding. See the full code in the Ringdroid *SoundFile* class. Don't forget, much like you saw when writing out .wav files, compressed audio formats such as .mp3 and .mp4 also have headers that must be constructed when writing out the final compressed audio file.

7.9   Audio Synthesis

One thing you will notice with apps that contain internally stored audio files is that the size of these apps can grow quite large. You saw that uncompressed files get big fast, and even when you encode audio assets, file sizes can still be large especially if you are encoding with reasonably high bitrates to ensure audio quality.

This is where audio synthesis comes into play. With the emergence of the Android smartphone, we now have the availability of audio synthesis engines on our mobile devices. These engines have the ability to play complex audio sounds that can be represented by simple, small-sized, text-based instructions.

Some of these synthesis engines have been around for quite a long time. Csound goes back to the 1970s. Table 7-12 shows a listing of the most popular audio synthesis engines available today, including those available on Android.

Table 7-12. Audio Synthesis Engines

Name	Purpose	OS	Cost/License	Latest Version
Chuck	Real-time synthesis, live coding, pedagogy, acoustic research, algorithmic composition	Mac OS X, Linux, Windows	Free/GPL	2014-12 ver 1.3.5.0
Csound	Real-time performance, sound synthesis, algorithmic composition, acoustic research	Mac OS X, Linux, Windows, Android, iOS	Free/GPL	2014-07 ver 6.03
Impromptu	Live coding, algorithmic composition, hardware control, real-time synthesis	Mac OS X	Free/Proprietary	2010-10 ver 2.5
Max/MSP	Real-time audio + video synthesis, hardware control	Mac OS X, Windows	Non-free/ Proprietary	2014-12 ver 7.0.1
Pure Data	Real-time synthesis, hardware control, acoustic research	Mac OS X, Linux, Windows, Android, iOS	Free/BSD-like	2015-03 ver 0.46.6
Reaktor	Real-time synthesis, hardware control, GUI design	Mac OS X, Windows	Non-free/ Proprietary	2014-09 ver 5.9.2
Super Collider	Real-time synthesis, live coding, algorithmic composition, acoustic research, all-purpose programming language	Mac OS X, Linux, Windows, FreeBSD, Android, iOS	Free/GPL	2013-04 ver 3.6.6

On Android, there are now three choices:

- Pure Data: Excellent stable library ported to Android by Google. Recommended as a general purpose synthesis engine for Android.

- Csound: Powerful synthesis engine. Higher learning curve and not quite as light a resource footprint as Pure Data, but can produce some amazing sounds. Chosen as the audio engine for the OLPC (One Laptop Per Child) initiative.

- Supercollider: An excellent choice for live coding. The Android library is not very stable at this time. It is an excellent synthesis engine, but unfortunately at this time there are just not enough Android resources available for me to recommend it.

Although these engines have been around for many years, the Android ports are fairly recent. If you want to use audio synthesis in your apps, it basically comes down to choosing between Pure Data and Csound. Table 7-13 shows a comparison.

Table 7-13. *Android Audio Synthesis Comparison*

Pure Data	Csound
Excellent Android support	Minimal Android support
Huge number of operators	Huge number of operators
Medium learning curve	High learning curve
Graphical based, GUI is easy to use	Document based, GUIs available (winXsound, cabbage, blue)
Composing is difficult, you have to build a GUI	Easy to compose in document-based file
No IDE	CuteCsound IDE
Limited GUI architecture	Expandable architecture
Small library size	Large library size

In summary, Pure Data is easier to learn, but Csound is more advanced. This is due to the Pure Data architectural decision that defines its GUI approach. Csound maintains a document-based approach, which makes it harder to learn and use, but it is extremely flexible and powerful in terms of what it can do.

Both engines can produce amazing sounds.

Pure Data Overview

Pure Data is a real-time graphical programming environment for audio. It was originally developed by Miller Puckett and the Android port was done by Peter Brinkmann and others.

There are two "flavors" of Pure Data available: plain vanilla and extended. Plain vanilla is the version that is supported in Android. The main difference is that the extended version includes changes that allow it to work better on desktop GUI platforms.

Pure Data uses patches to synthesize audio. A Pure Data patch is an ASCII text file that always ends with the .pd extension. There are many patches available online that can be played by Pure Data. And, of course, you can create your own patches. It is amazing what you can create using Pure Data. Just check YouTube for some examples of what the Pure Data community has created.

Pure Data is cross-platform and has been ported to almost every platform, including Windows, Mac, Linux, and of course, Android.

The easiest way to understand Pure Data and the patches it plays is to see it visually.

Figure 7-11 show the trivial Hello World example for Pure Data.

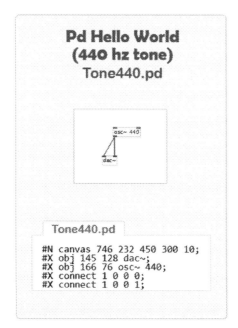

Figure 7-11. Pure Data Hello World example

In Pure Data, you create sounds by defining operators and then connecting them together. In the Hello World example, a simple oscillator operator produces a 440 Hz tone. This operator is connected to the ADC operator, which is the analog to digital converter that represents the hardware output of your device.

Patches can be saved. In the Hello World example, the *Tone440.pd* file is the Pure Data ASCII text file that represents the graphical patch. When this patch file is loaded into Pure Data and played, the 440 Hz tone can be heard.

You typically build Pure Data patches in a desktop GUI environment and play them back on an Android device with apps incorporating the Pure Data library. I recommend you install Pure Data on your laptop and do your GUI Pure Data editing in this environment. Then you can play patches you create on your Android device with the Pure Data Player app presented later in this chapter.

I am not going to teach you how to create PD patches here as it is beyond the scope of this chapter. However, there are many resources available to help you to learn the vast array of Pure Data operators and how to use them to produce all kinds of interesting sounds.

Figure 7-12 shows one such example. It is a complex Pure Data patch titled Readymade, written by Martin Brinkmann. You can load it into Pure Data on your desktop to see what it looks like and play it. You can also play it on your device using the Pure Data Player app.

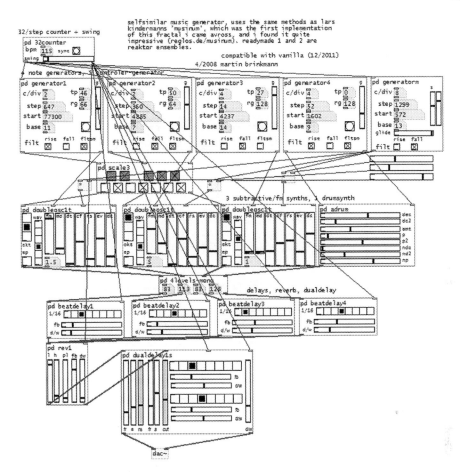

Figure 7-12. Complex Pure Data example

As you can see, this is a much more complex Pure Data patch. It creates some very interesting music and gives you a good idea of the power behind these audio synthesis engines.

Next, let's take a look at how to implement a Pure Data Player app on Android.

Pure Data Player App

Whether you create your own Pure Data patches or have pre-existing patches that you want to use for your audio, you need an app that supports Pure Data to play the patches.

It is hard to find a good Pure Data player, so I created this app by modifying the Pure Data Test app that comes in the Pure Data distribution. This app will work well for you if you do not need a graphical interface in your app and just want to use Pure Data to play sounds that you load into your Android App via .pd files.

If you need a graphical interface for Pure Data, I will cover the open source Circle of Fifths Pure Data app in the next section. It is an excellent example of how to achieve a graphical interface to Pure Data.

Figure 7-13 shows a snapshot of the Pure Data Player app.

Figure 7-13. Pure Data Player app

The app allows the user to select a Pure Data patch file. After a patch is selected, the .pd file will be loaded and then played. There is also a button to stop a patch that is currently playing and reload a new patch. The bottom button on the GUI allows the user to set the audio preferences, including mono/stereo output and sample rate.

There is a *TextView* at the bottom of the layout which shows Pure Data messages while the patch is running.

Pure Data Player Project

Table 7-14 shows the Pure Data Player project structure. It consists of the main activity *PdPlayer.java* and the main screen layout *main.xml*. Note there are two required libraries. More about the setup of these libraries later.

Table 7-14. *Pure Data Player Project Structure*

Sources	Resources	Libraries
PdPlayer.java	main.xml	pdcore.jar
CustomDialog.java	list_item.xml	androidmidi.jar
	load_dialog.xml	

The .pd files for the PD Player app are stored in the */sdcard/PDPatches* folder. If you want to play external .pd patches with the Pure Data Player app, just copy your .pd files to this directory.

You need the following libraries included in your Android Studio project:

- *PdCore*: A required library project that depends on *AndroidMidi*
- *AndroidMidi*: A low-level midi library required by Pure Data

Figure 7-14 shows the setup dependencies for Pure Data.

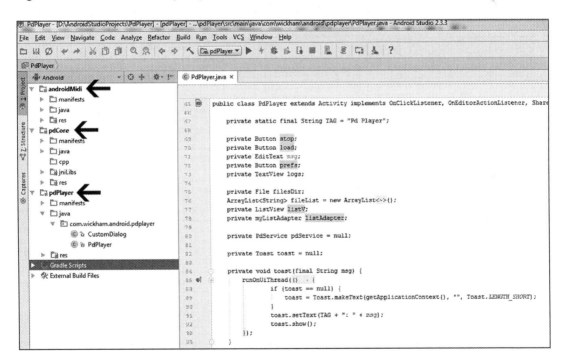

Figure 7-14. *Pure Data setup*

The project references contain several links to help if you have any trouble setting up Pure Data. Once you have Pure Data set up, using the library in your app to play audio is straightforward.

Pure Data Key Code

The core of Pure Data is a service called *PdService*. You will see it included in the Manifest file. *PdPreferences* is also part of the library and handles changes to the audio configuration.

PDPlayer.java

Interface to the Pd library is accomplished through the *PdBase* and *PdService* classes. The following code shows how to connect to the service and open a patch file:

```
private PdService pdService = null;
private final ServiceConnection pdConnection = new ServiceConnection() {
    public void onServiceConnected(ComponentName name, IBinder service) {
        pdService = ((PdService.PdBinder)service).getService();
        PdBase.setReceiver(receiver);
        PdBase.subscribe("android");
        PdBase.openPatch(patchFile);
    }
    public void onServiceDisconnected(ComponentName name) {
    }
};
```

In the *onCreate* method of the activity, you are required to initialize the audio parameters and bind the service. This is completed with the following code:

```
protected void onCreate(android.os.Bundle savedInstanceState) {
    AudioParameters.init(this);
    bindService(new Intent(this, PdService.class), pdConnection, BIND_AUTO_CREATE);
};
```

To control the audio output, you use *stopAudio* and *startAudio* methods. The *.initAudio* method uses stub parameters (-1 values) because those are automatically picked up by the *PdPreferences* class.

```
private void startAudio() {
    pdService.initAudio(-1, -1, -1, -1);
    pdService.startAudio(new Intent(this, PdPlayer.class), icon, name, "Return");
}
private void stopAudio() {
    pdService.stopAudio();
    pdService.release();
}
```

The PD Player app is a good example of play .pd patches that do not require a GUI interface. In the next example, you will see a Pure Data app that does require on a GUI interface.

Pure Data Circle of Fifths App

A well-known open source Pure Data example is the Circle of Fifths app. It allows you to explore guitar chords. It includes a graphical interface that is used to select a chord. When you press on a chord, Pure Data messages are sent to the Pure Data service to instruct it what to play.

Figure 7-15 shows the main GUI.

Figure 7-15. Pure Data Circle of Fifths app

PD patches for the Circle of Fifths app are stored in the */Resources/raw* folder as a compressed *.zip* file. They are opened, extracted, and loaded into Pure Data in the same way you saw with the previous app. The following code shows how to open the patch file:

```
File dir = getFilesDir();
File patchFile = new File(dir, "chords.pd");
IoUtils.extractZipResource(getResources().openRawResource(R.raw.patch), dir, true);
PdBase.openPatch(patchFile.getAbsolutePath());
```

When the surface is pressed, the data for the corresponding chord is sent to Pure Data using the PdBase.sendList command as shown in the following code:

```
Public void playChord(boolean major, int n) {
    PdBase.sendList("playchord", option _ (major ? 1 : 0), n);
}
```

Using this approach to send messages into Pure Data to play sounds allows you to build interactive apps with Pure Data.

I won't cover the code for the Circle of Fifths GUI here, but you can view the source to see how it is set up. Inside the Circle of Fifths project, you can view the GUI code inside the *CircleView.java* file. The Pure Data code is located inside the *CircleOfFifths.java* file.

Csound Overview

The Csound synthesis engine is available on Android. The following is a quick look at the Csound highlights:

- Csound is a mind-blowing computer music synthesis system based on Linux that was created in 1986.

- Csound was recently ported to Android (*Csoundandroid.jar*). The latest update is Csound 6.06. The CsoundObj API is used to interface with your apps (Java API).

- Like Pure Data, it is also cross platform. You can create sounds on your laptop or desktop and then play them on your Android device.

- The One Laptop Per Child project chose Csound as its sound engine.

- Csound patches consist of a Synthesis block and a Score block.

- There are several GUI front ends available for Csound.

- The default audio mode uses the OpenSL API offered by the NDK. There is a native shared library built using the NDK.

- There is a significant learning curve if you want to master Csound.

Csound .csd files

Csound performs all its magic with .csd files. These are text-based files that contain three sections as follows:

```
<CsOptions>      </CsOptions>
<CsInstruments> </CsInstruments>
<CsScore>        </CsScore>
```

As you did with Pure Data, let's take a look at a simple Csound file that allows you to play a tone. You are going to define the Csound instructions to accomplish the following:

- Set up an 880hz oscillator as instrument 1.

- Play instrument 1.

- Start playing instrument 1 at 0 seconds.

- Stop playing instrument 1 ending at 5 seconds.

The following is the code for Tone880.csd:

```
<CsoundSynthesizer>

<CsOptions>
    -odac -b240 -B16384
</CsOptions>
```

```
<CsInstruments>
    sr=48000
    ksmps=8192
    nchnls=2
    instr 1
    aSin        oscils      0dbfs/2, 880, 0
    out         aSin
    endin
</CsInstruments>

<CsScore>
    i 1 0 5
    e
</CsScore>

</CsoundSynthesizer>
```

This .csd file can be played by any Csound engine. Next, you will take a look at running Csound on Android.

Csound Setup

When you grab the Csound for Android project, it will include all of the projects listed in Figure 7-16.

1. Grab Csound for Android version 6 and import into your IDE.

2. Getting it built on Android Studio is much easier than Eclipse.

3. Csound-android-6.06.0 is available at the Csound SourceForge page.

4. See the *csound_android_manual.pdf.*

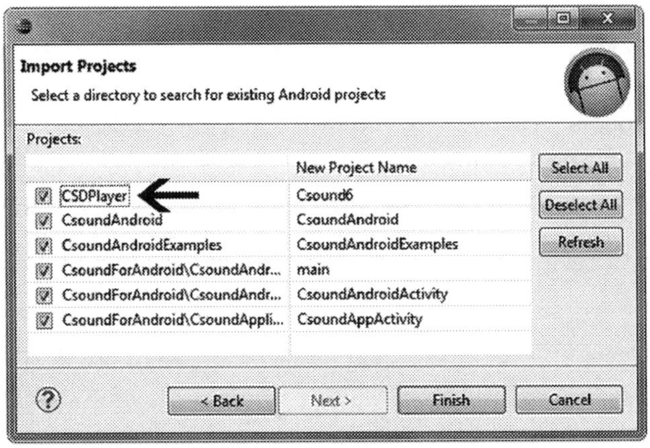

Figure 7-16. Csound setup

Csound App

The Csound Player app is the best way to get started exploring Csound. You can install the pre-built app and start playing .csd files.

Figure 7-17 shows the Csound Player app.

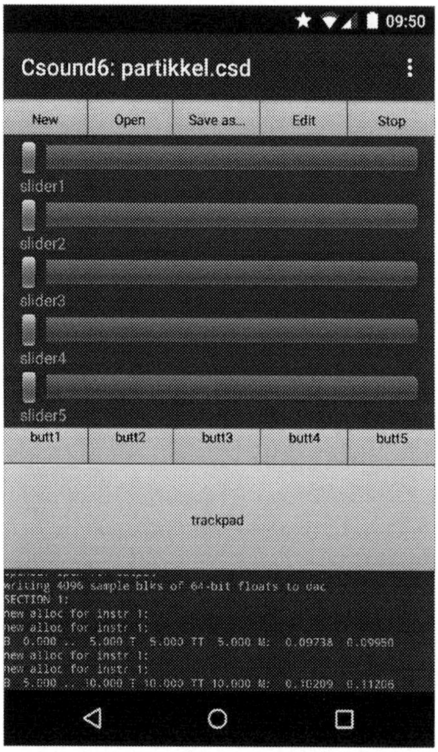

Figure 7-17. *Csound Player app*

The app contains a simple GUI interface with five sliders, five buttons, and an X-Y trackpad. Csound files have the hooks available to interface with these GUI widgets.

You can load internal .csd files or open external .csd files which you copy onto your device. Some of the internal .csd files are very impressive, so I recommend that you check them out. The internal files can be accessed using the overflow icon (three little dots) and selecting examples.

Like the Pure Data Player app, there is a *TextView* in the lower part of the screen that shows the Csound messages as the .csd file is played.

Csound Key Code

It is very simple to play a sound with Csound. There are many code examples in the Android release package. Several .csd patches are included in the Android CSD Player.

Like Pure Data, just decide if you need GUI control or not, and then proceed accordingly.

To interface with the Csound library, you simply set up a Csound object and then use the .startCsound and .stopCsound methods to control the audio.

CsoundHaikuIVActivity.java

One of the examples included in the app is a Csound file called HaikuIV. It is a nice sounding patch. The code for controlling the patch follows and is an excerpt from the file CsoundHaikuIVActivity.java:

```
public class CsoundHaikuIVActivity extends BaseCsoundActivity {
    protected CsoundObj csoundObj = new CsoundObj();
    public void onCreate(Bundle savedInstanceState) {
        String csd = getResourceFileAsString(R.raw.iv);
        File f = createTempFile(csd);
        csoundObj.startCsound(f);
    }
}
```

SimpleTestActivity.java

Interfacing to the GUI widgets is accomplished by adding widgets and listeners to your Csound objects. The SimpleTest Csound activity provides a good example of how to do this. It attaches a slider to control the sound.

```
String csd = getResourceFileAsString(R.raw.test);
File f = createTempFile(csd);
CsoundUI csoundUI = new CsoundUI(csoundObj);
csoundUI.addSlider(fSlider, "slider", 0. , 1.);
csoundObj.addListener(SimpleTest1Activity.this);
csoundObj.startCsound(f);
```

Note that some of the example .csd files use the GUI widgets so that you can interact with the sounds being generated, while many of them do not.

Csound Summary

Csound is really an amazing synthesis engine for Android. There is a huge library of effects available on Csound. It is an excellent choice if you want to write an equalizer or effects app. The engine supports virtually every kind of audio synthesis. Csound is a great choice if you want to write a synth or musical instrument. Learning the Csound language is not easy, but its instrument and scoring capabilities are unmatched.

7.10   References

Android References

- Android Audio Media Formats Support: `http://developer.android.com/guide/appendix/media-formats.html`

- Media Codec: `http://developer.android.com/reference/android/media/MediaCodec.html`

- Media Player: `http://developer.android.com/reference/android/media/MediaPlayer.html`

- USB Digital Audio: `https://source.android.com/devices/audio/usb.html`

- Audio Track: `http://developer.android.com/reference/android/media/AudioTrack.html`

- Audio Record: `http://developer.android.com/reference/android/media/AudioRecord.html`

- Audio Manager: `http://developer.android.com/reference/android/media/AudioManager.html`

- Media Recorder: `http://developer.android.com/reference/android/media/MediaRecorder.html`

- Media Extractor: `http://developer.android.com/reference/android/media/MediaExtractor.html`

- Media Format: `http://developer.android.com/reference/android/media/MediaFormat.html`

- Sound Pool: `http://developer.android.com/reference/android/media/SoundPool.html`

- Audio Format: `http://developer.android.com/reference/android/media/AudioFormat.html`

- Text to Speech: `http://developer.android.com/reference/android/speech/tts/TextToSpeech.html`

- Speech Recognition: `http://developer.android.com/reference/android/speech/SpeechRecognizer.html`

- Media Store: `http://developer.android.com/reference/android/provider/MediaStore.html`

- High Performance Audio Blog: `http://bit.ly/high-performance-audio`

Specifications

- OpenSL ES: `www.khronos.org/opensles/`

- OpenSL ES Specification: `www.khronos.org/registry/sles/specs/OpenSL_ES_Specification_1.0.1.pdf`

- JACK Audio Connection API: `www.jackaudio.org/api/`

- SWIG and Android: `www.swig.org/Doc2.0/Android.html`

- JSON (JavaScript Object Notation): `http://json.org`

- JSON Validation Checker: `http://jsonlint.org`

Third-Party Vendors

- Latency Results Compiled for Thousands of Devices: `http://superpowered.com/latency/#axzz3oxPTUDpq`

- Third-Party USB Audio Driver: `www.extreamsd.com/index.php/2015-07-22-12-01-14/usb-audio-driver`

- Samsung Professional Audio SDK: `www.youtube.com/watch?v=7r455edqQFM`

- Ring Droid: `https://github.com/google/ringdroid`

- Latency: `https://audioprograming.wordpress.com/`

- Google I/O 2013 High Performance Audio: `www.youtube.com/watch?v=d3kfEeMZ65c`

- JACK Audio Interconnection Kit: `www.jackaudio.org/`

Pure Data

- Pure Data for Android Wiki: `https://github.com/libpd/pd-for-android/wiki`

- Pure Data for Android: `https://github.com/libpd/pd-for-android`

- Pure Data HTML Manual: `https://puredata.info/docs/manuals/pd`

- Pure Data Modular Synthesis: `www.youtube.com/watch?v=p7XzBHoWOV4`

- Pure Data Downloads: `https://puredata.info/downloads`

- Pure Data Vanilla Patches: `www.martin-brinkmann.de/pd-patches.html`

Csound

- Csound: `http://sourceforge.net/projects/csound/`

- Csound Manual: `http://csound.github.io/docs/manual/index.html`

- Csound Manual: www.csounds.com/manual/html/index.html

- Csound Optimizing Latency: www.csounds.com/manual/html/ UsingOptimizing.html

- Csound for Android Paper: http://lac.linuxaudio.org/2012/ papers/20.pdf

- Csound Resources: http://iainmccurdy.org/csound.html

- Csound Web Player: http://csound.github.io/learn-csound-site/ pieces/trapped/index.html

- Csound Player APK: http://github.com/csound/csound/tree/develop/ android/CSDPlayer

- Csound Command Line Flags: www.csounds.com/manual/html/ CommandFlags.html

- Csound Book – Chapter 1: www.csounds.com/chapter1/index.html

Index

Get the eBook for only $5!

Why limit yourself?

With most of our titles available in both PDF and ePUB format, you can access your content wherever and however you wish—on your PC, phone, tablet, or reader.

Since you've purchased this print book, we are happy to offer you the eBook for just $5.

To learn more, go to http://www.apress.com/companion or contact support@apress.com.

Apress®